D1559888

INDIANS AND THE POLITICAL ECONOMY
OF COLONIAL CENTRAL AMERICA, 1670–1810

Indians and the Political Economy of Colonial Central America, 1670–1810

Robert W. Patch

University of Oklahoma Press : Norman

Also by Robert W. Patch

Maya and Spaniard in Yucatan, 1648–1812 (Stanford, Calif., 1993)
Maya Revolt and Revolution in the Eighteenth Century (Armonk, N.Y., 2002)

Library of Congress Cataloging-in-Publication Data

Patch, Robert.
    Indians and the political economy of colonial Central America, 1670–1810 / Robert W. Patch.
        pages   cm.
    Includes bibliographical references and index.
    ISBN 978-0-8061-4400-9 (hardback)
    1. Indians, Treatment of—Central America—History. 2. Forced labor—Central America—History. 3. Central America—Economic conditions. 4. Spain—Colonies—America—Economic conditions. I. Title.
    F1434.P36 2013
    972.8'03—dc23

                                                                        2013018148

1 2 3 4 5 6 7 8 9 10

To Stanley J. Stein and Barbara H. Stein
La grandeza del hombre es el flechazo, no el blanco

CONTENTS

Illustrations

MAPS

TABLES

Acknowledgments

Research for this book was made possible by a Fulbright Foreign Area Fellowship administered by the U.S.-Spanish Joint Committee for Cultural and Educational Cooperation, which allowed me to live in Spain for a year and a half and use Spanish archives. I would like to thank the Spaniards and Americans involved in administering and funding that fellowship. I thank the staffs of the Archivo General de Indias in Seville and the Archivo Histórico Nacional in Madrid for their help, and the many people in Spain who provided me with ideas, criticism, and comradeship. I also acknowledge the help and encouragement I received in Mexico from the Mexicans and Americans I knew there, who also contributed to my work with ideas and friendship. In the United States, I would like to thank my colleagues, students, and the many Latin Americanists I have known for their interest and encouragement. Stephen Webre and Bruce Castleman, as well as the anonymous readers of this manuscript, provided valuable criticism that contributed to a much better book. The manuscript received significant support from Alessandra Jacobi Tamulevich, acquisitions editor at the University of Oklahoma Press, who helped guide this book through the publishing process, and she deserves my thanks as well. The Academic Senate of the University of California, Riverside, provided me with consistent research support that contributed to the completion of this book. Needless to say, my family also deserves my heartfelt thanks for their support and encouragement.

Indians and the Political Economy of Colonial Central America, 1670–1810

Introduction

In an influential book written in the 1970s, Immanuel Wallerstein famously placed Asia and Latin America on the periphery of an early-modern world economy supposedly dominated by Western Europe.[1] Since that time, scholars from various regional perspectives have demonstrated that an opposite interpretation would be more accurate: China and India were actually the major manufacturing nations and exporters of industrial goods; Latin America was vital for world trade because it produced the silver and gold that were the lifeblood of the global economy; and Europe, far from being an industrial giant, had no industrial goods to sell in Asia. Europe therefore fought desperately for a share of Spanish silver in order to buy the industrial exports of China—which would take nothing but silver in return for its goods—and India. Moreover, Europeans needed Latin America's precious metals in order to purchase the Indian textiles that were necessary to exchange for the nutmeg and cloves of the Spice Islands. In short, Europe was more peripheral than central to a global economy based on Chinese silk and porcelain, Indian cotton textiles, Southeast Asian spices, African slaves, and Latin American precious metals.[2]

Latin America, therefore, was not simply a provider of raw materials from "coerced cash-crop" production (to use Wallerstein's phrase) for a globally dominant European economy.[3] On the contrary, it was one of the most industrialized parts of the world from the sixteenth to the eighteenth century—although less so than China—for it did

3

more than just produce the gold and silver that made world trade go around. The mining economy led to the development of backward linkages in the form of textile production, carried out to a great extent by Spanish-owned textile mills called *obrajes* that specialized in woolens.[4] However, the spinning of thread and weaving of cloth also took place in the traditional indigenous sector, which produced mostly cotton cloth. As a result of the backward linkages, regions as apparently isolated from the world economy as Chiapas, Yucatan, and Guatemala in fact were major export platforms that allowed northern Mexico and Honduras to specialize in precious metal production for export. When this system collapsed in the early nineteenth century, local leaders bemoaned the loss of so many jobs and so much wealth.[5]

While scholars have been able to analyze obraje woolen production in considerable detail, the study of the indigenous cotton sector is complicated by a political reality: Spanish colonial magistrates came to dominate a good deal of the production and marketing of Indian goods, including cotton textiles. This resulted from special historical circumstances: Because the colonial government could not afford to pay its officials respectable salaries, these officials, of course, found ways to supplement their incomes through various means, some of them illegal. At the same time, the power possessed by these local magistrates (*corregidores, alcaldes mayores,* or *gobernadores*), who ruled over provinces populated mostly by Indians, put them in control over a large part of the commercial exchange between the surplus-producing indigenous sector of the economy and the regional economy as a whole. Most foodstuffs, especially maize, beans, and squash, were unaffected and traded freely, although magistrates did profit from the resale of tribute goods like maize paid in kind. But valuable items that could be exported from the region, such as textiles and thread, as well as cochineal (a red dye used in textile manufacture), cacao, and raw cotton, tended to fall under the control of the local Spanish magistrates.[6]

Textile production therefore came to be carried out in a context in which government officials played a major role in stimulating manufacture and controlling commercial exchange between Indian producers and the wider world. Merchants were not legally prevented from engaging in trade with the Indians to acquire those goods. However, as will be seen, the power of office gave the magistrates an advantage that forced most merchants either to stay out of the Indian provinces or to make deals and work with the officials in order to get a share of the profits.[7]

The business activities that government officials carried out with the Indians were known as *repartimientos de mercancías*, *repartimientos de efectos*, or just plain *repartimientos,* a term that meant the allocation or allotment of merchandise, credit, or cash. These consisted of two kinds of operations: (1) the advance of credit or money by the magistrate to the Indians in return for future repayment in kind, that is, in marketable goods; and (2) the sale of goods on credit by the magistrate to the Indians, who paid the debt in the future in either cash or kind. Since the law prohibited all commercial dealings between government officials and the people under their jurisdiction, the practice was illegal, except for a brief period of legalization in the middle of the eighteenth century. Government officials also carried out a variety of business activities with non-Indians in the provinces that they ruled. These were also illegal. All such business was a manifestation of governmental corruption.

The illegal nature of the repartimiento system led to considerable controversy at the time and to historiographical controversy ever since. Most famously, Jorge Juan and Juan de Ulloa, Spanish military officers who carried out a secret inspection of South America in the 1740s, reported to the Spanish prime minister on what they called "the tyrannical government with which the corregidores oppress the Indians," and referred to the repartimiento as a system "so perverse that it appears to have been imposed as punishment on the people, for one could hardly imagine anything more tyrannical against them." The magistrates, Juan and Ulloa reported, exercised a commercial monopoly over the people under their control, and often sold them goods that were useless and unwanted. The indigenous people were being required to work so hard to repay their debts that "it cannot be denied that the Indians are in a situation crueler than that of the slaves." The origin of this injustice was "the insatiable greed that brought these officials to the Indies to govern."[8]

Juan and Ulloa's report was so devastatingly critical of the colonial system that it was kept secret until after independence, not being published until 1825. However, it circulated in manuscript form within the Spanish bureaucracy and inspired several generations of reformers who declared the repartimiento to be representative of corruption that the crown had to root out in order to establish good government and an honest bureaucracy. Judges could not be honest, it was believed, if they were carrying out business in the area of their jurisdiction. At the same time, it was seen as a system that exploited Indians, who were forced to buy goods at higher-than-market prices and to sell their goods at lower-than-market prices, to the point that it prevented them from participating freely in, and thus benefiting from, trade in the wider economy. On the other hand, the system also had its defenders, who pointed out that the Indians simply would not participate in the market economy without some form of coercion, and since the repartimiento also allowed the magistrates to make enough money to carry out their administrative duties, the system, while regrettable because it resulted in the mixture of private business with law enforcement and the administration of justice, paid for administration, provided the Indians with the means to pay their taxes, and did not over-exploit the Indians.[9]

Modern historiography has echoed these colonial disputes. Various scholars point out that the difference between what the Indians received and what the goods were worth signified a level of exploitation that simply could not have existed in a non-colonial economy. Coercion was applied to get the Indians to participate either through purchasing goods or paying their debts in kind—and collection sometimes included heavy-handed physical punishment like whipping and incarceration. The repartimiento, then, reveals the exploitative nature of Spanish colonialism.[10]

Other scholars, however, have gone deeper in their analysis of the significance of the repartimiento. Horst Pietschmann, in a study of Puebla, points out that the repartimiento was in essence a system of credit that allowed the Indians to purchase expensive and useful capital goods like mules, which the indigenous people could not afford to buy without credit and which they gradually paid for in installments.[11] Jeremy Baskes, in an in-depth analysis of Oaxaca, also notes that the repartimiento was the means of advancing credit to the indigenous people. The difference between the price at which mules were sold on the free market in cash—usually twelve to fifteen pesos—and what the Indians were charged—twenty-five pesos— was simply disguised interest being charged over what was usually a five-year period, which was the alcalde mayor's term of office.[12] Baskes and María de los Ángeles Romero Frizzi, who also studies Oaxaca, call into question the allegation that the products the Indians were forced to buy were useless. This may have been true at times, but was hardly the case with respect to mules, cattle, oxen, and metal tools. These were goods that the indigenous people clearly wanted and might not have been able to purchase without credit.[13]

Furthermore, my previous work about colonial Central America demonstrates that regardless of the exploitative nature of the system, the repartimiento served to integrate peasants into the wider colonial and world economy. Baskes and Arij Ouweneel make the same point regarding Oaxaca and central Mexico, respectively.[14] Many earlier scholars missed this point because they were focusing on the repartimiento almost exclusively as a manifestly immoral and corrupt system of colonial exploitation. Yet, worldwide economic integration is one of the reasons why it was important; it was the system's reason for existence and the explanation for its profitability.

Finally, Baskes argues that since Indians usually found ways to resist and counteract colonial over-exploitation, it would be surprising to find that they calmly accepted over-exploitation in the case of the repartimiento. In particular, he suggests that it is hard to believe that the indigenous people could have been compelled to accept allocations of goods, and indeed mules were so useful that the Indians actually *wanted* to purchase them. Baskes criticizes much of the modern scholarship on the repartimiento system because it accepts at face value the criticism made by Spain's eighteenth-century reformers, even though their accusations took place in the context of political disputes between those reformers and the defenders of the status quo. This results, he argues, in a jaundiced or one-sided interpretation based on late-colonial bureaucratic partisanship.[15]

Nevertheless, it is important to emphasize that Baskes, who has developed the most comprehensive reinterpretation of the repartimiento, does not deny that the relationship between magistrates and Indians involved coercion. As Marcello Carmagnani points out, Baskes helps take the discussion to a new level by removing it from judgments based on morality.[16] Nevertheless, Baskes notes that merchants collaborated with the officials because "alcaldes mayores . . . could use their political power to collect debts," and that when "peasants failed to pay promptly, the alcaldes mayores could be ruthless, resorting to violent means to collect their debts."[17] The controversial part of Baskes's argument, then, is that coercion was not needed to get the indigenous people to participate in the repartimiento system: "Put simply, the colonial state and its agents were not in the business of forcing peasants into the market through the repartimiento as has traditionally been believed," Baskes writes. Peasants participated voluntarily, and then, one supposes, like many debtors throughout the world, tried to avoid repayment. The role of the magistrates, therefore, was to use "political power" to collect debts, repayment of which was decidedly not voluntary.[18]

Because much of the existing knowledge about the repartimiento is based on documentation resulting from political conflict within the bureaucracy, it would be useful and informative to approach this topic from a different point of view by consulting different sources. This book will attempt to contribute to the debate about the repartimiento by using new sources as well as traditional ones. First, it will provide an insider's perspective by focusing, in chapter 4, on a particular magistrate—an alcalde mayor—and his activities at a particular point of time in a specific place, namely, Huehuetenango-Totonicapán (in the highest of the highlands of Guatemala) in the mid-eighteenth century. It just so happens that the records also involve that magistrate's business partner, and thus this source will give us the merchant's perspective as well. An insider's perspective will also be provided, in chapter 5, about the repartimiento in the lowlands of Central America, in Nicaragua. There, a governor carried out activities that tied the indigenous people into the world economy by helping to provide for the defense of the Spanish empire. These case studies will take the discussion out of the realm of generalities and into that of daily business and interaction with the indigenous people under the rule of government officials and in the commercial domain of a private merchant. This new perspective will not only provide insight into the realities of economic exchange between Indians and the outside world in the Spanish empire but also a better understanding of the complicated nature of commerce and government—the business of politics and the politics of business—in a region tied to the world economy through exports to other regions that produced the precious metals that were a driving force in the world economy in the era before the Industrial Revolution.

This book will also use a well-known source in a new way. That source is the documentation of the arguments in support of the repartimiento. Scholars have tended to overlook this source because the reports favoring the system then in existence were based on racist Spanish ideas regarding the Indians. Moreover, it has been assumed that support for the status quo was based on the self-interested desire to protect what was obviously a lucrative business for the people involved in the repartimiento, in which case the arguments in favor could be easily ignored. This book, however, will take these people's points of view and arguments more seriously. Of course, the supporters of the system were racist. But so, too, were the critics of the system, who favored imperial reform to root out corruption. Moreover, far from being merely apologists for the status quo and supporters of vested interests, the advocates of the repartimiento provide an explanation of *why* the system worked in the way that it did and why any "reform" would have had adverse economic and fiscal effects. On the latter point, history has proved them correct. The critics, in turn, provide us with a good explanation of *how* the system worked. By judicious use of both sources, a more balanced understanding of the repartimiento will emerge.

Back in 1985, Juan Carlos Solórzano Fonseca, the first to call attention to the economic significance of the repartimiento system in eighteenth-century Central America, called for more research on the topic because of its obvious importance.[19] This book is a step in that direction. It does not pretend to be a definitive account of government and the repartimiento system in eighteenth-century Central America. Rather, using heretofore little-used sources, it will provide a broader understanding of how and why the system operated in the way that it did.

Among these sources are what were known as *provisiones* and *títulos*—appointments and titles to office—made or given by the government in Spain to positions at the provincial level in Central America. These are crucial for understanding the functioning of the bureaucracy at the local level, where officials interacted directly with Indians. A second source that this book is based on are the numerous *residencias*—trials for conduct in office—that ended up being stored mostly in archives in Spain. These detail the variety and extent of the economic activities that provincial magistrates carried out with the indigenous people, thereby revealing important features of Indian economic activity that otherwise would escape from our view of history. It turns out that most of the magistrates on trial did not attempt to cover up those illegal activities. Rather, residencia judges whitewashed them; that is, they presented the activities as good or at least forgivable. A third source, the chance survival of inquests into specific magistrates, will allow us to understand the nature of indigenous commerce with officials through the experiences of the officials themselves.

Finally, reviews of policy, discussion of problems with the implementation of policy, and the formulation of new policy, especially regarding the repartimiento system in America, were all matters carried out at the top of the colonial bureaucracy by the Consejo de Indias (Council of the Indies). The documentary record left behind will also help clarify not just how the system worked but also why so many officials defended it, and will reveal in surprising detail just how much the people at the top knew about the abuses of the colonial system. Like the appointment records, residencias, and inquests, these policy documents are to be found mostly or entirely in Spain, in the colonial archives where the Council of the Indies sent them in case they were needed for future consultation. Although some scholars have used these documents, no one has attempted thus far to employ them in a detailed analysis of the repartimiento system in colonial Central America.

It will therefore be left to a future monograph to combine both Spanish and Central American sources in a new whole providing an even broader understanding of one of the most important economic and political themes of the colonial era. This book has more modest aspirations. It will attempt to show that the sources used in this study can take historical understanding and historiographical discussion to a higher level, thereby preparing the way for future research.

It is obvious that any study of the repartimiento system revolves around the indigenous people of Spanish America. Consequently, despite all the discussions of bureaucracy, bureaucrats, policy, and imperial reform, this book is first and foremost about the indigenous people of what was known as the Kingdom of Guatemala (Central America without Panama but with Chiapas included). They were the backbone of the economy and made the repartimiento system work, and where it worked well, the repartimiento succeeded because it used already existing indigenous structures of production.

Unfortunately, although the indigenous economy will be central to the themes discussed in this book, it is not possible to provide many details of the Indian point of view regarding the repartimiento system or of Spanish colonial policy. It would of course be desirable to present the native voice to balance that of the Spanish bureaucrats and businessmen whose point of view can be studied. History, however, must be written on the basis of evidence, and the surviving documents do not often include the indigenous voice. They were not drawn up for that purpose. They were left behind by a bureaucracy interested in carrying out the goals of the colonial regime. To be sure, some documentation in indigenous languages does survive and has been used to provide an indigenous perspective on history. However, these sources tend to be mostly about village politics and indigenous property ownership. They tell us a lot about the native people that is not in the Spanish documents, and in the past two decades, scholars using native-language sources have produced a revolution in our understanding of Indians during the colonial era.[20] But such sources do not provide much of an idea of what the Indians thought about the colonial regime that ruled over them and exploited them.

Some evidence of the indigenous voice, however, is revealed in the colonial Spanish archives. On many occasions, the Indian people rebelled against their rulers. They did not leave behind them a paper trail in their own language that might have incriminated them. They were far too wise to do that. However, the Spaniards did try to gather incriminating evidence, and to do so, interrogated indigenous people implicated in the rebellions. One might think that records like this, drawn up precisely for the purpose of getting the Indians to incriminate themselves, would reveal very little of the indigenous perspective. However, in my previous book about Mayas in eighteenth-century Guatemala and Yucatan, I was able to demonstrate that such documentation in fact contains what James Scott has called a "hidden transcript," and that a close reading of interrogations and accompanying Spanish reports tells us a great deal about indigenous thinking about colonialism. On occasion, it even tells us something about what the Mayas felt about the repartimiento system.[21]

This hidden transcript shows, first, that the indigenous people largely accepted what scholars refer to as the moral economy: they resigned themselves to taxation and other forms of exploitation but only at agreed-upon limits. When the Spanish authorities surpassed those limits, rebellion sometimes resulted. The Indians took steps to reduce the level of agreed-upon exploitation when rumors abounded that the Spanish government in the colonial capital had taken steps to make it easier for them to pay their taxes. This, of course, would have made it unnecessary for them to accept repartimientos from their magistrates to pay their debts. When rumors such as this were rampant, the native people did indeed resist the exploitation carried out by their local corregidores or alcaldes mayores. They were, in a sense, renegotiating the terms of the moral economy.[22]

The revolts also reveal that the indigenous people accepted what can be called the moral polity: their leaders agreed to collect taxes and organize forced-labor drafts in return for Spanish recognition of the right of the Indians to govern themselves in their own villages. When Spanish authorities interfered with this indigenous political autonomy, once again rebellions sometimes resulted. Usually this happened when a corregidor or alcalde mayor interfered with village elections by trying to put into office people more willing to do his bidding. The very attempt to do this, in turn, reveals that the native elite were by no means always compliant. And one of the matters that frequently came up in these disputes was the payment of debts owed as a result of the repartimiento.[23]

Acceptance of the moral economy and polity did not mean, however, that the indigenous people resisted the demands of the colonial system only when those demands were arbitrarily increased. In reality, not all resistance was simply reactive. Sometimes the Indians themselves took the initiative and tried to renegotiate the terms of their acceptance of colonialism. People from some villages became known for being continually recalcitrant and uncooperative, and the Spanish noted their tendency toward being "troublemakers." The indigenous people sometimes objected to the forced labor being required of them and tried to get the state to lower the requirements. On at least one occasion villagers even burned the thread that they were supposed to deliver to their magistrate as part of their repartimiento debt. This was a sure sign that the repartimientos carried out by the magistrates were disliked and on occasion resisted.[24] The native people's voice was not heard, but actions revealed their thinking.

The records of revolts also show that indigenous women were often at the forefront of riots and rebellions. They were not asked for their opinion regarding the repartimiento system, which was based to a great extent on female labor, but they often pushed the men to take action in defense of their perceived rights. Spanish soldiers entering recalcitrant villages found themselves in unpleasant situations, for the native women sometimes tried to unhorse them or sprayed them with urine. Colonial authorities therefore found women to be especially troublesome, defiant, and insolent, even when on trial, and did not hesitate to have them whipped.[25]

At times the indigenous people even rejected their unequal status in the colonial regime and claimed to be the equal of Spaniards. When they had the chance, they humiliated Spanish magistrates and did their best to annoy them. They were adept at using what are called the "weapons of the weak" by never missing an opportunity to drag their feet, pretend not to understand what was being demanded of them, insist that unwanted orders be put in writing (both to annoy and to delay the Spaniards), and sabotage the government's efforts to reestablish order in other jurisdictions. They sometimes even demonstrated a remarkable degree of solidarity with other indigenous villages—if not all, then at least with those speaking the same language. Consequently, although the native voice was rarely heard, native actions sometimes spoke louder than words.[26]

All of this helps debunk one of the great myths of colonial history: that Spanish colonialism was like a steamroller that smashed everything in its path and shaped the indigenous people's economy and society to serve its exploitative, and frequently extractive, interests.[27] To be sure, colonialism was destructive both physically and culturally. However, scholarship has also demonstrated the dynamism, vitality, and creativity of the indigenous people under colonial rule.[28]

This indigenous agency had historical significance. It meant that Spanish colonialism, far from overwhelming everything like a steamroller, had to adapt to the nature of indigenous society. One of the main themes of this book is the process of adaptation through which the colonizer learned to take advantage of already existing structures of production that were part of Indian civilizations. That meant that where indigenous society had a productive economy, Spanish colonialists learned to exploit it. But where the Indian economy was unproductive, the indigenous people were useless as producers, and the Spaniards had to introduce new structures of production. Thus, from the Spanish point of view, regardless of racist ideas, not all Indians were alike. Some were worth more than others and were worth preserving. The Spanish could not easily transform people who were unproductive and close to subsistence into surplus-producers. This had important implications for the survival of Indians in America. It demonstrates that for the Spanish colonists, indigenous society was a factor to which they had to adapt. What they did, in short, depended to a great extent on what they found.

Another factor that required adaptation on the part of the colonial regime was geography. This will also be a major theme of this book. Scholarship has demonstrated convincingly that geographical factors shaped and sometimes determined the historical development of colonial society.[29] The repartimiento, based on indigenous labor, and one of the key colonial mechanisms for adapting to the already existing indigenous economy, also demonstrates the interaction between colonialism and geography. Cattle, sheep, wheat, and sugar—all of Old World origin—could not be raised everywhere in the Kingdom of Guatemala. Cattle raising was the most widespread, but it was sometimes squeezed out by certain kinds of profitable agriculture. This was reported in 1770 in San Salvador, where increased output of indigo came at the expense of cattle raising and cheese production.[30] Some areas could produce wheat better than others, and sheep prospered in some regions but not in others. Geography also affected production of the important native crops like cotton, cacao, and indigo. Cotton could be grown in most provinces but not in all. Cacao and indigo were limited mostly to the warm and sometimes tropical lowlands. So, too, was production of sisal fiber, extracted in Yucatan from *henequén* and in Nicaragua from *cabuya*.

Finally, gold and silver were largely absent in Central America except for parts of what is now Honduras. This lack of precious metals undoubtedly helped save the Indians from the horrors connected to mining in colonial Peru, for it is impossible to believe that the Spanish government would not have implemented a massive forced labor system like the Andean *mita* if rich deposits of gold or silver had been found in Central America. Even so, the silver economy of Honduras affected the development of the Kingdom of Guatemala in a variety of ways, as will be shown. But the Spanish, although in possession of advanced mining technology, could not create a mining economy where no gold or silver existed. Like the indigenous people, geography was something that could not be made to conform to the desires of the Spaniards. The Spanish colonists adapted to geography because they could not force the geography to adapt to them; what they found determined what they did. By adapting, the Spaniards exploited the resources available and then created a wide network of trading relationships that linked practically all of the regions of the kingdom to each other as well as to the world economy. The repartimiento, as will be shown, was one of the major mechanisms for accomplishing the economic integration of local, regional, and international markets; systems of labor; and geographically diverse environments.

Still another factor affecting the development of colonial Spanish America was disease. Once again, although the Spanish invaders brought diseases with them, they had no control over the results. All over America, indigenous people died by the millions from new diseases. In Central America, the same was true. As time went by, however, the people in the highlands tended to survive better than those in the lowlands, for once tropical diseases became endemic, the indigenous people in lower altitudes did not easily recover from decline. In many places, they continued to decline in number until the very end of the colonial period.

All of this had important historical implications. The Spanish could organize the large highland populations through the repartimiento system, but could do little with existing structures of production where there were few people to exploit. New structures, such as sugar plantations, could be introduced, but they had to rely almost entirely on non-indigenous labor. As a result, some areas imported African slaves and developed mixed-race populations while others could not afford to do so. The latter areas—Escuintla (on the southern Pacific coast of Guatemala) and Costa Rica being the best examples— therefore would be affected hardly at all by the repartimiento. They were also undesirable locations from the Spanish point of view, and thus had few Hispanic immigrants or settlements. The disease environment, like geography, could not be changed to fit the wishes of the colonial rulers. Once again, colonialism was limited by factors beyond Spanish control.

Thus, colonial history, far from being merely the story of Spanish abuse, was a complicated interplay of human, geographical, and pathogenic factors. The repartimiento was affected by these factors and reflected their importance. As a result, the history of the rise and decline of the repartimiento will reveal many of the inner workings of Spanish colonialism in America. At the same time, it will provide evidence of the indigenous response—including resistance— to the colonial project that resulted from the Spanish invasion of Central America.

CHAPTER 1

PEOPLE AND TAXES IN THE EIGHTEENTH CENTURY

At the heart of the colonial economy and of the colonial system were the indigenous people, conquered by the Spanish and incorporated into the world economy through the mechanisms of colonialism. The demographic decline of the Indians had contributed to decreased production of Central America's exports in the sixteenth century, and demographic stagnation restrained all efforts to increase economic growth in the following century.[1] It is to be expected, therefore, that the indigenous demographic expansion of the later colonial period— perhaps from the 1680s on—would contribute to economic growth in the eighteenth century, and this was indeed the case. The Indians made up the great majority of the population, and they were, first and foremost, the major producers of goods they and the entire colonial society consumed. They were also, of course, the major source of labor for enterprises run by the Hispanic elite and by an increasing number of other non-Indians in Central America. Almost all economic activity, therefore, depended in one way or another on the Indians.

I

Overall population statistics are scarce, of dubious quality, and contradictory (see appendices). The most important source is the count of tributaries, but the value of this source is diminished by the changing definition of tributary. Before 1756 all adult Indian males and females

Map labels:

Gulf of Mexico

Caribbean Sea

YUCATAN

TABASCO
New Spain
Tacotalpa

UNEXPLORED

Ciudad Real
CHIAPA

VERAPAZ

Puerto Caballos
Trujillo

SOCONUSCO
GUATEMALA

Comayagua-Honduras

Pacific Ocean

Santiago

Comayagua
Tegucigalpa
TEGUCIGALPA

UNEXPLORED

San Salvador
SAN SALVADOR
Sonsonate
San Miguel

Gulf of Fonseca

Leon
Lake Managua
Realejo

Granada
Lake Nicaragua

COSTA RICA
NICOYA

1. VALLEY OF GUATEMALA
2. CHIQUIMULA DE LA SIERRA
3. ATITLÁN (SOLOLÁ)
4. HUEHUETENANGO-TOTONICAPÁN
5. QUEZALTENANGO
6. SUCHITEPÉQUEZ
7. ESCUINTLA-GUAZACAPÁN
8. SONSONATE
9. SUTIABA
10. REALEJO
11. SÉBACO-CHONTALES
12. NICARAGUA

0   100   200 Mi.
0   100   200   300   Km.
N

Kingdom of Guatemala: Political Jurisdictions

18

were counted as tributaries. After 1756 only Indian males were counted.[2] Then, in 1788, mulattoes and free blacks were included in the count.[3] The numbers of the latter two were quite small in the Central American highlands outside of the capital city of Santiago de Guatemala, and thus tributary counts for the highlands continued to be mostly the enumeration of Indians. In the lowlands, however, there were more blacks and mulattoes and thus their inclusion as tributaries greatly dilutes the proportion of Indians. Nevertheless, the overall trend is clear.[4] The number of tributaries and the resulting estimated Indian population in what are now Guatemala, Chiapas, and El Salvador before 1756 are as follows:

Table 1.1

NUMBER OF TRIBUTARIES AND ESTIMATED POPULATION IN
GUATEMALA, CHIAPAS, AND EL SALVADOR BEFORE 1756

Year	Tributaries	Estimated indigenous population
1687	79,645	318,500
1720	87,056	348,200
1746	91,123	364,500

After 1756, the figures are as follows:

Table 1.2

NUMBER OF TRIBUTARIES AND ESTIMATED POPULATION IN
GUATEMALA, CHIAPAS, AND EL SALVADOR AFTER 1756

Year	Tributaries	Estimated population
1770	94,668	435,500 (Indians only)
1773	90,543	416,500 (Indians only)
1797	97,024	446,300
1803	91,402	420,449

Data analyzed by other scholars suggest that in 1750, what is now Guatemala, minus the capital city, had a total Indian population of 154,517 and a non-Indian population of 10,786 (that is, 6.5 percent of the total). The two groups together therefore numbered 165,303. The areas with the largest proportion of non-Indians were Chiquimula,

Quezaltenango, and Chimaltenango, with the largest concentrations of non-Indians found in Chiquimula (with 39.7 percent of the non-Indians), Los Amatitanes (23.6 percent), and Quezaltenango (14.8 percent). The total population was officially 361,204 in 1778 and 365,178 in 1800.[5]

The rest of the kingdom's population was also increasing. The four jurisdictions in what is now Nicaragua (Sutiaba, Matagalpa or Sébaco-Chontales, Realejo, and Nicaragua) and the two jurisdictions of Honduras (Tegucigalpa and Comayagua-Honduras) saw their tributary populations grow as follows:

Table 1.3
NUMBER OF TRIBUTARIES AND ESTIMATED POPULATION IN
NICARAGUA AND HONDURAS, 1773 AND 1797

	Year	Tributaries	Estimated population
Nicaragua	1773	7,351	33,800
	1797	11,573	53,200
Honduras	1773	6,018	27,700
	1797	7,194	33,100

In the case of Nicaragua, however, the sharp increase in numbers is due to the inclusion in the statistics of blacks and mulattoes, who made up a large part of the population. These people were also very significant in Honduras.

The work of other scholars sheds considerable light on the eighteenth-century population of Central America south of Guatemala. In San Salvador in 1798, Spaniards and other non-Indians numbered 69,836 (51.21 percent) and Indians 66,515 (48.78 percent). In 1807, the total of non-Indians was 94,103 (57 percent) and the Indians were 71,175 (43 percent). The Indian presence was inexorably diminishing in what is now El Salvador. In modern-day Nicaragua, the story was the same. By 1776, when the total population reached some 103,943, non-Indians outnumbered indigenous people in all provinces.[6] The situation was even more marked in Honduras, where by 1777, mulattoes, blacks, mestizos, and Spaniards made up 80 percent of the population. Only nine years later, however, the statistics showed a total adult population of 65,008, with the Indian population

35.2 percent of the total.[7] An 1804 report gave the total population as 127,620. Of these, 35,392 (28 percent) were Indians, almost half of whom lived not in villages but on Spanish haciendas or in mining camps.[8] Village Indians had become a small minority.

Finally, Costa Rica stood out as the least Indian province in the kingdom. Population figures are almost nonexistent, because for most of the colonial period the indigenous population was exempt from tribute, and some of the estimates are difficult to believe, given what is known about the rest of the kingdom.[9] More credible estimates suggest that in 1700 the Spanish and mestizo population numbered almost 3,000, and that there were only 2,252 Indians under Spanish control.[10] In 1803 the total number of Indian tributaries was 328, which would have meant an indigenous population of about 1,500 people subject to the colonial regime.[11]

An important factor having an impact on the population of the Kingdom of Guatemala was the great pandemic of smallpox that hit the North American British colonies in 1775 and soon spread to Central America.[12] One scholar has declared this to have been "the major epidemic of the century" in the kingdom.[13] In the 1780s, smallpox killed 10 percent of the population in Honduras, 9 percent of the Indian population of Nicaragua, and more than ten thousand Indians, about one-third of the population, of the highland Guatemalan province of Los Amatitanes-Sacatepéquez, in the Valley of Guatemala.[14] These provinces seem to have lost the most people to the epidemic, but the scarcity of records means that other areas might have suffered just as much. Without smallpox, population counts everywhere would have been higher. Eventually, of course, ideas and science concerning disease also arrived in Central America and mitigated the demographic impact of epidemics. By the 1790s, knowledge of the smallpox vaccine was available, and the first inoculations began no later than 1795 on the orders of President Bernardo Troncoso. In 1803 the royal government printed and distributed throughout the kingdom a quantity of pamphlets informing the people about the invention of the smallpox vaccine.[15]

Of course, there were local or regional variations in a process that was never the same everywhere. In what is now Chiapas, the highland *alcaldía mayor*, or high magistracy, of Chiapa witnessed significant growth, while the lowland province of Soconusco saw a population decline. There was also a significant decline in the two Pacific coastal provinces of San Antonio Suchitepéquez and Escuintla. This strongly suggests that the whole northwestern Pacific coast of the kingdom suffered from significant incidence of tropical disease, although the smallpox pandemic of the 1770s and 1780s may also have played a role. Demographic expansion was substantial in the four Guatemalan highland provinces of Quezaltenango, Huehuetenango, Atitlán, and Verapaz despite the impact of smallpox. The population ostensibly increased in the jurisdictions of San Salvador and Sonsonate (together forming modern-day El Salvador), even though both of those provinces were located to a great extent in a tropical or semitropical environment. Indeed, San Salvador, on paper at least, had the largest demographic expansion in the entire kingdom. However, this is to a certain extent an illusion, for much of the increase was undoubtedly not growth at all but just the result of counting the mulatto and black populations as tributaries when they had been excluded before. The indigenous population of El Salvador may actually have declined. The lack of good information leaves this issue unresolved.

In the highland Valley of Guatemala, the two provinces of Chimaltenango and Los Amatitanes experienced demographic growth during the first half of the eighteenth century. However, the greater population density of the area made the people more susceptible to epidemic disease, and this proved mortal in the second half of the century. The smallpox pandemic hit especially hard in Amatitanes.

On balance, nevertheless, the indigenous population as a whole was increasing in most parts of the kingdom. The general trend toward demographic expansion, interrupted by occasional epidemics, helped lay the basis for the increased production and availability of labor that made economic growth possible. As a result, Bourbon Central America—that is, the Kingdom of Guatemala in the eighteenth century—experienced significant economic expansion and capital accumulation. From the point of view of many people then and now, therefore, the Bourbon era was a time of prosperity.[16]

It is important to note that while the indigenous population was increasing overall during the eighteenth century, the non-Indian population was increasing at an even more rapid rate, not just in El

Salvador, Honduras, and Nicaragua, but also in Guatemala. It was not the result of urbanization, for the total population of the capital city, Santiago, did not grow significantly during the first three quarters of the century, and neither did its non-Indian population.[17] Growth therefore took place elsewhere, in rural areas and in the smaller urban centers such as Quezaltenango, which benefited from the influx of many weavers who fled the capital after the earthquake of 1773. The kingdom's non-Indian population had been growing for some time, but this surge was not officially recognized, as the law prohibited anyone but Indians from living in the villages. Nevertheless, despite the law, the non-Indian population living in the villages, especially in the important ones, was growing. It was also growing on landed estates. Eventually, many of these people wanted to establish legally recognized settlements. In the last third of the eighteenth century, the government began to legalize a number of towns—*villas*—for the non-Indians. Some of these had already been in existence and were simply recognized at this time, while others were new settlements altogether.[18]

Increasingly, the people in these settlements were called *ladinos*. The word *ladino* had originally been used to refer to an Indian who could speak Spanish. Eventually the term was extended to non-Indian Spanish-speakers as well, although in the colonial period it never included the Spanish or creole (American-born Hispanic) population.[19]

II

Although the growing population stimulated economic development because of greater demand for goods, internal factors were not alone in contributing to economic growth. External demand for the goods of Central America resulted in increased production for export. Silver continued to be exported from Tegucigalpa and Comayagua-Honduras, and production increased dramatically after 1724, when the government lowered taxes on production and on mercury (a chemical element that when mixed with silver ore resulted in increased output) and acted to provide more forced labor for the mines. Many indigenous communities in Honduras were forcibly relocated to the mining camps, and increased numbers of Indians from the *corregi-miento* of Chiquimula de la Sierra, in northeastern Guatemala, were involuntarily recruited and sent to Honduras. The corregidor of Chiquimula de la Sierra accomplished this by paying the tribute debts of the Indians and then requiring them to pay off their debt to him by working in the silver mines of the neighboring province. The magistrate who was most successful in rounding up workers was rewarded by receiving first a rare reappointment to his position, and then a new appointment as governor of Nicaragua with promotion to the rank of colonel.[20]

In other parts of Guatemala, criminals were sentenced to work in the mines along with the Indians at one-quarter the wages paid to the ostensibly free indigenous workers. Positive steps to attract workers were also taken, for the crown agreed to exempt Indian mine-workers from tribute. These steps produced quick results. Within twenty-five years the number of silver mines increased from one to seven, while two new gold deposits began to be worked. Registered silver output rose from 136,715 pesos in 1733 to 327,750 in 1739. Production thereafter declined significantly because frequent wars cut the industry off from the supply of mercury, and the labor supply continued to be insufficient. By the 1750s, average annual production had declined to 166,388 pesos.[21] Thus, after an initial bonanza in the mid-eighteenth century, which certainly stimulated the region's economy, stagnation returned and remained characteristic of the silver economy throughout the rest of the colonial period.

Cacao had been the most important Central American export in the sixteenth century, but production had fallen off drastically by the end of that century. The most important producing areas were Sonsonate, Soconusco, and San Antonio Suchitepéquez, and secondarily parts of Nicaragua and Costa Rica.[22] The demand for cacao was greater than the supply, and in fact quantities were being imported into Central America from Guayaquil and Caracas in the seventeenth century. The city council of the capital fretted about these imports competing with Central American cacao in the important market of New Spain.[23] In the eighteenth century there was a decrease in production in Suchitepéquez, in part because the Indians of the region were no longer required to pay their tribute in cacao.[24] Meanwhile, production was increasing in Nicaragua, where haciendas rather than indigenous peasants accounted for the most output.[25] The same was true in the cacao-producing region along the Caribbean coast of Costa Rica, which had witnessed significant growth in the late seventeenth century. But labor shortage in the latter region continued to plague the industry because of the small number of Indians who could be forced to work for the Spanish landowners. The cacao haciendas of Costa Rica therefore were dependent on imports of African slaves,[26] but these were not sufficient in quantity to result in extensive growth of production. With all these obstacles, cacao therefore could not serve as the driving force behind commercial expansion and exports in the last century of colonial rule.

By far the most important export crop of the Kingdom of Guatemala in the eighteenth century was indigo. The dyestuff had a long history in Central America and had been exported to Europe since shortly after the Spanish invasion. But the labor shortage that afflicted all branches of the economy also had an impact on indigo production, which stagnated in the seventeenth century. Production apparently began to pick up in the late seventeenth and early eighteenth centuries, precisely when the population began to increase. Exports of indigo through Honduras and from the Guatemalan Caribbean coast continued to stagnate, according to government records, and during the first half of the eighteenth century, shipping into and out of those traditional areas sometimes ceased altogether. But this does not mean that the economy as a whole, or indigo production in particular, was stagnant, for a considerable quantity of smuggling not included in official statistics went on along the Honduran coast. Governors of Honduras and merchants from Guatemala shamelessly engaged and invested in smuggling. Just as importantly, however, exports overland to New Spain (Veracruz and Puebla) and by sea to Peru and Cuba expanded. Much of this was in the form of indigo, which was greatly in demand not only in Europe but also in the textile industries of Mexico and Peru. The exports also included Guatemalan textiles; Guatemalan merchants frequently entered into commercial deals with local magistrates to gain access to cotton cloth to sell in New Spain. Overall, then, the Central American economy was recovering from its seventeenth-century slump even before the indigo boom that was so notable after 1750.[27]

The increase in indigo production took place mostly in the area around San Salvador, which became far and away the most important center for the industry for the remainder of the colonial period.[28] By the middle of the eighteenth century, indigo was transforming the commercial export economy and making an important impact on the kingdom's internal commerce as well. The *consulado* (merchant guild) of Guatemala later estimated that in the late eighteenth century, the value of internal trade in indigo totaled four and a half million pesos, while exports were valued at three and a half million.[29] Indigo production and trade had important social and economic effects throughout Central America.

One of the most important of those effects was the economic stimulation of other regions of the kingdom. As a direct result of the demands of the indigo industry, and indirectly, of the Honduran mining industry, more and more land and labor in the province of San Salvador were taken out of production of food, cotton, and cotton clothing and diverted to producing the dye. Similarly, in Honduras, entire villages of Indians were moved closer to the silver mines and ended up abandoning production of some subsistence goods. The concentration on indigo and silver was possible only because other sources of supply became available. The livestock economy of Nicaragua expanded to meet the growing demand for meat in San Salvador.[30] The demand for cotton clothing was so great that production of cotton was stimulated in the Pacific coastal lowlands of Suchitepéquez and in Verapaz, located in the middle altitudes of northern Guatemala. Meanwhile, production of cotton textiles for San Salvador and Honduras was stimulated all over the highlands, and even resulted in the importation of cheap cloth all the way from China.[31]

Increased production of cotton, cotton cloth, and cattle was therefore a backward linkage of increased production of indigo and silver. It was the result of regional specialization: the areas that emphasized exports could do so only because other areas were able to provide them with what was needed to survive. In this way, most of the indigenous people of the Kingdom of Guatemala were tied into the world economy indirectly by being tied into the kingdom's economy directly. Indigenous production therefore remained the sine qua non of the colonial regime.

The reverse side of the export economy was the flow of imports from Europe, South America, and Asia. The most valuable goods were those brought from Europe. Sometimes these were made or produced in Spain, which shipped wine, olive oil, iron tools, and paper to its colonies. Luxury textiles of silk, wool, and linen were also shipped from Spain but were usually of non-Spanish origin, having been manufactured in France, Great Britain, the Low Countries, Italy, and Germany.[32] Some goods came in legally through the Guatemalan and Honduran ports on the Caribbean (Puerto Caballos, Santo Tomás, and Trujillo). Others were smuggled in through the coast of Mosquitia, Honduras.

The merchants who controlled Central America's imports and exports also wanted to be able to bring in goods from Peru, although the crown had prohibited such trade in the 1620s. In 1659 the Santiago city council supported the request for legalization of trade with Peru, which went on despite prohibition and consisted mostly of exports of indigo and imports of wine.[33] Once it had become clear that Spanish production was insufficient to provide the Kingdom of Guatemala with wine, which was necessary for Mass as well as for ordinary consumption, the crown legalized trade with Peru in 1680. Central America was permitted to import wine and olive oil from Peru up to the value of two hundred thousand ducats or up to forty thousand casks of wine. But in 1713 the crown once again banned such trade in an attempt to protect the Andalusian producers who they hoped would monopolize the market. This step almost resulted in riots, and the government therefore chose not to enforce the law.[34]

It had also been a long-standing desire of Central American merchants to import goods from China. The first known request to do so was made by the Santiago city council in 1575, and permission was granted temporarily in 1590.[35] In this way, Guatemala got some access to the luxury silk and porcelain being carried across the Pacific from Manila to Acapulco on the famous *Nao de Manila* (Manila ship—usually mistranslated as the Manila galleon). Then, trade with China was officially made illegal, but it was carried on anyway throughout the eighteenth century by large-scale merchants in Mexico City who controlled access to the luxuries from Asia.[36] The nature of that trade changed, however, in the last half of the century, when cheap, light cotton textiles became the most important goods from China sold in Central America. This cloth was for consumption not by the colonial elites but by the urban poor and by those who worked on the indigo plantations of San Salvador and in the mines of Tegucigalpa.[37]

The Guatemalan merchant community frequently requested permission to establish a commercial corporation to stimulate commerce. One such request emphasized commerce with Peru.[38] Another petition to the crown in 1756 sought authorization for the establishment of a commercial corporation to increase Central America's trade with Europe, South America, and Asia. This latest effort was a response to a new policy introduced by the crown: the stimulation of the economy of Catalonia. In 1747 the crown had authorized Catalan merchants to import raw cotton duty-free from Guatemala for four years and thus provide industrialists with the material needed for making cotton textiles.[39] The government then authorized Catalans to send ten *registros*—individual ships, outside of the normal fleet system (which consisted of convoys sent exclusively to Cartagena and Veracruz)—to bring cloth to the Kingdom of Guatemala. Guatemalan merchants soon found that Catalans were becoming dominant in the trade between Central America and Spain, and to counteract this they formed a commercial corporation.

The founders of the corporation requested that their company be given a monopoly on trade between Spain and the Kingdom of Guatemala (thereby eliminating the Catalan competition, although that was unmentioned). They also wanted permission to trade with Havana and directly with New Spain, by land or by sea, to ship indigo, *achiote* (annatto, a spice and food dye), and bales of textiles to the viceroyalty to the north. Furthermore, the merchants wanted to be permitted to import cloth from China, cacao from Guayaquil, and various goods from Peru. They planned to export to South America spices, glass, and pottery, not only from Guatemala but also from Japan. Drinking-water on the ships was to be kept in barrels, which the government would promise not to inspect (thereby permitting smuggling, although that also was unmentioned). In return, the company would agree to provide the trading posts in the mines with tools and cloth worth fifty thousand pesos per year to stimulate silver production. It would also ship mercury, Bulls of the Crusade (indulgences for sale in America), and stamped paper, for official and legal use, free of charge from Spain, arm their ships (apparently without cannons) with one hundred rifles, provide a fully equipped ship to be used by corsairs, and build a road to the new Spanish fort of Omoa on the northern Honduran coast. The company would be capitalized with one million pesos from the sale of commercial shares at five hundred pesos each. Yet, despite endorsement by the *audiencia* and by two presidents, the proposal was never approved.[40]

Nevertheless, the commerce of the Kingdom of Guatemala became an important part of Spanish imperial trade. Between 1747 and 1761 the value of exports to Spain of staples (that is, excluding precious metals) averaged 1.6 million pesos annually. This compares favorably with exports from the viceroyalties of New Granada and Peru, which sent staples valued at one million pesos each, and was more than half of the three million pesos from New Spain.[41] Moreover, when in the 1770s war with Great Britain drastically reduced the Spanish colonies' trade with Spain, Guatemalan indigo became even more important because, unlike cacao, it could be stored for a long period of time. It was therefore in great demand in Mexico City by merchants, who warehoused it while waiting for the opportunities that would emerge once the war had ended.[42] The Kingdom of Guatemala was also important enough to be favored in the reforms introduced for the purpose of breaking the monopoly of the consulados of Mexico City and Cádiz, for the crown eventually authorized the establishment of the Consulado of Guatemala. This was set up in 1793 and continued its activities long after independence.[43]

The Spanish government played a significant role in shaping economic development in the eighteenth century. Realizing that many branches of the economy were stagnant, the new Bourbon dynasty, which took power after the death of the last Hapsburg king in 1700, pursued policies designed to stimulate economic growth. A major goal of these measures was to increase royal revenues by encouraging commercial expansion.[44] The Bourbon monarchs also introduced political changes to root out corruption, improve administrative efficiency, increase Spain's control over its overseas possessions, and once again raise revenues. All of these policies regarding the eighteenth-century economy, commerce, and politics became known as the Bourbon Reforms. As we shall see, some of these policies were successful, others were failures, and most were contentious.[45]

III

The overriding importance of the economy of the indigenous people was recognized early in the colonial period. Indian production was the basis of the *encomienda* system, which was the primary way in which a surplus was extracted from the conquered or subject people and delivered to the Spanish conquistadors as a reward for their services to the crown.[46] An encomienda at first was a grant to a private individual—either a conquistador or someone with a good deal of political influence—of the right to demand forced labor and goods from the Indians. By the second half of the sixteenth century, this had been reduced to the right to demand goods and money, which became increasingly common as the economy became more and more monetized. Payments were called tribute.

Until the late colonial period, Indian males between the ages of eighteen and fifty and females between eighteen and fifty-five were required to pay tribute. In practice, this worked out in most places to payments in money or kind worth two pesos per year. Officials in the indigenous village government and people engaged in important work for the Church were exempt.[47] Once the crown had succeeded in taking control of tribute throughout the kingdom by abolishing the encomiendas, a process begun in the sixteenth century and largely complete by the early eighteenth century,[48] the Indians no longer paid goods and money to individuals but to the king's representatives in America.

Although the government acted quickly in the sixteenth century to deprive *encomenderos* (the recipients of encomiendas) of the right to extract labor from the indigenous people, forced labor was by no means ended. On the contrary, it continued under a new name, the *repartimiento de indios* (draft of Indian labor) and was placed under government control.[49] Unlike in New Spain, where the repartimiento of agricultural labor (but not mine labor) was ended in 1632, in Central America it lasted, with varying intensity, for the entire colonial period. The repartimiento de indios consisted mostly of grants of short-term laborers to a landowner for agricultural work, although it was also used on so-called public works. In the provinces of Chiquimula de la Sierra and Tegucigalpa, Indians were forced to work for low wages in the mining industry. In many cases, the labor draft resulted in the requirement for a specific village to provide a certain number of workers for short-term work on a specific hacienda or haciendas. For example, during an inquest in 1720 it was revealed that the Indians of the villages of San Cristóbal Amatitan and San Juan Amatitan, in the central valley, each were required to provide twenty workers to the nearby wheat farm (*labor de panllevar*) of Barillas during the harvest season.[50]

This, however, was only what was owed to one farm, and no mention was made of possible obligations to other estates. Several inquests between 1670 and 1680 revealed that the seventy-seven villages in the Valley of Guatemala, which had a population of some seventy thousand people, were required to provide laborers every week (six days a week, no labor being required on Sundays and religious holidays) for the wheat-producing estates, the owners of which numbered between 94 and 110. Included among the estate owners were the Dominican, Augustinian, and Jesuit religious orders. The individuals who received the labor were all classified as Spanish, with the exception of one *indio ladino* (a Spanish-speaking Indian). No Indians were supposed to be sent to work on sugar estates, but in practice this rule was sometimes violated. In practice, one-fourth of all able-bodied men were required to work one week per month for an eight-month period, and during the month all able-bodied men ended up working in the wheat fields of the Spaniards. In some cases they were required to work one week during all twelve months of the year. For a day's work each Indian was paid one real, while the landowner had to pay a tax of one-half real to provide revenue to maintain the Spanish fort on the San Juan River in Nicaragua. Assuming the repartimiento de indios was limited to eight months, an Indian spent at least eight weeks of the year (or some forty-plus days, subtracting holidays) working for the Spanish landowner, as well as taking care of his own fields. The repartimiento de indios therefore absorbed between 15 and 20 percent of the peasants' labor. This was a heavy exaction indeed.[51]

Nevertheless, forced labor drafts were less onerous outside of the central Valley of Guatemala and in San Salvador, where there was increased need for labor on the indigo plantations. In most of the kingdom, tribute was the main burden that the colonial regime placed on the indigenous people.[52] One would expect the government to have paid the most attention to tribute, because, as one president put it in 1737, tribute was "the principal nerve that the Royal Treasury has in these Kingdoms, for it has more interest in this branch of revenue than in any other."[53] In the early eighteenth century, tribute accounted for 78.5 percent of royal income.[54]

However, as the century progressed, tribute declined in importance as other sources of revenue yielded greater quantities of money. Sales taxes (*alcabalas*) derived from commercial transactions grew as internal commerce and exports increased dramatically. Payments to the treasury resulting from silver production began to increase substantially in the 1740s and continued to grow even more rapidly in the 1750s, although silver mining started to decline in the next decade and stagnated for the rest of the century. Eventually, however, the tobacco monopoly (*estanco de tabaco*), established in 1765, became the most important of all sources of royal revenue. By 1805–1809, fully half of royal income was derived from the government control and sale of tobacco. Meanwhile, revenues from Indian tribute peaked in the 1740s and thereafter declined not only in importance but also in quantitative yield. By 1769, tribute accounted for only 32.2 percent of total royal income in the kingdom. By then it had been surpassed by sales taxes, which accounted for 39.2 percent.[55] By 1805–1809, tribute made up only 18.4 percent of royal income.[56] The importance of tribute would probably have been even lower had the government succeeded in introducing a rum monopoly. The crown tried this, but the measure proved so unpopular—it had led to large rebellions in South America—that the government eventually gave up.[57]

Tribute revenues overall declined once the government began to permit payment exclusively in cash rather than in cash and kind, as had been the case previously. Under the old system, the goods that

Indians were required to deliver in kind were assessed at sixteenth-century prices but resold at the higher prices of the eighteenth century, thereby resulting in more actual revenue for both the government and the magistrates in charge of tribute collection. This began to change in the 1740s, when the government gradually began enforcing a new law allowing the commutation of payments in kind to cash.[58] This had an important impact after 1756, when the government began to implement a kingdom-wide change that exempted women from tribute. This measure was expected to yield more revenue, because all males over the age of eighteen, not just those who were heads of families, were made subject to tribute. In reality, the fiscal gain was more than offset by the loss resulting when women no longer paid their share in resellable goods like thread and cloth. The overall result was the gradual decline in tribute revenues. The new policy that commuted all tribute to money payments had been introduced in order to reduce the exploitation of the indigenous people by the provincial magistrates. It apparently accomplished its goal; it was later reported that the economic interests of those officials who had formerly profited from the resale of tribute goods had been adversely affected.[59]

The extreme importance of tribute to royal finances during the middle colonial period explains why the crown, over and over again, allowed its magistrates to carry out repartimientos—business with the Indians—despite laws prohibiting them, and the decline of tribute in turn helps explain the crown's willingness to abolish the repartimientos. The justification of the alcaldes mayores and corregidores was always the same: it was the repartimiento that allowed tribute to be collected, and without the repartimiento, tribute would not be collected. The crown put a higher priority on tax revenues than it did on good government for almost all of the colonial period.

Tribute counts were supposed to be carried out every three years. However, in 1743 it was reported that in the case of the villages of the Valley of Guatemala, the counts were fifteen years old. In 1763 the chief official of the royal treasury charged with tribute collection complained that, according to his records, new counts had not been carried out in twenty or even thirty years in some places, while most tribute counts in use were eight years old.[60] In the same year of 1763 another report informed the crown that some villages in Chiapa had not had a recount since 1703, and in most provinces the most recent counts had been done before 1750.[61] Four years later, the curate of a village in the corregimiento of Chiquimula reported that a tribute count there had not been carried out for nineteen years.[62]

The problem of tribute collection led to political conflict. Normally, alcaldes mayores and corregidores were responsible for turning in the tax revenues, but the two alcaldes of the *cabildo*, or city council, of Santiago acted as magistrates in the wide area of the city's jurisdiction, which included the central Valley of Guatemala. Thus there were no royal magistrates to ensure tribute collection, and for decades it had been left in the hands of Indian village governors appointed by the president. However, in 1742 the president reorganized village government and abolished the position of governors. He then instructed the city's alcaldes to collect tribute as if they were alcaldes mayores or corregidores. This plan failed because the city officials could not possibly carry out tax collection on top of their other duties, and moreover, Santiago's alcaldes, unlike alcaldes mayores and corregidores, were not held personally responsible for tribute. Taxes fell into arrears. By 1751 the debt stretching back to 1715 totaled 223,832 pesos. Collecting back-taxes was said by Spanish officials to be impossible "because of the Indians' poverty and their inclination to liberty, laziness, and vice."[63]

To solve the problem, the president and the audiencia argued for the establishment of two new *alcaldías mayores* (high magistracies) that were to have jurisdiction over the Indians of the valley in order to collect tribute. However, since this would have taken power away from the city council, it vehemently resisted. This led to intense political conflict between an audiencia dominated by European Spaniards and a city council dominated by American Spaniards. The king eventually sided with the audiencia and authorized the establishment of the two new alcaldías mayores governed by magistrates who were responsible for tribute collection. This decision was a major irritant to the American-born elite for the rest of the colonial period.[64] But tribute collection at times took priority over other political concerns.

Tribute collection was never an easy task or an exact fiscal operation. A royal scribe in charge of keeping the records lamented in 1763 that

Indian government officials as well as Spanish alcaldes mayores always hid people to prevent them from being put on the rolls, collected taxes from those people anyway, and then kept the money for their own benefit. Some Indians took refuge on haciendas, where the landowners hid them to ensure a labor supply. In places like Chiapa and San Salvador, it was common for the same counts to be used over and over again without any attempt to carry out new ones.[65]

The government attempted on multiple occasions to come up with a better way to count the Indian population in order to tax them. In 1763 President Alonso Fernández de Heredia pointed out that the counts were supposed to be made by the alcaldes mayores and corregidores, but those magistrates did not get paid extra to carry out what was a very tedious task. Therefore, he pointed out what others before him had pointed out: the alcaldes mayores and corregidores normally just used the old counts, and if the population increased, they just collected from the new people and kept the money for themselves. The Indian village officials did the same. To avoid this and get an accurate count, the president introduced a new method. He appointed a new salaried official, the *apoderado del señor fiscal* (a person legally empowered to act in place of the *fiscal* of the audiencia), who carried out a new tribute count, completed in 1768 after Fernández de Heredia had left office. The result was a higher count, which of course meant more money for the crown. As a result, the next president in Guatemala, Martín de Mayorga, and the royal accounting office and the fiscal of the Consejo de Indias in Spain all reported favorably on the new method.[66]

Charles III, however, not informed of these good results, objected to the plan because it involved the appointment of a new official with a high salary. He therefore issued a *real cédula* (royal order) on December 7, 1776, that terminated the former president's innovation and ordered the audiencia to appoint one of its judges to carry out the new tributary count. Since the *oidor* (judge) appointed to do this was already receiving a salary, the king's plan would not cost the government any money. In Guatemala, the president and the audiencia objected to this idea, however, for the task of carrying out the count single-handedly by one official going from village to village would take ten years. The oidor so appointed would in effect be nothing but a tributary counter, leaving the court with one less judge at a time when its business was substantially increasing.[67] Good government, in short, once more would be given a lower priority than tax collection.

The king still did not like the plan that had just proved to be effective, and therefore in 1779 he suggested a compromise: instead of one judge being assigned to carry out the count, two or three should be assigned, thereby avoiding the necessity of paying a new official to do it. Once it was clarified that the tribute counts did not need to be done every three to five years, as President Fernández de Heredia had argued for, but only when the audiencia felt it necessary, agreement was reached.[68] The judges in effect did not have to carry out a count unless they wanted to. It turned out that they rarely, if ever, wanted to. Tribute counts and collection thus remained as sporadic and defective as always, despite a great deal of attention to the matter and the direct involvement of the king. On the other hand, the *oidores* thereafter devoted themselves to what they were trained for, the law, rather than to wandering around counting people who did their best to avoid being counted. Thus, in the end, tax collection did not take priority over good government.

Nevertheless, a good deal of thought was still being put into tribute collection, and in 1780 the idea emerged of making blacks, mulattoes, and mestizos, as well as those Indians theretofore exempt, subject to tribute. It was felt that the need to pay taxes would force these people to work more.[69] The proposal finally went into effect after the establishment of the intendancies in the late 1780s, although at the suggestion of the intendant of Nicaragua, Juan de Ayssa, the government refrained from calling the tax "tribute." Ayssa had politely pointed out that although the imposition of tribute was "most just," his knowledge of his province suggested that "perhaps it would be best not to push this point too much." Nicaragua was filled with an "exorbitant number of mulattoes" compared with the rest of the population, and this fact, as well as "their particular character, social relations, and ideas," made it imprudent to upset them, especially since they were necessary as militiamen for the defense of the province against marauding Carib Indians and of the Pacific coast as far south as

Panama. The colony, in short, depended on "the industry and dedication of these colonists."

The problem, Ayssa pointed out, was that "In this case it is not the impost itself but rather the term tribute that is odious to the mulattoes, because convinced as they are, although falsely, of the superiority of their class to that of the Indians, whom they judge for no good reason to be vile because of their status as tributaries, they are strongly offended by any appearance of equality between them."[70] In Spain, both the accounting office and the fiscal of the Consejo de Indias accepted the recommendation and thanked the intendant for his "wisdom." However, the government found it difficult to invent a euphemism, and so the new impost became just another tax.[71]

Tribute collection in some cases had to be suspended altogether because of natural disasters. If a disaster was significant, it was reported to officials in Spain for their approval of tribute relief. An outbreak of measles (sarampión) in 1743 caused the government to grant tribute relief to many villages in the Valley of Guatemala.[72] The same disease hit villages in Suchitepéquez shortly afterward, and the government responded in the same way.[73] An unidentified disease struck the village of San Juan Chamelco in highland Verapaz in 1761, resulting in tribute relief.[74] An epidemic of measles ravaged the village of Ostuncalco in Quezaltenango between 1772 and 1774, and as a result 941 Indians died. Among them were 326 of the village's 621 tributaries. The villagers were excused from paying tribute for an entire year.[75]

The measles epidemic seems to have died out during the last quarter of the century, but other diseases killed people by the thousands. In 1771 "plague" broke out in the Totonicapán section of the province of Huehuetenango-Totonicapán, and the villages of San Lorenzo Masatenango (which suffered the loss of more than 800 people), Santa Ana Malacatán, and Santa Bárbara Malacatán (130 and 342 fatalities, respectively) were badly affected and given tribute relief.[76] In 1774 the villages of San Mateo and Quezaltenango, in Quezaltenango province, and San Francisco el Alto, in Totonicapán, were also devastated by "plague." San Mateo, a small village, lost 22 of its 60 tributaries, while the large village of Quezaltenango lost 356 tributaries and a total of 459 adults.[77] In San Francisco El Alto, the death toll reached 310 tributaries and more than a thousand women and children. In the case of the latter village, tribute relief was not quickly forthcoming, for the alcalde mayor refused to reduce its payment, which in effect meant that the living were being asked to pay for the dead. Once the *apoderado del fiscal* had confirmed the number of deaths—which had increased since the first report—the crown granted tribute relief for all of 1775 and half of 1776.[78] Later in the century there were reports of tertian fever (*tercianas*, a variety of malaria) in the villages of Salamá, Rabinal, and Cubulco in Verapaz, and of a malignant fever—perhaps typhus—called *tabardillo* in Jocotán, Camotán, and San Juan Hermita in Chiquimula in 1801–1803. These outbreaks also resulted in tribute relief.[79] Many other eighteenth-century epidemics in the kingdom have been discussed by other scholars.[80]

The continent-wide pandemic of smallpox in the 1780s also resulted in requests for tribute relief. The government granted the devastated province of Comayagua-Honduras relief from the tax payment due at Christmas, and the village of Agualteca in particular was relieved of tribute for the whole year. Comayagua had only 5,121 tributaries before smallpox struck, so the epidemic guaranteed that the province would have a small population for some years to come. It also impeded the spread of Spanish control over the province, where the Xicaque Indians resisted the arrival of missionaries for fear of the spread of future contagions. In Spain, meanwhile, the king ordered that in the future, matters such as the epidemic in Los Amatitanes, which, as noted, killed more than ten thousand people, could be handled by the authorities in Guatemala, who should immediately lower tribute assessments and order a new count of tributaries. Thereafter, the audiencia did not have to request permission from Spain to grant tribute relief.[81]

Disease and epidemics were not the only forms of natural disasters. On October 8–9, 1762, there occurred what the audiencia reported to have been "one of the gravest of calamities and notable misfortunes that the inhabitants have suffered and experienced in the 242 years that have passed since the Conquest of this Kingdom." Torrential rains caused massive flooding and washed away the entire village of San Miguel Petapa in the alcaldía mayor of Los Amatitanes, Valley of Guatemala. The surviving villagers, among them a large number of ladinos, had to find a new site for their settlement, and to give them time to recover from the disaster, the audiencia granted them tax relief for two full years.[82] This eventually led to the establishment of an entirely new ladino settlement.[83] And in 1775 the village of San Juan Tecuaco, in Escuintla, suffered a fire that destroyed forty houses, as well as the maize stored inside, and then lightning sparked another fire that burned down the village church. The audiencia investigated and granted two years of tribute relief, which the fiscal of the Consejo de Indias, declaring those measures to be humane and wise, approved.[84]

Two other forms of natural disaster that wreaked havoc were earthquakes, for which Guatemala is famous, and locust plagues, which are less famous in history but nonetheless destructive. Earthquakes, of course, were always a threat. The big one of 1773, which forced the abandonment of Santiago and the founding of a new capital at modern-day Guatemala City, is well known.[85] But other major seismic events took place during the century. The great earthquake of 1717 caused so much damage to the capital that the authorities considered abandoning the site and founding a new capital elsewhere. It was decided, however, to stay put and rebuild. Thus Santiago had another fifty years of existence. The earthquakes of 1773 devastated not just the capital but other places in Guatemala as well. The province of Chiquimula was badly damaged, and not only did the government grant the village of San Juan Baptista Comalapan tribute relief for 1774, it eventually extended the relief for six more years to give the Indians more time to rebuild their shattered village.[86] The earthquake of October 14, 1774, that struck Honduras badly damaged the cathedral in Comayagua.[87] In 1775, Pacaya volcano erupted in the central Valley of Guatemala, causing the collapse of all the houses in the village of San Cristóbal Amatitanes. The audiencia granted the villagers relief from half their tribute payments for two full years to give them time to rebuild.[88]

Locust plagues occurred with considerable frequency in the second half of the century. They not only caused famines but also, less obviously, resulted in the large-scale destruction of the all-important indigo crop. That occurred, of course, only if the locusts afflicted El Salvador. Thus the terrible locust plague in Chiapa and in the newly created alcaldía mayor of Tuxtla between 1765 and 1770 did not affect the export economy but caused considerable damage to the maize crops and caused a local famine. Some small villages had to be abandoned; the survivors moved to larger settlements. The shortage of food was so extreme that the government granted a full year of tax relief to virtually all the villages in both Chiapa and Tuxtla.[89] At the same time, the locusts consumed the crops in three villages in Huehuetenango, and there the government granted the people two years of tax relief.[90]

More ominous from the government's point of view was the appearance of locusts in San Salvador at the same time as they were devastating the maize crops in Chiapa, Tuxtla, and Huehuetenango. No record of tribute relief has been found, but the impact on indigo production, and hence commercial taxes, was severe. It was later reported that between 1769 and 1771 most of the indigo plants were destroyed, and the alcalde mayor, who had loaned eighty thousand pesos to the indigo planters, could not collect any of the debts owed to him.[91]

The locust infestation of the late 1760s and early 1770s was part of a Mesoamerica-wide plague of locusts that affected people outside of Central America.[92] Recovery was swift, but in the late 1790s the locusts returned with a vengeance. Around 1797 a new infestation began and continued to afflict the region for more than eight years. Food shortages immediately resulted, and the president was compelled to take steps to "avoid the effects of famine which in another time . . . annihilated Chiapas," referring to the crisis of 1769–71. Wheat was imported from Chile, and tribute relief had to be provided to some villages. In Chiquimula, for example, villagers reported that the locusts had destroyed not only their maize but also their banana trees and other fruit trees and sugarcane fields.[93]

Needless to say, natural disasters disrupted life and hindered tax collection. Recovery from the earthquake of 1773 was long and drawn out, and the steps taken by the government sometimes caused even more disruption. Archbishop Pedro Cortés y Larraz bitterly opposed the decision to move the capital and abandon Santiago because it meant that debts to the Church in the form of liens on houses soon to be abandoned would lose all value.[94] Yet Indians were also affected by the decision to leave, because the president ordered not just the city but also its surrounding indigenous settlements (which the chief executive called *aldeas* as opposed to *pueblos*, the term commonly used to refer to Indian villages). This was done to ensure the new city an ample supply of *molenderas* (women who grind corn). It may not have occurred to any Spanish official that the Indians might not want to move. In fact, the villagers of Almolonga, Jocotenango, Utateca, San Felipe, and Pastores refused to move, claiming that if they did so they would end up without adequate common lands and would have to abandon their fruit trees. Archbishop Cortés y Larraz took the Indians' side and claimed that the alcalde mayor of Sacatepéquez, charged with carrying out the transfer of the people, had threatened to send mounted troops into the villages to cut down the trees and to use "powder and shot" to get the Indians to comply. The fiscal of the audiencia, however, ordered the move to go forward, noting that new trees could be planted at the new site, and in any case, the Indians could not be permitted to live in a dangerous location.[95]

Despite the mortality and disruption of life caused by epidemics, earthquakes, and locust plagues, the population of the Kingdom of Guatemala grew substantially in the eighteenth century. The increased population was the basis of the economic growth during the last century of colonial rule, and it created more commercial opportunities. Merchants, landowners, and tax collectors were all ready to get their share of the increased commercial prospects. At the same time, however, the nature of the economy and of the colonial system created opportunities for regional government officials. This led large numbers of office-seekers to request positions in Central America. Their commercial dealings with the indigenous people are the main theme of the rest of this book.

CHAPTER 2

Government Officials
and the Colonial State

Colonialism has been justified in the mind of colonial authorities
everywhere because it supposedly improves the life of the people
living under colonial rule. For the Spanish, this improvement meant
not just acceptance of the "one true religion," that is, Roman Catholi-
cism, but also the rule of law and the dispensation of justice. The
bureaucracy existed to implement the law, including, of course, laws
regarding taxation. But the colonial state was only as good as the
men who staffed the bureaucracy, and these men were real-life individuals, not bureaucratic abstractions. As a result, the colonial state
was characterized on the one hand by commitment to the improvement of the native people and to the rule of law, and on the other by
a bureaucracy staffed by people who pursued their own interests,
often contradictory to the state's abstract ideological goals. As a
result, the native people did not live in a state in which the law was
supreme, and they often suffered as a consequence. To understand
the contradictions of the colonial state, it will therefore be necessary
to analyze the individuals who staffed the bureaucracy and who lived
in a real, material world, rather than an idealistic one.

I

The bureaucracy that ruled the Kingdom of Guatemala grew slowly
during the first century of colonialism. By the late seventeenth century,

it had taken on the structure that would be maintained with only minor changes until the 1780s. The kingdom as a whole was governed by an *audiencia* (high court), located in the capital of Santiago de los Caballeros (modern-day Antigua, Guatemala) and composed of five oidores (judges), a fiscal (the equivalent of an attorney general in the United States or a king's counsel in England), and a president. A staff of trained lawyers served as clerks for the court and represented a pool of talent from which many future judges were drawn. Presidents almost never voted in audiencia proceedings because, with one exception, they were not trained lawyers. This was the situation since 1659, when in response to the threat of attacks by buccaneers, the crown had begun a policy of appointing a military officer rather than a lawyer as the chief executive officer and head of the audiencia. The president served as the governor of a large part of central Guatemala, and in that capacity he exercised considerable power. In addition, he held the temporary title and rank of captain general. Presidents were almost always professional soldiers with considerable experience, and as captain generals they commanded all military forces in the kingdom except for those under the command of the captain general in charge of the Honduran coast.[1]

The various Central American provinces were ruled by officials called governors, alcaldes mayores (high magistrates), and corregidores (magistrates).[2] These positions did not entail a chain of command; governors did not have corregidores or alcaldes mayores serving under them, for all three posts were the lowest-level salaried bureaucrats in the areas in which they served. Moreover, although one might think magistrates and high magistrates would aspire to a *gobernación* (governorship), in fact, as we shall see, few did, and few wanted to. Indeed, one of the fundamental characteristics of the Spanish imperial bureaucracy was the nonexistence of a ladder that anyone could ascend.

Gubernatorial positions entailed significant military duties, and consequently governors were appointed in those provinces where the threat of invasion or piracy was significant. Thus northern Honduras, southeastern Nicaragua (which guarded the San Juan River, the route of invasion from the Caribbean), Costa Rica, and Soconusco were all ruled by governors. The rest of the provinces were run either by alcaldes mayores or corregidores. Functionally, these two offi-cials were exactly alike; different titles existed because at the time of the creation of the posts, the provinces to which alcaldes mayores were assigned were considered to be of greater importance. As time went on, even this original difference between the two positions was largely forgotten, and in fact the terms "alcalde mayor" and "corregi-dor" became almost interchangeable. Frequently the crown itself was uncertain as to which kind of magistrate was to be posted to particular provinces. The only important difference between the two positions was that the salary of an alcalde mayor was usually twice that of a corregidor.[3]

In addition to the magistrates, a total of six officials of the royal treasury (Real Hacienda) served in the provinces. Honduras and Nicaragua each received two of these people, while Sonsonate and Costa Rica each received one. Also on the government payroll were several detachments of soldiers, stationed near Lake Nicaragua, and, once a fort had been constructed, at Omoa (on the Gulf of Honduras), to guard against pirates and invasion. All other salaried officials were posted to the capital, where they worked either for the royal treasury or for the audiencia.

Everyone else who worked for the government in the provinces was unsalaried. Each magistrate usually hired a secretary and one or more assistants, called *tenientes* (lieutenants), and paid for them out of his own pocket. However, precisely because these people were not salaried, they were not even considered to be members of the royal bureaucracy. They were hired and paid by the magistrates themselves and were therefore considered to be nothing but the henchmen of their employers.

The largest concentration of bureaucrats was found in the capital, where the audiencia and its staff were located and where the govern-ment had its treasury offices: the Real Hacienda (royal treasury) and the Tribunal de Cuentas (royal auditing agency). Also in Santiago were the Aduana (customs agency), the Correo Real (post office), and eventually the Real Moneda (royal mint) and the Real Renta de Tabaco (royal tobacco office, a state-run monopoly). Outside the capital, however, bureaucrats were few and far between. In the late seven-teenth century, a total of four governors, eight alcaldes mayores, six corregidores, and six treasury officials—twenty-four people in all— administered the kingdom's eighteen provinces. The detachments of soldiers in Honduras and Nicaragua were stationed in two of the least-populated provinces and in any case were concerned with foreign, rather than domestic, threats to security. The small size of the bureaucracy was maintained over time. In the 1740s only twenty-five officials—four governors, nine high magistrates, six magistrates, and six treasury employees—were sufficient to rule nineteen provinces. In the 1750s two more high magistracies were created, and one more in 1770. However, because one of the corregidor posts was simultaneously eliminated, salaried officials ruling over the twenty-one provinces still totaled only twenty-seven people as late as the 1770s. This study will concern itself almost entirely with the provincial officials, rather than those located in the capital, because the provincial magistrates were at once the executive officers and the judges who ruled directly over the vast majority of the population.

During the period of imperial reform under Charles III (1759–88), the size of bureaucracy in the kingdom increased somewhat. In the 1780s the crown created intendancies in what is now Chiapas (Chiapa, Tuxtla, and Soconusco), El Salvador, Comayagua-Honduras, and Nicaragua. Besides the intendant, each new intendancy in turn included a subordinate official called a *teniente letrado–asesor* (legal lieutenant and assessor), who was a trained lawyer.[4] That meant a total of eight new positions, although these were not at the lowest level, for other people were below the intendants. The crown left the corregimientos (magistracies) and alcaldías mayores (high magistracies) in Guatemala, as well as the one in Sonsonate, untouched. Costa Rica remained a gobernación. The establishment of the intendancies did not result in the elimination of the magistracies below them, for most of the already existing corregimientos and alcaldías mayores within the jurisdictions of these intendancies became what were known as *subdelegaciones* (subdelegations); the gobernaciones, in turn, were merged with the intendancies. A few new subdelegations were created (one in San Salvador, one in Nicaragua, and five in Comayagua-Honduras, the region with the smallest population and the greatest opportunities for smuggling). The number of lowest-ranking salaried officials within the royal bureaucracy thus reached thirty-two (twenty-six

magistrates and six treasury officials) in the last decades of the colonial period. What was new in the provinces with intendancies was
the addition of the eight new posts—intendants and tenientes letrados–
asesores—superior to the subdelegados.[5] Despite this expansion, the
bureaucracy running Central America in the late eighteenth century
was still extremely small by modern standards.

While the crown succeeded over time in maintaining a small state
apparatus, it was also successful in keeping down the salaries of
the officials who served the state. In the late seventeenth century,
the presidents earned 5,000 *escudos* (the equivalent of 5,000 pesos)
per year. This scale remained in effect until 1760, when the salary was
raised to 8,000 pesos.[6] The lower-level magistrates did not do nearly
so well. In the late sixteenth or early seventeenth century, governors
earned between 600 and 2,400 pesos annually,[7] and alcaldes mayores
earned between 331 and 800 pesos. The salaries of corregidores were
not even recorded because the latter officials were assigned an income
according to the whim of the president. Later, the Council of the
Indies in Spain established salaries for the lesser magistrates at a
level of about half that of the major ones. These pay scales were still
in effect when the Spanish monarchy passed from the Hapsburgs to
the Bourbons in 1700. Thereafter, some officials were given pay raises,
but most were not. In effect, as table 2.1 demonstrates, two of four
governors, five of nine alcaldes mayores, and all five corregidores
were being paid in the 1760s what their predecessors had been
paid—and in some cases even less than what their predecessors
had been paid—a century and a half earlier. When inflation is taken
into account, the crown in fact had lowered the real salaries of the
majority of its officials.

In the Kingdom of Guatemala, the Spanish crown thus enjoyed
considerable success in keeping the bureaucracy small and bureaucrats' salaries low. However, this does not mean that an effective
government was operating in the kingdom. On the contrary, the Bourbon monarchs eventually became so concerned over the defects of
the system of government that it chose to abandon the old policy of
the Hapsburgs and introduce a reform program involving a modest
expansion of the bureaucracy and a considerable increase in the salaries of some officials. This change was introduced because the costs

of the old system had come to outweigh the benefits. A clue to the nature of those costs is found in the willingness of prospective officeholders not only to accept extremely low salaries but even to pay for their offices.[8]

The sale of magistracies began in the 1670s, when the government of the last Hapsburg king, Charles II, introduced the measure in a desperate attempt to tap all possible sources of revenue. Technically, of course, the offices were not sold; a post was granted to a worthy subject who had performed what was euphemistically called a "monetary service" for the crown. The appointment was called a *beneficio* (benefit), and unlike positions in the royal treasury, post office, mint and audiencia, it was not a lifetime appointment but for a specific term of office.[9] A president was to serve for eight years, while governors, alcaldes mayores, and corregidores had five-year terms. "Benefits"—a euphemism for the sale of office—also differed from outright sales of offices in that the offices so granted included the power of jurisdiction, that is, the right to dispense justice. Nevertheless, since the granting of a "benefit" was made in return for money (or something else of value), I shall refer to the procedure as the sale of office.

The granting of the posts of president, governor, alcalde mayor, and corregidor was directly related to the crown's need to raise money for wartime expenditures. Consequently, when Spain was at peace, the crown stopped granting "benefits" and began giving the posts away to veteran soldiers as rewards for valor and as compensation for bodily injury received in His Majesty's service. The disguised sale of offices thus ceased in peacetime, even in the latter years of the reign of Charles II. But unfortunately for those who wanted to improve the honesty of government officials, Spain in the seventeenth and eighteenth centuries was frequently at war. As a result, offices were more commonly sold than given away. At one point or another, all royal offices were up for sale. This included that of president–captain general, a post sold to Jacinto de Barrios Leal in 1686 for 80,000 pesos, thereby making the post of president of the Audiencia of Guatemala the most expensive presidency in the Spanish empire.[10] In the following century, the post was resold at least two more times. First, in 1711 Francisco Rodríguez de Rivas, an officer with thirty-two years of service in the Spanish Navy, paid 4,500 doubloons (the equivalent

Table 2.1

SALARIES OF PROVINCIAL MAGISTRATES IN THE
KINGDOM OF GUATEMALA, 1673–1797

Province	Year	Salary (pesos)
Chiapa (AM)	1677	800
	1728	800
	1764	800
Ciudad Real (AM)	1777	1,000
Tuxtla (AM)	1777	1,000
Soconusco (G)	1677	600
	1724	600
	1767	600
Quezaltenango (C)	1738	331
	1762	331
	1777	330
Huehuetenango-Totonicapán (AM)	1703	331
	1738	331
	1764	331
	1777	330
	1795–97	330
Atitlán-Tecpanatitlán (AM)	1703	661
	1738	661
	1777	661
	1795–97	661
Chimaltenango (AM)	1777	1,000
	1795–97	1,000
Sacatepéquz-Atitanes (AM)	1777	1,000
	1795–97	1,000
Verapaz (AM)	1677	770
	1738	1,275
	1768	1,265
	1777	1,275
	1795–97	1,275
Chiquimula de la Sierra (C)	1738	661
	1769	661
	1777	660
	1795–97	660
San Antonio Suchitepéquez (AM)	1677	700
	1703	1,158
	1769	1,158
	1777	1,158
	1795–97	1,158
Escuintla-Guazacapán (AM)	1700	331
	1736	331

Province	Year	Salary (pesos)
	1761	331
	1777	331
	1795–97	330
Sonsonate (AM)	1677	600
	1749	600
	1764	600
	1795–97	992
San Salvador (AM)	1676	500
	1724	827
	1761	1,000
	1777	827
Comayagua-Honduras (G)	1675	1,000
	1748	3,000
	1769	3,000
Tegucigalpa (AM)	1701	400
	1744	400
	1765	400
	1777	661
Sébaco-Chontales (C)	1738	275
	1766	250
	1777	250
Sutiaba (C)	1693	300
	1738	250
Realejo (C)	1722	537
	1738	537
	1756	537
Realejo-Sutiaba	1777	787
Nicaragua (G)	1699	1,200
	1755	2,000
	1763	2,000
Nicoya (C)	1677	240
	1738	275
	1764	275
	1777	275
Costa Rica (G)	1673	2,400
	1738	2,400
	1765	2,400

Source: AGI, Guatemala 275; 276; 277; 440; 441, Títulos y provisiones, undated, Lista de los corregimientos y alcaldías mayores del Distrito de la Real Audiencia de Guatemala; 442; 443; 601, Expedientes diarios 1778–80, no. 9, Plan remitido por la Audiencia de Guatemala sobre la rebaxa que debe hacerse de sus salarios a los corregidores y alcaldes mayores de aquel Distrito para aumento de sus sueldos a los subalternos que han de crear en aquel Tribunal, 1777.

AM = Alcaldía Mayor   C = Corregimiento   G = Gobernación

of 18,000 pesos) for the presidency, which he occupied from 1717 to 1724.[11] In 1733 Tomás de Rivera Santa Cruz paid the same amount and served from 1742 to 1748. Rivera was the son of a former chief officer of the royal treasury in Mexico City (a post that cost 20,000 pesos) who later became president of the Audiencia of Guadalajara (New Galicia). A former student of the University of Mexico and of law schools in Guadalajara and Mexico City, the younger Rivera was possibly Mexican-born and probably the only president of the Audiencia of Guatemala in the eighteenth century who held a law degree.[12] The other presidents of that century received their appointments as a reward for service. The two who bought the post turned out to be perhaps the most corrupt presidents in the history of the kingdom.

Also periodically up for sale were the positions as oidores of the audiencia. The first such sale was attempted in 1709, when a judgeship was sold to Nicolás de Ulloa Calleja for 6,000 pesos. There must have been some embarrassment regarding the deal, for the buyer asked that neither the sale nor the selling price be mentioned in his title.[13] In any case, the title was almost immediately withdrawn, as will be explained below.

The first sales of judgeships that actually went through took place in April and May 1710, when no less than three positions on the court were sold to people who would occupy their positions once the serving judges had either resigned, retired, or died. First, Tomás de Arana, a graduate of the University of Mexico and a lawyer on the staff of the Audiencia of Mexico, paid 6,200 pesos for the post of oidor. As in the case of Ulloa Calleja, the purchaser requested that the title make no mention of the sale.[14] Just eighteen days later, another judgeship was bought by José Rodezno for 5,000 escudos (5,000 pesos). Rodezno was a native of Mexico City and, like Arana, a graduate of the University of Mexico. His father had served in Mexico City as the accountant of the royal treasury who handled sales taxes, and his maternal grandfather had been a Knight of Calatrava who had served the king for many years in Flanders and in Italy. Rodezno paid an additional 2,000 pesos for the right to marry in Guatemala, judges normally being prohibited from marrying into local families to avoid a conflict of interest.[15] Finally, two weeks later, Felipe Antonio de Lugo, a native of Potosí (Peru), paid 6,000 escudos (5,000 in cash in Spain and another 1,000 upon taking up the post in America) for still another judgeship. Lugo held a doctorate in law, and like Arana and Rodezno, was a graduate of the University of Mexico.[16]

Still more positions on the audiencia were sold during the next year. First, on August 20, 1711, Ambrosio Tomás de Santaella Melgarejo paid 7,000 pesos to be the fiscal of the audiencia with the right to become oidor when that position became available.[17] Just two days later, Domingo de Gomendio Urrutia paid the same amount for appointment as judge.[18] It was not until 1740—a gap of twenty-nine years—that the next sale of a position on the audiencia took place. In that year, Juan José Martínez Patiño paid 8,000 pesos for the next position as oidor that became available.[19] That was the last time a judgeship on the Audiencia of Guatemala was sold.

Some of these people may have proved to be good jurists. Lugo was promoted in 1722 to be an oidor of the Audiencia of Mexico. This was one of the most prestigious positions in the world of judges. A year later, Santaella Melgarejo was also promoted to the Audiencia of Mexico, where he served as the criminal prosecutor (*fiscal del crimen*). Gomendio Urrutia served as oidor in Guatemala until his death around 1735. Rodezno retired to Mexico City in 1741, and although he had been described as a good servant of the king who, it was said, had not allowed his own interests to affect his rulings, he was given the usual pension of half-salary, rather than the full salary he had requested.[20]

Arana and Martínez Patiño, on the other hand, suffered a different fate. They both served on the court until 1745, when the royal government abruptly fired them and two other judges as well, and in addition suspended President Rivera Santa Cruz—one of the two presidents who had bought his post. Even worse, Arana was fined and deprived of a pension. Martínez Patiño was exiled, and all the fired judges were subject to immediate residencias (trials for conduct in office). The crown made this decision because of "the disorders, excesses, abuses and discord" on the court. Those who were fired were said to be "the principal leaders of and accomplices in the already mentioned disturbances."[21]

Despite the allegations against the four judges, including the two who had bought their posts, none of them was found guilty of any of the major charges brought against them during their residencias.[22] On the other hand, the two presidents who purchased their offices were given exceptionally severe sentences. Francisco Rodríguez de Rivas was found guilty of accepting a huge quantity of bribes in return for making appointments to the offices of governor, corregidor, alcalde mayor, village magistrate, and more, and for granting special economic privileges such as participation in the meat market. He also bribed an audiencia judge, engaged in illegal commerce with the Kingdom of Peru, appointed some of his relatives to carry out repartimientos with the native people, overcharged the king for the construction of some ships built to patrol Lake Nicaragua, underpaid the garrison stationed at the fort on the Honduran coast, failed to investigate charges of financial fraud against the commander of the fort at Granada (Nicaragua), fired twenty-one militia officials so he could replace them with his hangers-on, failed to maintain discipline among the soldiers stationed in the capital, paid large salaries to the men he appointed to military positions, and interfered with municipal elections in the capital. He was fined eighty thousand pesos, exiled from America for five years, declared unfit to hold future office, and ordered to take the first ship from Veracruz to Spain so he could appear before the Council of the Indies.[23] This was not a slap on the wrist.

The kingdom's only lawyer-president, Tomás de Rivera Santa Cruz, may have been even worse. He took bribes or demanded payment in return for various favors:

> to delay proceedings against magistrates who were late delivering tribute payments from the Indians
> to allow the Dominicans and Franciscans to collect illegal payments from the Indians
> to appoint people, including his relatives, to office
> to prevent the secularization of some Dominican benefices
> to interfere with the appointment of judges to conduct residencias of the magistrates
> to provide the owners of haciendas with Indian workers
> to allow gambling in the military barracks
> to permit illegal participation in the meat market

to award the meat contract to someone other than the lowest
   bidder
to allow the illegal sale of alcoholic drinks
to permit smuggling
to allow his cronies to sell tribute goods at artificially high prices
to confirm elections in the Indian villages

He refused to pay the required pensions to the former encomenderos or the salaries of the garrison at the fort on the Honduran coast
unless they paid *him* first to do so. Most bizarre of all, he was accused
by the former corregidor of Quezaltenango of committing an inde-
cent act when three Indians from that province presented him with
a request that they not be required to come to the capital every year
to have their appointments confirmed (an opportunity used by the
president to demand money from them). The corregidor spoke to
Rivera on behalf of the Indians, and later related that "as soon as I
spoke the first word, he turned his back to me showing me—with all
due respect—his behind, and with his two hands lifted up his frock
from behind, leaving me talking to the part of his body that he sits
on." This charge was thrown out because the testimony of Indians
was judged to be unacceptable against a Spaniard, leaving only the
word of the corregidor against that of the president.

Rivera, like Rodríguez de Rivas before him, was fined eighty thousand pesos and declared unfit for further office. As a result, his request
for a position on the Audiencia of Mexico was turned down. Moreover, his property was impounded, as was that of his closest associates. Once again, this was not a slap on the wrist.[24] President Pedro
Rivera, who served in the office between Rodríguez de Rivas and
Tomás de Rivera Santa Cruz, had advised the crown against selling
the post, because to recover his investment and make a profit, a
president would have to commit a variety of injustices.[25] But the
second sale had already been made, and the warning proved accurate.
It is no wonder that the post of president was never sold again.

The record of sales of judgeships and the presidency was therefore mixed. Several of the judges were apparently good servants of
the king, but two others were probably not, while the two presidents
who bought their positions were disasters. Several conclusions can

be drawn from this brief survey of the sale of the highest offices in the kingdom. First, sales of these positions were in fact rare and were concentrated in the period of 1710–11. During the period of the sale of offices (1670–1750), one of the two presidencies sold was bought during those two years, as were five of the six judgeships. Presidents served for eight-year terms, and one of the presidents who bought his post was removed after only six years, so the sale of a presidency did not commit the crown to misrule for very long. Oidores, on the other hand, served lifetime appointments and left office only because of retirement, promotion, death, or expulsion. This meant that the sale of a judgeship had lasting impact.

Nevertheless, over the eighty-year period, most of the judges serving on the audiencia received their posts without purchasing them, as did all but two of the presidents. Since the crown could easily have sold them if it wanted to, it obviously did not want to. It was out of desperation that so many high offices were sold in 1710–11, a period that corresponded with the War of the Spanish Succession, when Philip V was driven out of Madrid and was desperate to raise cash for his armies.[26] Moreover, the desire to obscure information about the sale and selling price of titles reveals that the people involved were not comfortable with a system in which the offices were for sale. In short, there really was a commitment to the rule of law. Had there been no such commitment, all the offices would have been sold all the time. The sale of offices was considered to be an evil, although at times a necessary one.

This commitment to judicial integrity is revealed in the above-mentioned unsuccessful attempt by Nicolás de Ulloa Calleja to purchase a judgeship. A Mexican-born Spaniard (creole) from Oaxaca, a graduate of law schools in Mexico City, and a lawyer on the staff of the Audiencia of Mexico, Ulloa Calleja was in Madrid in 1709 when he paid 1,500 doubloons for the position of oidor on the Audiencia of Guatemala. Once the crown had approved the sale of the office, the buyer celebrated by going on a three-day drinking binge. He was later found carousing somewhere in Andalusia. When the Council of the Indies found out, it wrote to the king, Philip V, the first Bourbon monarch of Spain, saying that "this subject is unbridled in his behavior and given to the vice of drunkenness" and therefore unsuitable as a judge. The council thought it "indispensable to our obligation to consider all the problems and damage in the lives and property of men who are subject to a person so possessed by a vice and exposed to venality and errors" that would follow from decisions made while drunk. King Philip, however, wrote in the margin of the council's letter, "I am now aware of this; nevertheless the decision will be carried out." He was sticking to his decision to appoint the man in question.

The councilors, however, would not relent. They sent the king a second letter stating that the council had "seen with pain" the monarch's decision. With such a judge, they pointed out, the king's vassals would receive justice not on earth but only in "the Court of God." The council understood the exceptional needs of the moment, noting that "in cases of evident necessity the law permits even the sale of Holy Chalices to aid and defend the State, and in this decision the Council concurs." But no legal authority would defend the sale of the right to dispense justice to someone of the character of this candidate, for the result would be innumerable lawsuits alleging that the judge's decisions had been affected by drunkenness. Then the council came to what was for the councilors the crux of the matter: "The act of greatest sovereignty for kings is that of depositing their own authority in a vassal so that with respect to lives, property, and honors he practice all that pertains to the Sovereign, and the most heroic act of the vassal is to follow blindly another man invested as Minister of his King." This time Philip gave in to the council's wishes and revoked the appointment. The money was returned to Ulloa Calleja, and when he demanded repayment with interest, the crown agreed. He got back his money plus 8 percent.[27]

This case was not unique, for in other instances the Council of the Indies likewise requested and then reiterated vehemently its position in favor of canceling the appointment of unsuitable persons to the Audiencia of Mexico.[28] Since the councilors had all served the last Hapsburg monarch, it is clear that there existed an underlying belief in the rule of law regardless of what dynasty ruled Spain. This was true despite the mockery often made of justice, as was so notoriously the case in efforts by well-meaning officials to abolish the horrid forced-labor draft for the Peruvian mines and, in the case of Guatemala, the repartimiento de indios on the landed estates of the central valley in the seventeenth century.[29] Bureaucracy was not devoid of good intentions, but good intentions often lost out in the face of necessity or expedience, especially when resisted by vested interest.

The sale of the highest offices also reveals that the buyers were frequently men who had either grown up in or been born in America. The practice, although a necessary evil in the eyes of the government in Spain, clearly opened up the system to participation of people with close ties to the crown's American kingdoms. Was there discrimination against these people? Possibly, because the record-keepers apparently felt the need to explain in great detail why these particular "Americans" were qualified for the offices they were purchasing. That is why more is known about them—their family background, their academic careers—than about most people whose appointments were sent to the Council of the Indies for its approval. The council, it seems, needed to be convinced. On the other hand, while one might assume that the American-born were excluded from these highest offices once they were no longer sold, after 1750, in fact in 1755, Felipe Romana, a native of Bogotá, was appointed fiscal of the Audiencia of Guatemala, and he served on the court for almost two decades. Americans were not really excluded from the most important offices even in the late colonial period.

II

When dealing with the highest offices, therefore, the crown stuck to its commitment to good government and the rule of law, yielding to necessity on only a few occasions. Its record at the lower levels, however, was not so good. Dishonesty was almost certain to result from the sale of posts in the royal treasury, especially because these positions, unlike those of president or provincial magistrate, were granted with lifetime tenure. These posts were sold anyway, in some cases, from the early seventeenth century on. In the era of the Bourbons, the sale of treasury positions ceased during peacetime, but as noted, war was frequent and so, too, were sales. Once again, many positions were sold during the bad years of 1710–11. The prices for these offices varied. The most expensive treasury positions were those in the

Guatemalan capital, where in the 1690s the position of chief accountant sold for 3,500 pesos, while that of treasurer sold for 2,500 pesos.
In 1712 the cost of the latter had risen to 3,500. By 1743 the chief
accountancy sold for 4,000 pesos, while in 1750 the position of
treasurer sold for 4,600.[30] In short, prices kept rising. There were
few sales, however, because the positions were virtually for life and
thus tended to stay in one man's hands for an extended time.

Treasury positions outside the capital were, of course, cheaper. The
post of chief accountant of Nicaragua sold for 1,000 pesos in 1686
and for 1,500 in 1703, while the treasurer position sold for 1,000 pesos
in 1688 and 1,200 in 1710. Neither post was sold in the rest of the
century.[31] The treasurer position in Honduras was sold once for 500
pesos, in 1694, while no one seems to have wanted to be chief accountant there. When the post became vacant in 1715, no one applied.
The Council of the Indies then managed to scrounge up three applicants, but none of them offered to pay anything. Similarly, no one
wanted to buy the position of treasurer in Costa Rica.[32] Clearly,
Honduras and Costa Rica offered few economic opportunities to
compensate for the poor living conditions in those provinces. In Costa
Rica, for example, there was little commerce and such a severe shortage of hard currency that as late as 1782 the government permitted
people buying positions on the city council to pay in cacao rather
than in silver.[33]

The only exception to the generally poor prospects for treasury
officials outside the capital was the post of *oficial real* (royal official—
a rank lower than chief accountant and treasurer) in Sonsonate. That
part of what is now western El Salvador was economically valuable, as we shall see, especially because of cacao. The post was given
away in 1701 in return for the cancelation of a debt owed by the
government of 4,000 pesos. A debt of 8,000 pesos was similarly paid
off with an appointment to the post in 1703. The post became available again in 1723 but was granted free of charge then and for the rest
of the century.[34]

It is hard to imagine that the buyers simply wanted to get prestigious jobs with mediocre salaries. They bought the posts to participate
in graft. Treasury officials knew of many ways to turn their positions
into profit-making enterprises. They took bribes to undercount

production of taxable goods and to look the other way in the face of smuggling. They even became smugglers themselves. They collected tribute goods and then underreported the money brought in by the sale of those goods. The loser, of course, was the royal government itself, which ended up with less revenue than what would have been collected and reported by honest officials.

Nevertheless, treasury posts were not the most lucrative in the kingdom. This is proved by the career of Diego Rodríguez Menéndez, who had served as corregidor of Sutiaba (Nicaragua), a post he had purchased for 1,500 pesos in 1693, before he paid 3,500 pesos in 1696 to become chief accountant in the royal treasury office of Guatemala.[35] He was still in that office in 1711 when he paid 1,000 doubloons (4,000 pesos) to serve as alcalde mayor of Huehuetenango (with the right to name his cousin as his replacement if he died before taking office). Only two years later, while still waiting to take up the post in Huehuetenango, he paid 3,500 pesos for the alcaldía mayor of Atitlán-Tecpanatitlán (Sololá), to be occupied in the distant future, and then another 4,500 pesos for the alcaldía mayor of Verapaz, to be occupied in the still more distant future. He was not required to give up his lifetime position as chief accountant, and so to solve the problem of occupying two—or more?—posts concurrently, he was given permission to appoint a temporary substitute to hold down his job at the treasury in his absence.[36] The annual rewards of holding any of the three choice alcaldías mayores of Huehuetenango, Atitlán, or Verapaz must have been greater than what he could get in a year using his position in the treasury. On the other hand, there is no evidence that he actually assumed any of the alcaldías mayores he had bought, for Rodríguez Menéndez apparently never faced a residencia. It is likely that he simply appointed an associate to serve for him. But with or without an associate, his activities in the alcaldías mayores must have occupied much of his time, for it is known that he hired a replacement to carry out his duties at the treasury. It is of course possible that his replacement as chief accountant was better at the job or more honest than he was. The opposite seems more probable, however, for the interim appointee had every reason to make money even faster than a normal officeholder because he would be in office for a limited time. The level of graft, therefore, was more likely to increase than to decrease. Whatever the case, good government was unlikely when treasury positions were sold and then the purchasers carried on their own business activities, or went off and occupied other positions to carry on enterprises elsewhere.

Nevertheless, once again, it is important to note that most of the time, the people who occupied positions at the royal treasury did not purchase their posts. They received their positions free of charge. But because some of the posts were not considered worth buying, the men who held them probably had to work hard at entrepreneurial activities outside the law just to make ends meet. Once again, it is hard to imagine that this produced good government.

III

In the Kingdom of Guatemala, the most numerous posts outside the capital, and at the same time those most often sold, were those of magistrate, high magistrate, and governor. They were not sold at auction, however. Rather, the state as seller and the would-be official as buyer gradually worked out accepted selling prices. Sometimes this required negotiation, and when the money offered for these positions was considered insufficient, the Council of the Indies, which handled the appointments, provided some hints. For example, when a would-be officeholder offered to buy the alcaldía mayor of Huehuetenango in 1706 for 3,500 pesos, the council in Spain demurred, noting that the position was "known to have brought in a larger sum in the past [since] this post, like others in that Kingdom, was greatly sought after." When the applicant raised his offer to 4,000 pesos—still short of the 5,500 pesos for which the magistracy had sold in 1697—he was appointed forthwith.[37]

Not all positions could be so easily sold—for reasons to be made clear later. The high magistracy of Escuintla (covering the southeastern Pacific coast of modern Guatemala) was sold twice in the 1690s and once more in 1709, but for the most part, few people wanted the post, and those assigned to it almost always asked to be transferred or relieved. No one ever offered to buy the governorship of Costa Rica—despite its high salary—or the magistracy of Realejo (on the northwestern Pacific coast of Nicaragua), frequently sacked by pirates. Other posts were sold for small sums. The corregimiento of Sébaco (in modern northern Nicaragua) went for a mere 400 pesos, while that of Chiquimula de la Sierra (eastern highland Guatemala) and the gobernación of Nicaragua sold for up to 1,000 pesos, and the magistracy of Sutiaba (northwestern Nicaragua) brought in 1,500 pesos. On the other hand, some positions sold for small fortunes. The gobernación of Soconusco, the corregimiento of Quezaltenango, and the alcaldías mayores of Huehuetenango, Atitlán, Suchitepéquez, Verapaz (all in modern-day Guatemala), and San Salvador sold for between 4,000 and 6,000 pesos. Soconusco, in fact, was the seventh most expensive gobernación in the Spanish empire, while Huehuetenango was the fifth most expensive alcaldía mayor.[38] Most expensive of all in the Kingdom of Guatemala was the high magistracy of Chiapa,[39] which sold for more than 9,000 pesos. This made Chiapa the third most expensive alcaldía mayor in the Spanish empire.[40]

Some posts were so valuable that the government used them as assets or even as collateral for loans. In 1677 the crown tried to use the gobernación of Soconusco as part of deal in which a group of merchants were to be given that post in return for a loan to the government of 280,000 pesos. It was never explained how the men would have shared responsibility for administration, and in any case, the deal fell through.[41] In 1682, however, the crown succeeded in using the same post to raise 6,000 pesos in a loan at 8 percent interest, and in addition the government was paid 6,000 pesos in cash.[42] In the same year, the alcaldía mayor of Chiapa was sold in return for a cash payment of 4,000 pesos and a no-interest loan of 2,000 pesos.[43] In the following year, the high magistracy of Suchitepéquez was sold for 6,000 pesos plus a 6,000-peso no-interest loan, while that of Verapaz went for 4,000 pesos and a 1,000-peso no-interest loan.[44] And in 1685 the alcaldía mayor of Chiapa was sold for 4,000 pesos plus a 2,000-peso loan at 8 percent.[45] Such practices became less common under the Bourbons. Still, in 1731 the crown granted the alcaldía mayor of Chiapa and the corregimiento of Quezaltenango, as well as the gobernación of Tlaxcala (in New Spain) to Isidro de la Mesa y la Madriz as repayment for the forced loan of 35,345 pesos that he had made to the crown back in 1714. He never occupied any post in Central America, however, for he eventually named people to serve in his place.[46]

The government also accepted payment in kind, or at least of particular kinds. In 1686 the gobernación of Honduras was given to Sancho Ordóñez in return for two patrol boats, which he was to deliver for service on the Ulúa River (in Honduras) within eight months of taking office.[47] In 1692 the governorship of Soconusco was awarded to Nicolás de Rioja y Zúñiga in return for raising and equipping at his own cost a force of 420 infantry to serve in the war in Europe.[48] In 1703 the crown appointed Juan Mier del Tojó, a merchant of Seville and a member of the consulado of that city, to the post of alcalde mayor of Atitlán in return for having provided a fire ship used in Vigo against the attacking English fleet.[49]

Posts were also used as compensation for damages, as when in 1680 the corregimiento of Nicoya was given to Joseph de Albelda to compensate him for land in Panama City that the crown requisitioned for unspecified use.[50] The crown also awarded magistracies as compensation for other posts that were being eliminated. When the position of accountant of the Santa Cruzada (the body that sold indulgences to raise money for Church and state) was abolished in 1751, Cristóbal Gálvez Corral, whose family had purchased the post in the 1690s and who himself had paid 26,000 pesos to succeed his father as accountant in 1729, was awarded the alcaldía mayor of San Salvador with the right to occupy the magistracy for ten years and appoint substitutes to serve in his place should that be necessary. Gálvez Corral undoubtedly requested that specific post, for he had already served as high magistrate of San Salvador in the 1730s and certainly knew the business.[51]

Since almost all magistracies were granted for five-year terms, the payment of large sums of money meant—as table 2.2 demonstrates—that the purchaser frequently paid more than he would receive in salary during his entire tenure in office. To make matters worse, other costs made these posts even more expensive in practice. Since 1631, the crown had required all prospective salaried officeholders to pay in advance one-half of the first year's salary. This payment, called the *media anata*, was eventually made subject to a surcharge of one-third, for what were called emoluments—the perquisites of office—and then the total was taxed an additional 18 percent for shipping the money from America to Spain. This last impost was instituted to take into account the large number of offices being sold to people already in the colonies. Once introduced, however, this 18 percent was inevitably applied even to people who bought their positions while in Spain; these purchasers were thus charged for shipping that never took place.

Taxes and other charges ended up taking some 78.5 percent of an officeholder's earnings in his first year, or about 16 percent of the cumulative five-year salary. Net incomes, however, were further reduced by other expenses. A majority of magistrates received their appointments while in Spain and had to travel to America to take up their posts. Yet the crown paid nothing for travel expenses. Then, once in the colonies, the official had to demonstrate generosity—that is, provide gifts—to the judges of the audiencia in order to be allowed to take the oath of office. This must have been a substantial cost, which is why the crown provided an alternative for those who received their appointments in Spain: they could take the oath in Cádiz and avoid paying bribes to the members of the audiencia if they paid fifty pesos to the Convent of San Telmo in Seville.

Expenses did not cease once the appointee took up his post. Because the crown provided no funds to cover administrative costs, these were borne entirely by the officeholder himself. Moreover, bureaucratic duties and the large extent of territory under his jurisdiction required the official to hire at least one secretary and sometimes one, two, or even three lieutenants to preside over official business in distant locations. Magistrates also had to contribute sums from their own pockets to help equip the local militia and were even expected to lead the community in charitable work like founding or maintaining hospitals and churches.

All told, the monetary burdens placed on officeholders were such that their salaries were widely reputed to be insufficient even to defray administrative expenses, let alone provide a living for the official and his family. Moreover, personal disaster threatened those who purchased these posts. Officeholders might be driven from office

Table 2.2
CUMULATIVE FIVE-YEAR SALARIES OF MAGISTRATES
COMPARED WITH THE COST OF OFFICES, 1688–1749 (IN PESOS)

Magistracy	Year	Salary*	Amount paid for post	Year	Salary*	Amount paid for post
Chiapa (AM)	1697	3,372	7,400	1747	3,372	9,200
Soconusco (G)	1688	2,529	6,500	1740	2,529	5,100
Quezaltenango (C)	1697	1,395[a]	5,500	1743	1,395	4,500
Huehuetenango-Totonicapán (AM)	1697	1,395[b]	5,500	1747	1,395	5,800
Atitlán-Tecpanatitlán (AM)	1697	2,809	6,000	1748	2,786	4,600
Verapaz (AM)	1694	3,246	4,500	1749	5,375	5,635
Chiquimula de la Sierra (C)	1697	2,786[c]	2,000	1745	2,786	1,150
Suchitepéquez (AM)	1697	2,951	5,500	1747	4,881	5,175
Escuintla-Guazacapán (AM)	1693	1,395[d]	1,000	1736	1,395	0
Sonsonate (AM)	1686	2,529	2,500	1749	2,529	1,955
San Salvador (AM)	1697	2,108	4,500	1746	3,486	4,600
Comayagua-Honduras (G)	1689	4,215	5,500	1740	4,215	3,000
Tegucigalpa (AM)	1697	1,686	3,000	1744	1,686	1,800
Sébaco-Chontales	1708	1,159[a]	400	1744	1,159	400
Sutiaba (C)	1693	1,265	1,500	1735	1,265	1,500
Realejo (C)	1720	2,264	0	1746	2,264	0
Nicaragua (G)	1695	3,513	1,000	1741	3,513	1,000
Nicoya (C)	1690	703	1,200	1732	1,159	2,750
Costa Rica (G)	1692	7,026	0	1733	7,026	0

Source: AGI, Guatemala 275, 276, 277, 440, 441, 442, 443.

AM = Alcaldía Mayor
C = Corregimiento
G = Gobernación
*After taxes.
[a]Based on salary as of 1738.
[b]Based on salary as of 1703.
[c]Based on salary as of 1724.
[d]Based on salary as of 1704.

either by Indian rebellions or by the opposition of powerful local elites.[52] There was also the possibility of the buyer dying before completing his tenure in office and thus before recouping his investment. Dangers rare in Spain were present in Central America. The magistrate of Chiquimula, for example, was badly injured in the earthquake that struck his province in 1765. Hundreds of people died, and at least one village priest was badly injured.[53] Earthquakes did not respect gender, class, status, or ethnic lines.

To prevent such misfortune, purchasers frequently requested, and received, the right to name replacements. The crown readily assented to appointing substitutes chosen by the purchaser if the latter for some reason failed to take up his post. This assent, of course, usually required an additional "monetary service," as when the heirs of Luis de Ayala, who had bought the corregimiento of Quezaltenango in 1689 for 4,500 pesos but died before taking office, were required to pay an another 1,000 for the right to name a replacement.[54] Similarly, when Diego Olaya Vivanco, a resident of Mexico City, chose not to serve as governor of Soconusco, which post he had bought in 1708 for 5,000 pesos, he had to pay an additional 600 pesos in 1712 for the right to name a replacement, namely, Joseph Damián Fernández de Córdoba, city councilman of Santiago.[55] And Juan Joseph de la Rea, named governor of Nicaragua in 1711, paid 1,300 pesos four years later so that his cousin, Gaspar de la Rea, could take up the position.[56]

In addition, purchasers usually took precautionary measures to protect their families in case they died in office. The normal procedure was to include in the terms of purchase the right to name successors. Thus, when Francisco Franco paid 3,500 pesos in 1707 for the alcaldía mayor of San Salvador, he was given permission to have his heirs name his replacement in the event of death or inability to serve.[57] In the following year, Manuel de Porras bought the high magistracy of Tegucigalpa for 2,800 pesos and named his brother as his replacement in case of death.[58] In 1713 Juan Rodríguez de la Gala, who bought the magistracy of Quezaltenango for 4,000 pesos, was given the right to name his son to replace him.[59] And when Joseph de Argárate bought the alcaldía mayor of San Salvador in 1724 for 4,000 pesos, he named his wife to name someone to replace him, should that become necessary;

it did, for Argárate died and his widow then named Pedro de Echevers to the post.[60]

Buyers sometimes spelled out the succession in detail. When Manuel de Lacunza bought the alcaldía mayor of Suchitepéquez for 4,500 pesos in 1731, he named Guillermo Martínez Pereda and Manuel Muñoz, in that order, to succeed him. All three men eventually served in the post, for the first two died in office.[61] And when Joseph Salgado y Artunduaga purchased the corregimiento of Sutiaba for 1,500 pesos in 1735, he was given the right to appoint "any of his brothers, or whoever marries [his sister] Doña María Manuela de Salgado Artunduaga, or if all else fails Don Pedro Fajardo or Don Thomas Sunsín" to replace him.[62]

Purchasers thus learned to protect their investments. Such measures became more important as time went on, for eventually those who bought posts had to wait longer and longer before taking them up. This was because the demand for positions in Central America, as in Peru,[63] was greater than the supply, and the crown soon discovered that it could sell the same post more than once by selling "futures," that is, the right to succeed to a post after prior purchasers had served their time. In other words, buyers formed a queue while the government drew up a waiting list.

As a result, there was frequently a considerable time-lag between the purchase and the assumption of office. The high magistracy of Suchitepéquez, for example, was sold in 1731 for 4,500 pesos, but the buyer, Manuel de Lacunza, had to wait eight years before taking up his post,[64] while Manuel Antonio de Lazalde, who bought the same position for the same sum in 1738, had to wait ten years.[65] Isidro Díaz de Vívar, who bought the alcaldía mayor of San Salvador in 1734 for 4,000 pesos, had to wait almost fifteen years before taking office.[66] The prospect of waiting so long led Bernabé de la Torre Trassierra, who paid 4,600 pesos for the alcaldía mayor of San Salvador in 1746, to request permission to go to Brazil and Peru and finish up some business affairs there while he waited. War delayed his return, and as a result Domingo de Soto Bermúdez, who bought the same post for the same amount in 1750, was allowed to assume office first. Torre Trassierra finally succeeded in taking up his post in 1757, only to be removed from office in 1760 as a result of political conflict with the city councils of the province. All of his property was impounded as well. He was eventually exonerated and his property was returned, but this was only in 1768.[67] This official therefore had a long, if not illustrious, career.

Such long periods of waiting, however, were sometimes nothing but a minor inconvenience, for some buyers put their time to good use by taking up other offices. Diego de los Ríos, the brother of the governor of Cádiz, bought the future governorship of Soconusco in 1688 for 6,500 pesos, but before assuming that post, he first served as high magistrate of Cholula (New Spain), which he had purchased at an earlier time.[68] In 1709 Manuel de Porras bought the alcaldía mayor of Escuintla for 1,000 pesos because he would have to wait years before assuming the alcaldía mayor of Tegucigalpa, which he had purchased the year before for 2,800 pesos with the right to name his brother as his replacement.[69] Juan Rodríguez de la Gala must have been thinking of the distant future when in 1713 he purchased the corregimiento of Quezaltenango for 4,000 pesos with the right to name his son as his replacement; he had just been named alcalde mayor of Tabasco (New Spain) and had yet to take up that post.[70] The same could be said of the chief accountant of the royal treasury in Guatemala, Diego Rodríguez Menéndez, who, as we have seen, at one time held the right to serve in no less than three high magistracies once the incumbents had left office.

The only factor preventing the sale of future positions a century in advance was peace. For when Spain was no longer at war, the sale of most of these positions ceased. As a result, no one new joined the queue, and the waiting list got shorter. Appointments were then made to supposedly deserving individuals, usually soldiers who received the posts in lieu of pensions. This was true even for some of the most valuable positions. The governorship of Soconusco, which sold for 5,000 pesos in 1708, was awarded in 1716, without a "monetary service," to Captain Francisco Antonio Pimentel Sotomayor, who had served as a company commander in Havana for almost thirteen years.[71] Similarly, the magistracy of Quezaltenango, which sold for 4,000 pesos in 1713, was awarded free of charge three years later to Pedro de Andueza, who had served in the Presidio of Manila for seventeen years and in addition had good personal connections at court.[72] The high magistracy of Suchitepéquez brought the crown 4,500 pesos in 1711 but was granted for no payment in 1717 to Miguel Pérez de Velasco, a resident of Havana, who had helped rescue the king's silver when the treasure fleet went down in a hurricane in 1715.[73]

The resumption of hostilities, especially with Great Britain, forced the crown to resume the sale of offices. The alcaldía mayor of Verapaz, for example, having been sold for 4,500 pesos in 1694 and then given as an award for military service in 1702, was sold again for 4,500 pesos in 1712, 1713, and 1718.[74] Similarly, the above-mentioned gobernación of Soconusco, corregimiento of Quezaltenango, and alcaldía mayor of Suchitepéquez, given as rewards for military service in 1716–17, were all sold in the next round of appointments. The next period of peace led once more to the awarding of posts: between 1722 and 1725 the high magistracies of Suchitepéquez, Verapaz, Tegucigalpa, and San Salvador and the magistracy of Quezaltenango were awarded without "monetary service."

In 1750, shortly after the end of the War of Jenkins' Ear, the king, Ferdinand VI, as was customary, stopped the sale of offices. The result was another round of appointments made for military service just before the Seven Years' War (1756–63): between 1753 and 1758 the alcaldías mayores of Verapaz, Tegucigalpa, Sonsonate, and even Chiapa—the most expensive post of all—were all granted free of charge (except, of course, for the usual taxes).[75] War with Great Britain started again in 1762, but this time the new king, Charles III, broke with tradition and refused to resume the sale of offices. This meant that after 1750 the magistracies and governorships were no longer sold and a new era of imperial history had begun. Before 1750, however, many posts were occupied by people who had purchased them, and in some cases the queue of office buyers endured longer than the peace. Thus it took years before the last officials who had purchased their positions finally left office.

IV

Bureaucrats—said to be faceless and insensitive—are people everyone loves to hate. Nevertheless they were real, flesh-and-blood people who behaved as they did because of their culture and the system in which they had to operate. Since a bureaucracy is never better than the bureaucrats who serve in it, an understanding of the colonial state requires a deeper understanding of the servants of the state. This is especially important because of misleading or erroneous interpretations of bureaucrats' actions. In the case of Spanish America, for example, Benedict Anderson has argued that these people's career patterns produced the creole nationalism that eventually led to the founding of the post-Independence nation-states. He argues that, because individual functionaries moved from place to place as they moved up in the bureaucracy, they thereby became acquainted with provinces other than their own and met other functionaries who were making similar discoveries about themselves—and about the political-institutional unit that would eventually become their nation.[76] This interpretation is worth testing empirically, because the testing process itself reveals a great deal about the reality of bureaucracy and its relationship, if any, to future political and institutional development.

In early-modern European bureaucracies, positions were seen not merely as the opportunity to serve the king but also as rewards for service or as benefits for one's friends and relatives. In the case of the Spanish colonial bureaucracy, the great majority of the people who held the positions in America were not "functionaries" who had joined the colonial office as young men hoping to make a career by holding a series of posts at successively higher levels. As has been shown, there were very few levels that one could ascend. At the lowest level of salaried officials, there were seventeen, then nineteen, and finally twenty-six lowest-level units, that is, corregimientos, alcaldías mayores, gobernaciones, and subdelegaciones. This constitutes a very small bureaucracy indeed, considering the size of the Kingdom of Guatemala.

An examination of the bureaucrats who held these offices during the period when most of these lowest-level units were sold (1670–1750) and then during the late colonial period (1750–1810) reveals that most of the bureaucrats were middle-aged or even somewhat elderly men who had already served the king, usually as soldiers, for one, two, or even three decades. Pedro de Andueza, named corregidor of Quezaltenango in 1716, had served as an officer of the garrison at the Presidio in Manila for seventeen years before returning to Europe. The son of a servant of the dowager queen of Spain (widow of Charles II), Andueza went to Bayonne to meet her, and she recommended him for the post that he eventually received.[77] Juan Francisco Real, appointed to replace Andueza in 1724, had served for twenty years in the king's royal guard.[78] The two men appointed to serve as corregidores of Realejo in the 1740s were also longtime servants of His Majesty: Cristóbal Ignacio de Soria, named in 1746, had served in the Spanish Navy for twenty-five years; his successor, Pedro Aparicio, had served as a soldier for fourteen years. Aparicio's successor, Pedro Mauricio Sala, appointed in 1756, was only a second lieutenant but had served as an instructor of mathematics at the Royal Military Academy and was the son and grandson of important soldiers and diplomats.[79]

While these men were well-connected as well as usually long-serving, others received posts after having served in combat. Francisco Tomás del Castillo Ruiz de Vergara had been a soldier in his native Canary Islands and then in Flanders, was promoted in 1700 to *sargento mayor* (the equivalent of a modern-day major) of the Presidio at Callao (Peru), and then fought the English at the Puerto de Santa María during the Anglo-Dutch invasion that unsuccessfully tried to capture Cádiz. Having been recommended by Captain General the Marqués of Villadarias, he was named alcalde mayor of Verapaz in 1702.[80] Pedro Lastiri, named to the same post in 1755, was a captain of infantry who had served in the wars in Italy, France, and the Mediterranean and in addition was the son of a distinguished soldier.[81] Fernando de Torres Villavicencio, like the above-mentioned Castillo Ruiz de Vergara, had fought at the Puerto de Santa María during the Anglo-Dutch invasion after having already fought the "Moors" in Morocco and the English at La Coruña and Gibraltar, as well as in Catalonia. He was named alcalde mayor of Suchitepéquez in 1703.[82] Fernando Isidro de Saavedra, appointed to the same post in 1722, had been serving the king since at least the 1680s. He served for seven years as a captain in the king's army in Milan and then went to Mexico City, where he was promoted to sargento mayor and in 1695 raised a company of troops for service in the Philippines. He continued to serve in Mexico at the same rank until he was forced to retire as the result of a cutback on military expenditure. Since he was of advanced age, he was given the position in Guatemala as the equivalent of a pension, to provide for him and his family.[83] Finally, Narciso Barquín de Montecuesta, appointed to the same post in 1742, had served for many years in New Spain and had fought well in two campaigns in northern Mexico that resulted in the conquest and pacification of Indians. For this he had already been awarded a corregimiento in New Spain with the title of *capitán a guerra* (war captain). He was therefore one of the not very numerous individuals who succeeded in being named to a second governmental post.[84]

Among the officeholders was a small group of men who received their appointments not because of their own service but because of that of family members. In this way, some soldiers managed to cash in on their own accomplishments by having their sons or other relatives appointed to the bureaucracy.[85] The practice therefore did not violate the basic principle that offices were rewards for service. It was also consistent with the belief that virtue was hereditary and ran in the "blood" (a word that is sometimes mentioned in the summaries provided to the Council of the Indies); the assumption was that appointing close relatives was likely to produce the same quality of service. Since at least the early sixteenth century, it was common practice in the Spanish Navy for people related through kinship to recommend each other for posts and occupy numerous positions.[86] This proved that a family was truly in the king's service, and it is no surprise therefore to find the practice continuing within the royal bureaucracy in the eighteenth century. In fact, unabashed nepotism, based on the presumption that virtue was hereditary, was a characteristic feature of all early-modern European societies and was exemplified by the careers of Lord Nelson and the Duke of Wellington.

The prospects for career advancement for these government officials, however, were slim. Of a total of 315 men who held office as magistrate, high magistrate, or governor in the Kingdom of Guatemala between 1676 and 1810, just 25 percent succeeded in getting more than one posting. However, only 5 percent—twenty people over a period of more than a century!—were appointed to anything more than twice. This meant that three-quarters of the men left the bureaucracy after serving, at most, one five-year term of office. A great number of them, however, either died in office before filling out their five years or occupied their positions for less than five years because they were filling out the terms of those who had died in office or who had voluntarily stepped down. For the great majority, therefore, the career pattern was not "in and up" but "in and out." There was no movement from province to capital to province to capital in a series of posts. Most bureaucrats started and ended their careers where they started, and the handful that got more than two postings in fact ended up at the same level but in a different location.[87]

It is important to note, moreover, that some of the officials who served in Central America had also served elsewhere in the Spanish empire. They did so in what are now different countries. For example, in 1688 the son of a count in Spain was appointed to hold two posts in America consecutively, first the alcaldía mayor of Cholula (Mexico) and then the gobernación of Soconusco. In 1731 a man owed money by the crown was paid off with posts in Tlaxcala (Mexico) and in Quezaltenango, Guatemala. In 1771 the outgoing high magistrate of Texcoco (Mexico) was appointed to be governor of Soconusco. And in 1774 the highly regarded post of alcalde mayor of Chimaltenango, near Guatemala City, was given to a man who had been a corregidor in Peru. Lists of applicants for posts in the Kingdom of Guatemala included people who had served throughout the Spanish empire.[88] Some had served in or would eventually be sent to the Philippines, Bolivia, Colombia, and Cuba, as well as Texas, Florida, and, as already mentioned, Mexico and Peru.

People with this experience were not very likely to develop a strong sense of creole nationalism within the confines of what are now the modern nations of Latin America. On the contrary, they were just as likely, and probably even more likely, to develop an empire-wide sense of loyalty and identity. Neither the American-born creoles nor the European-born *peninsulares* (people born in the Iberian Peninsula) were restricted in their service to a single region and thus could not have felt spatially "cramped," as Anderson has argued. Gerhard Masur's assertion—which served as the basis of Anderson's interpretation—that "the hammer of Spanish administration had forged nationalities whose inclinations were inward rather than outward" has no basis in fact.[89]

Unfortunately, it is impossible to determine with any precision the proportion of officeholders who were creoles or peninsulares. Ironically, however, the lack of information is not important, for as we have seen, very few people could possibly have had career patterns that might have led to creole awareness. Moreover, it is by now widely known that creole consciousness had emerged in many places as early as in the sixteenth century, and in virtually all places by the seventeenth. This is long before the crisis of Independence. Discrimination against the American-born, especially in the ecclesiastical establishment, was of long standing and yet did not lead to massive political disaffiliation. Within the royal bureaucracy, many Spanish-born people undoubtedly also felt disdain for the members of creole society, but this did not result in the wholesale exclusion of the American-born from office. One suspects that in part this was because for some eighty years—1670 to 1750—the lowest positions were frequently sold, thus enabling creoles to get into the bureaucracy by purchasing offices. After that, however, the evidence suggests that the number of creoles who succeeded in getting positions as provincial magistrates declined. This was due to discrimination not just in favor of the Europeans but also against the Americans.

Furthermore, in the late colonial decades—from the death of Charles III in 1788 to 1821—very few people, whether of European or American origin, served in more than one post in the Kingdom of Guatemala. This was a time when tensions between creoles and peninsulares were reaching a crisis point, as was revealed in 1800 in secret documents presented to the Council of the Indies, in which the aspirants to posts in Central America were carefully identified as being either of European or American origin.[90] The council nonetheless continued to appoint a few Americans as corregidores and alcaldes mayores. Discrimination, therefore, did not result in complete exclusion. However, as in the case of the bureaucrats of Buenos Aires in the late colonial period, it did result in the overwhelming dominance of Europeans in the bureaucracy, as over and over again outsiders were brought in to occupy positions for which the locally born felt themselves qualified.[91] This, rather than outright exclusion, led to resentment among some Americans.

In any case, during the very late colonial period, from 1790 to 1820, a total of only eight people were appointed to more than one position in Central America, and only one of these managed to get a third. Two of the group had first been appointed to office during the reign of Charles III. There is no information as to whether they were creoles or peninsulares. Three others received their first appointments during the reign of Charles IV. Of these, one was identified as a European Spaniard, and another was a Caballero de Santiago and therefore probably, but not certainly, a European Spaniard. The origin of the third was not given. Finally, three other officials were appointed to more than one post in 1810 or after. Of these, one had served in Spain at the siege of Zaragoza in 1808 and therefore was probably a European Spaniard, while the origin of the second was not given. This means that only the last person can clearly be identified as a creole.

Therefore, even if all the officials whose origins cannot be positively identified are added to the creole group, at most seven of the people who held more than one office between 1788 and 1818 were American-born. It is probable, however, that the number was no more than four. This is why the lack of certainty regarding the European or American origins of the officeholders is not of great significance. Four, or at most seven, was simply too small a number of creoles or possible creoles to have experienced the career pattern of "absolutist functionaries" (Anderson's term) moving from post to post and from province to province. Needless to say, their impact on the formation of creole nationalism could not have been very important. It probably was not important at all.

An investigation of the royal officials who served in the bureaucracy thus reveals that there was no career ladder that officials gradually climbed. As a result, there was little or no movement "upward"; practically everyone who served in more than one post in fact moved "laterally," that is, from one corregimiento, alcaldía mayor, or gobernación to another. The only higher ranks that these lowest-ranking salaried officials might have aspired to—with the exception, soon to be discussed, of judge—were those of governor or president–captain general. However, the people appointed as governors in the Kingdom of Guatemala were almost always active-duty senior military officers, because the posts involved the command of military forces stationed in the province to repel British invasions or raids by pirates or corsairs. Very rarely did a magistrate or high magistrate get appointed as a governor. Most of them probably did not even want to, because three of the four governorships were not very lucrative. As already noted, that of Costa Rica was so devoid of business opportunities that no one ever offered to buy it. Those in Honduras and Nicaragua, while worth purchasing, were not among those posts sold at high prices. This was because of their limited commercial opportunities. Only the governorship of Soconusco, one of the major cacao-producing regions in Mesoamerica, was considered a plum position, and some of the people who held that post went on to be magistrates or high magistrates elsewhere. This was hardly moving up a ladder. It was lateral movement in pursuit of personal economic interest, wherever that may have taken them. Only near the end of the colonial period—when moving up from corregidor or alcalde mayor to governor was possibly seen as a promotion—would it become possible to talk of the existence of a bureaucratic ladder.

Since exceptions often provide insights into the rules in force, it will be worthwhile to examine a rare example of someone who held an extraordinary number of positions in the bureaucracy in Central America. The person who broke all records for holding posts was José González Rancaño, a peninsular Spaniard who first acquired a position in 1730, when he bought the corregimiento of Chiquimula de la Sierra (in eastern Guatemala). At the time, he was living in Cádiz, where many magistrates lived when they purchased an office in America. González Rancaño apparently had a military background, for while serving as magistrate of Chiquimula de la Sierra he was called upon as someone with experience for the purpose of putting down an Indian uprising in the province of Verapaz. He did so without the need to resort to force, and succeeded in restoring order.[92] González Rancaño was so successful in rounding up workers for the silver mines in nearby Tegucigalpa that his term of office was extended for an additional five years.[93] His next appointment, in 1748, was as governor of Nicaragua, and to operate effectively in a position of command over troops, he was given the military rank of colonel—a rank that in his case was specifically limited only to America. He served as governor of Nicaragua between 1751 and 1756, and during that time fought a small campaign against the Indians on the Caribbean coast. Next, he was appointed interim governor of Costa Rica, and in 1764 he became the high magistrate of Atitlán (Sololá).When his term was running out, he made a special request to the government: either reappointment to his post or five hundred pesos for each of his four daughters to provide them with dowries.

The accounting office of the Council of the Indies, however, recommended against the request. It pointed out that although González Rancaño had performed adequately, his service had not been so exemplary as to warrant such special treatment. Moreover, the accounting office report noted that he had already been amply rewarded, and drew attention to "the numerous lucrative positions he has held without any interruption, and he continues to enjoy one of the juiciest [*más pingües*] alcaldías mayores of the Kingdom of Guatemala." The report concluded with the recommendation that posts should be shared out among the many meritorious candidates rather than be monopolized by a favored few.[94] Nevertheless, the Council of the Indies eventually decided to reward González Rancaño, not with his request for dowries for his daughters or reappointment as high magistrate of Atitlán, but with reappointment to the post as magistrate of Chiquimula de la Sierra, which of course was where he had started thirty years earlier.[95]

This career reveals many of the realities of the bureaucracy in the eighteenth century. First, positions were rewards for service already performed, not for people intending to make a career as bureaucrats. Even the purchase of an office was euphemistically called a "monetary service." Second, since there were many worthy candidates (no fewer than fifty-six people applied in 1763 to be magistrate of Chiquimula de la Sierra, which was not even one of the most lucrative posts in the kingdom),[96] the rulers believed it best to share the offices out to reward as many as possible. This meant that it was a violation of accepted procedures to keep reappointing the same people; hence the normal practice of "in and out." Third, the royal government knew very well that the positions were used for personal enrichment, and hence the candid observation that González Rancaño currently was holding one of the most lucrative posts, the implication being that he had already had ample opportunity to feather his nest. Fourth, the royal government, perhaps surprisingly to those who have never seen its archives, sometimes had a heart and was willing to bend the rules when it thought it humane to do so. Finally, this was clearly an example of an extraordinarily successful or lucky bureaucratic career, as was recognized at the time.

Yet González Rancaño had ended up exactly where he had started. In a modern bureaucracy, this would be the sign of an unsuccessful career. In fact, in the middle of the eighteenth century the exact opposite was true, because bureaucratic careers were not "modern." In any event, this case was rare, as three-quarters of officeholders never held more than one post in the colonial bureaucracy.

At the same time, it should be noted that for most of the colonial period, the provincial magistrates were cut off from any opportunity to advance up a ladder by joining the ranks of the audiencia. Entry into the legal profession required training that could only be acquired in professional law schools, and therefore it was closed off to practically all of the people who held positions in America as magistrate, high magistrate, or governor. Most of the latter, of course, were soldiers, not lawyers. For governors, therefore, there was no possible access to positions at the audiencia capital, with the exception of the position as president–captain general. Consequently, the career ladder of the lawyers and judges was disconnected from the magistrates, high magistrates, and governors who served as the lowest level of salaried bureaucrats.

On the other hand, as will be shown in chapter 6, in the late colonial period the Spanish crown may have been moving toward the establishment of a modern bureaucracy characterized by a career ladder. In the case of the Kingdom of Guatemala, in the 1790s the government began to treat the various ranks in the bureaucracy as steps of a ladder that a functionary could ascend. In a sharp break with tradition, it began to appoint some trained lawyers as corregidores and alcaldes mayores, and then some of these officials were appointed to higher posts, including the new one of intendant. These bureaucrats with legal training then could aspire to a judgeship on an audiencia. This meant the emergence of a system in which people joined the royal service as lawyers seeking a career as colonial bureaucrats and hoping to move up a career ladder as time went on. This situation existed, however, very briefly, and most importantly, only for the very small number of people with law degrees. After 1800 the policy was abandoned, and once again the people receiving appointments as provincial magistrates were people with military backgrounds who had limited hope of moving laterally from one position to another and no hope of moving vertically.

The only exception to this rule was the case of José de Estachería, whose career is the subject of chapter 5. After distinguished service in the Seven Years' War, he was appointed governor of Nicaragua and then moved up to become the president–captain general of the Audiencia of Guatemala in 1782. He got the promotion, however, not only because of the military ability he had displayed during the war against the English but also because he was well connected to the Gálvez family, one member of which, José de Gálvez, happened to be the man at the head of the colonial office in Spain. Most governors, alcaldes mayores, and corregidores lacked such connections and never had the opportunity to show any military prowess. They therefore rarely got more than one opportunity to serve their king in the colonial bureaucracy.

V

Despite the sale of the offices of magistrate, high magistrate, and governor, people who were appointed to those posts free of charge outnumbered those who purchased their offices. This was true even during the period from 1670 to 1750 when the offices were being sold. However, this fact is misleading, for a number of the positions were rarely or never sold and had high turnover rates among the officials who had the bad luck to be appointed. Inclusion of these posts should not blind us to the reality that many offices were held longer by people who had bought them than by people who had not. This was especially true of the really valuable posts with large Indian populations like Chiapa, Huehuetenango, Verapaz, Atitlán, Quezaltenango, Soconusco, and San Salvador. For most indigenous people, therefore, the government official who ruled over them between 1670 and 1750 was likely to be someone who had bought the office to make money at their expense.[97]

The system therefore was based on the likelihood of profit to be made at the expense of the indigenous people, and in fact, many of the people who held offices as alcaldes mayores or corregidores and made money by doing so founded families that became members of the social elite in eighteenth-century Guatemala.[98] This could not have resulted in good government, as the crown was well aware. Even when those posts were not sold, as was the case after 1750, the indigenous people accounted for a significant part of tax revenues either in the form of tribute or in the production of exportable, and thus taxable, goods. In short, the colonial bureaucracy, like the society of Spanish colonists, was based on the Indians, the sine qua non of the Kingdom of Guatemala.

CHAPTER 3

Indians and the Colonial State

Indigenous Economies, Government Officials, and the Business of Government

Needless to say, people did not invest large quantities of money to buy posts or live in what were often considered godforsaken places merely because of their loyalty to the king. Magistrates exercised political power that was easily translated into personal gain. The nature of commercial opportunity, however, depended on local economic, social, and geographic conditions. Local economy, society, and geography therefore must be analyzed in order to explain why some posts, like Costa Rica, could only be given away, while others, like Chiapa, could be sold for a small fortune. The problem will be addressed, therefore, by analyzing each province in turn along the axis running northwest to southeast from the Isthmus of Tehuantepec—dividing New Spain from the Kingdom of Guatemala—to the Isthmus of Panama.[1]

I

Chiapa

It is convenient to begin with Chiapa, the northernmost province of the kingdom.[2] The alcaldía mayor of Chiapa, occupying the central highlands and part of the northern lowlands of the modern state of Chiapas, was the most expensive magistracy in Central America, and, as noted in the previous chapter, was the third most expensive alcaldía mayor in the entire Spanish empire. Therefore, an explanation of its high magistrate's business activities will illuminate those elements of local economy and society that were crucial in determining why some provinces were valuable and others were not.

To the modern observer, the value of Chiapa in the colonial era is somewhat mysterious. The region does have resources for productive agriculture, especially in the Grijalva Valley, but most of the native inhabitants lived in mountainous regions of limited agricultural potential. Moreover, Chiapa was completely lacking in gold and silver, and produced only small quantities of cacao and the natural dye called *grana* (cochineal). Thus the province did not have much in the way of the natural resources considered by Europeans to be the true criteria for determining wealth. Even by modern Mexican standards, Chiapas (the modern Mexican state that includes the colonial provinces of Chiapa and Soconusco) is one of the poorest states of the Mexican Republic.

These modern observations, however, are misleading. In the context of the seventeenth and eighteenth centuries, Chiapa had one of the most precious of all resources: human beings. The population was certainly not poor in the opinion of the Maya people—most importantly, the Tzeltal and Tzotzil—who lived there and maintained long-standing cultural traditions. Chiapa in fact contained a well-organized, stable, and socially stratified society and a productive and complex economy. The Mayas had been living in the region for millennia and had been producing a substantial surplus to maintain an elite. After the conquest, Spaniards became the new elite, but the colonists were not so unintelligent as to wreck the tribute-producing society that had been and continued to be the basis of civilization in America. The Mayas, then, were the proverbial geese laying golden eggs. Colonialism adapted to the already existing structures of production and prospered by channeling the surplus away from the Indian peasantry and into the coffers of Church, state, and local Spanish elite.

Chiapa, which in 1746 comprised ninety-two Indian settlements containing 13,646 tributaries (more than fifty-four thousand native people),[3] presented government officials with considerable commercial opportunity. By the late seventeenth century the high magistrates were conducting a variety of profitable business activities with the Indians. They made money from the tribute system by taking advantage of the difference between the values at which tribute was assessed and market prices. In theory, Indians were required to pay part of their taxes in maize, and the magistrate was supposed to sell the grain and deliver the proceeds to the royal treasury. In practice, however, the alcalde mayor bought the tributary maize himself—working through intermediaries—at artificially low prices, and then sold the grain on the market for two or three times what he had paid for it. Treasury officials complained that the king, as well as the Indians, was a loser in these operations, but in fact little could be done because the magistrates used their political power to prevent competitive bidding for tribute goods. The crown eventually acted to remedy some of these abuses, and in the 1740s tribute was commuted to money in order to prevent alcaldes mayores from acquiring maize at artificially low prices.

Another business operation of the alcalde mayor of Chiapa was the acquisition of wheat at lower than market prices. If given a choice, the Mayas usually would not produce wheat at all, because maize, the traditional grain that the native people preferred to eat, was a more reliable and productive crop. In addition, maize was intimately connected to indigenous religion and to the Indians' sense of identity; they believed that humans were made of maize. The magistrates got around this resistance by loaning money to the peasants to help make their tribute payments in cash, and then demanding repayment in kind, that is, in wheat. This operation was known as a *repartimiento*. In this case, the alcalde mayor gave out money in return for goods to be delivered at a later time. In practice, however, one suspects that the Indians frequently got little or no cash, for in some cases all that happened was that tribute was paid for them, because they were usually short of cash. The high magistrate thus got them into debt and used the tributary system to buy wheat before the harvest at artificially low prices in order to resell it at a profit. Magistrates also used repartimientos to acquire some tobacco, cochineal, and cacao. The latter two, which were exported, eventually became even more important for the magistrates than the wheat business. Cochineal, sent to Spain, was produced by Indians in the highlands, and to acquire it the alcalde mayor had to spend more than two thousand pesos per year, but by the end of his five-year term he was reported to earn more than twelve thousand pesos in profits. He acquired the cacao, later exported to Oaxaca and possibly to points further north, by advancing cash to the native people living in the northern lowlands near Tabasco. The business was said to yield ten thousand pesos of profit over five years.

By far the most important business of the alcaldes mayores of Chiapa was the repartimiento to acquire thread and cloth. Just to get this going, it was reported in the 1760s that the magistrate needed to acquire between four and six thousand arrobas (between fifty and seventy-five tons) of raw cotton per year. This required the outlay of between two and three thousand pesos for the purchase of raw cotton. The cotton business was intimately connected to the tributary system. The indigenous people had to pay tribute, but as with the wheat business, sometimes the magistrate paid it for them, thereby getting the native people indebted to him. Other times he distributed cash for advance purchase of the goods. All of this required the alcalde mayor to spend at least five thousand pesos per year. He distributed raw cotton to the village leaders, who passed it out to the indigenous women for spinning. The Indians paid their debts to the alcalde mayor in cotton thread—made from the raw cotton given to the women—and textiles. This was in effect a kind of putting-out system. However, unlike similar structures of production in Europe, this putting-out system was involuntary and resulted from the colonial relationship between Spaniards and Indians. The Mayas had no choice in the matter: the magistrate routinely paid their tribute, thereby getting them into debt, and provided them with the cotton they would use to pay off that debt. The repartimiento and tributary systems thus overlapped, and debt collection was the same as tax collection. To be sure, taxation is unpopular and involuntary almost everywhere, and thus the repartimiento system tended to hide its coercive nature by embedding itself in the tributary system. Nevertheless, the indigenous people sometimes failed to pay their debts and taxes, and when this happened, the magistrate had the option of arresting and flogging the village leaders.

By the middle of the eighteenth century, the magistrates of Chiapa had introduced still another kind of repartimiento. This involved the sale of goods on credit to the indigenous people. The business sometimes consisted of the sale of machetes, a certain number of which were allocated—hence the term "repartimiento"—to the villages. In this case the Indians were incorporated into the market economy not as producers but as consumers. This practice, referred to as a *repartimiento de efectos*, was most common in central Mexico and Peru. In Central America, this variation apparently occurred late in the colonial period. It may have become possible only after the other form of the repartimiento—sales *by* the Indians—had raised the level of commercialization to the point that the native economy could bear the additional burden of consumption. In fact, in the 1760s it was reported in many provinces that the sale on credit of goods to Indians was a new activity, one which was generating some resistance. By that time, high magistrates in Chiapa were selling the Mayas not only machetes made in Puebla but also hats from Oaxaca and mules—about two hundred per year—raised in Chiapa itself. Magistrates bought the mules for fourteen pesos each and sold them to the Indians for twenty-five pesos. The difference in price covered the cost of credit (that is, interest), losses caused by default (the volume of which is impossible to estimate) or by the death of mules before they could be sold, and profits.

A minor business of the alcalde mayor of Chiapa, but a major activity elsewhere, was the sale of his own cattle to the slaughterhouse that provided beef to local consumers. Each year the city of Ciudad Real (modern-day San Cristóbal de Las Casas), the capital of the province, allowed the high magistrate a whole month during which he was the only one permitted to sell meat in the market. However, Ciudad Real was a small settlement with few meat eaters, and since the Mayas of Chiapa consumed little beef, the alcalde mayor probably did not make much money from this business. It was estimated that it brought in only about two hundred pesos per year.

In summary, Chiapa yielded profits because magistrates could use their positions to sell goods to the Indians and acquire wheat, maize, cochineal, cacao, and above all, cotton thread and cotton textiles. The grains were shipped to Santiago, and presumably to other urban centers, for sale. Much of the thread at first ended up in Santiago, although by the 1760s the high cost of transportation had induced the alcaldes mayores to open a factory in Ciudad Real. The workers wove the local thread into *naguas* (petticoats), which had higher value added than thread and thus could be shipped more profitably. The textiles, cacao, and cochineal sometimes went long distances before reaching their markets. Most of these goods were sent to Oaxaca by mule along the road from Guatemala to New Spain. However, taking cotton textiles and cochineal to Oaxaca was like carrying coals to Newcastle, for Oaxaca itself was a major producer and exporter of those same goods.[4] Mexico City merchants worked hand-in-glove with alcaldes mayores and merchants in the southernmost province of the Kingdom of New Spain, acquiring cotton textiles to ship to the mining camps of northern Mexico, and cochineal and cacao to export to Spain.[5] Chiapa's products were part of this flow of goods to the north or across the Atlantic. The province's skirts—called *chiapanecas*—were even imitated in Mexico.[6]

Business activities like these allowed the alcalde mayor of Chiapa to earn profits on such a scale as to justify the outlay of considerable sums to buy his post. His annual salary was only eight hundred pesos throughout most of the seventeenth and eighteenth centuries, but according to a secret report by the president of the audiencia in 1738, the annual profits earned by the high magistrate of Chiapa totaled twelve thousand pesos.[7] At an inquest carried out in 1765–66, a well-informed witness calculated annual profits of the magistrates to be more than fourteen thousand pesos.[8]

Soconusco

The province of Soconusco was in some ways the opposite of Chiapa.[9] Because of the considerable humidity and rainfall along this part of the Pacific coast, Soconusco was an excellent locale for growing cacao but an unhealthy one for human beings. Most of the native people died in the first fifty years after the conquest, and as a result this cacao-producing region went into decline.[10] Nevertheless, enough Indians— Motocintlec and Chicomuceltec Mayas, as well as some non-Maya

Tapachultec Zoques—survived to work the cacao trees to make the governorship of Soconusco a very valuable post indeed. In 1746 the royal treasury recorded a population of 3,709 tributaries—about fifteen thousand Indians—settled in twenty villages. The non-Indian population was small and included mostly mulattoes.

The governor exploited the natural resources of the province by carrying out repartimientos to acquire goods. Indians were required to pay their tribute in cacao instead of money, and governors also lent money or paid tribute for the indigenous people in return for future payment in vanilla beans. Some cacao was then shipped to Santiago, but the larger part was exported to Mexico City. Some was then reexported to Spain, where it was destined for the royal household. The salary of the governor was six hundred pesos per year throughout the entire colonial period, but the secret report of 1738 estimated that the governor's real annual income was about eight thousand pesos—that is, more than thirteen times his salary. However, the profits to the governor declined sharply after the 1740s, once the crown implemented the reform allowing the indigenous people to pay their tribute in money rather than in cacao.

Quezaltenango

The highland province of Quezaltenango, inhabited mostly by Mam and K'iche' Mayas, was similar to Chiapa.[11] In the 1740s its twenty-one villages contained 4,983 tributaries, or almost twenty thousand Indians. The non-Indian population was small early in the century, although it would become more significant in size after people displaced by the 1773 earthquake moved in. Most of the non-Indian people lived in the town of Quezaltenango. In the 1760s some twenty Spanish families and an undisclosed number of mestizos lived there. All of the non-Indians were said to be engaged in one way or another in the buying and selling of textiles.

The province's corregidores engaged in operations to acquire wheat and maize, and at least one magistrate made some extra money by allowing people to engage in illegal gambling. However, as in Chiapa, the major business came to be the repartimiento of cotton thread, textiles, and cacao. Since the latter could not be produced in the highlands, the Indians had to cross the mountains to trade for cacao in the bordering alcaldía mayor of Suchitepéquez, on the Pacific coast. The need to repay debts by making payments in cacao must have cost the Indians dearly in time and money. This type of repartimiento was carried out early in the eighteenth century, but later on seems to have died out. On the other hand, magistrates succeeded in replacing cacao as their main business by selling cotton cloth and iron hoes through repartimientos. The tools were made in Santiago and sold to the Indians, supposedly to stimulate agriculture.

The corregidores of Quezaltenango also conducted other kinds of repartimientos to take advantage of local ecological and economic conditions. Because the province lay at one of the highest altitudes in Central America, sheep raising was possible. Sheep were unknown to the Mayas before the Spanish invasion, but the Indians eventually raised them in considerable numbers. Magistrates therefore advanced the producers money to buy lambs and especially wool. The latter, in turn, was "put out" to the Indians for spinning and weaving. The repartimiento for woolen thread, always carried out through the indigenous government officials, was an important part of the business activities of the corregidores. Repayment of debts by the Indians was usually scheduled at the same time that tribute payments were due. In effect, the indigenous people therefore paid a great deal of their taxes in kind even if allowed to pay in cash. In Quezaltenango, the repartimiento system, which included both sales to and advanced purchases from the Indians, thus facilitated tribute collection.

The magistrates of Quezaltenango marketed their grains, thread, textiles, and wool in Santiago, although some of the goods—especially the cloth and thread—were sent to Mexico on the overland route through Chiapa and Oaxaca. Many of the mule drivers who carried the goods were indigenous people from the province of Quezaltenango itself. The secret report of 1738 estimated that the corregidor earned around ten thousand pesos per year, that is, approximately thirty times his annual salary of 331 pesos. To earn that money, however, during his tenure he had to invest between eight and ten thousand pesos, because every year he had to buy two hundred sheep, a considerable quantity of woven cotton cloth, hoes, and 2,500 pounds (250 bales, or *fardos*) of raw cotton that he had to acquire from outside the province. The corregidor began to recoup his investment in his third year in office.

Huehuetenango-Totonicapán

The province of Huehuetenango-Totonicapán, inhabited mostly by K'iche' and Mam Mayas, as well as by small numbers of Jacaltec, Kanjobal, Chuj, and Ixil Mayas, was located in the highest of the Central American highlands, in what is now northwestern Guatemala.[12] In 1746 its fifty-four villages contained 6,810 tributaries, or more than twenty-seven thousand Indians. The non-Indian population was much smaller than in neighboring Quezaltenango.

The most important business activities of the alcalde mayor were repartimientos to acquire cotton thread. Every six months, more than forty tons of raw cotton were "put out" to the Indians for spinning. Cotton was distributed to the villages in hundred-pound bales, each of which yielded twenty-five pounds of thread. Each woman was allocated between eight and ten pounds of raw cotton, and all together the women of the province produced more than ten tons of thread for the magistrate every six months. Bales of raw cotton cost between 4 and 5 pesos, and the alcalde mayor paid the Indians 6 pesos 2 reales per bale, or 2 reales per pound, for the spinning. His total costs came to between 10 pesos 2 reales and 11 pesos 2 reales per bale, but the twenty-five pounds of thread that he acquired was then sold for 15 pesos, giving him a return of between 33 and 46 percent on his investment. That was not pure profit, of course, for it included the cost of credit and some losses resulting from default by the Indians. Magistrates also engaged in repartimientos to acquire cloth, allocating thread and money in return for future payment in textiles of all kinds. However, this latter activity was said to be in decline in the 1760s because the crown had exempted several of the largest villages from this repartimiento.

The alcalde mayor of Huehuetenango also engaged in other commercial activities. The high altitude permitted sheep raising, and thus the magistrates carried out repartimientos to acquire wool, which was then sometimes allocated for spinning and weaving. They also carried out repartimientos to acquire wheat, virtually monopolized the sale of cattle in the province, and sold to the Indians all sorts of agricultural tools, some cotton cloth brought in from elsewhere, and even the cards needed to comb wool. The cattle business was said to be quite lucrative, thereby suggesting that meat consumption was higher here than in Chiapa. In the 1760s the alcalde mayor was said to be selling more than six hundred head of cattle per year. The high magistrate had the unusually low annual salary of only 331 pesos, but he made few complaints. His income from business was estimated by the president in 1738 to be twelve thousand pesos, that is, thirty-six times his salary. In the 1760s it was reported that the alcalde mayor needed to invest more than thirty thousand pesos to carry out all of his business activities, but if successful, profits could total thirty thousand in five years. He started to earn profits from his investment during his third year in office. It was best if the magistrate invested his own capital or had a business partner, for if he had to borrow from local merchants, the latter charged between 15 and 20 percent interest on loans.

The repartimiento was always carried out during June and December, when tribute payments were due. As a result, the Indians received the money to pay their tribute. It was reported by insiders that the magistrate did not need to employ "fuerza" (force, that is, coercion) to carry out his business, and this may have been the case, although the informants were of course supporters of the system. The linking of the repartimiento with tribute meant that business and government worked hand in hand, thereby facilitating commercial transactions between the magistrates and the indigenous people. It should also be noted that at least one alcalde mayor tried to bypass the village government and sell goods on credit directly to the Indians through repartimientos, but this did not succeed. His failure highlights the crucial role that indigenous officials, who were in charge of collecting tribute, played in the repartimiento system; their participation was the sine qua non for a magistrate's commercial success. The next chapter will analyze the role of a particular alcalde mayor of Huehuetenango and discuss in greater detail the reality of repartimiento in the province.

Atitlán-Tecpanatitlán

The highland province of Atitlán-Tecpanatitlán, inhabited by Tzutujil, Cakchikel, and K'iche' Mayas, was the heart of one of the most commercialized regions in Central America.[13] Although it occupied only a small area, the province included forty villages which in 1746 contained some 7,049 tributaries, or more than twenty-eight thousand Indians. As in the case of Huehuetenango, the non-Indian population was small. The native people produced a wide variety of goods and sold products in local markets and in Santiago, and the resulting high level of commercialization meant that magistrates could carry out repartimientos to sell to the Indians. Like most of the other highland provinces, the high magistracy of Atitlán (called Sololá in the late eighteenth century) offered enterprising officials great opportunities. In fact, as we have seen in the previous chapter, the Council of the Indies once denied a pension to a former alcalde mayor of this province because he already held "one of the juiciest alcaldías mayores of the Kingdom of Guatemala."[14]

The magistrates' business activities were diverse. Here, cattle were the most lucrative business, for it was said that more than a thousand head of cattle could be sold in the province's four meat markets due to the demand for meat during Indian festivals, and an additional hundred head could be sold on the hoof. As elsewhere, the alcalde mayor made money by carrying out repartimientos of cotton and cash in return for thread and cloth. Over five years he could acquire more than thirty-one tons of cotton thread. He also paid in advance to acquire wheat and even chickpeas (*garbanzos*—this was the only province in which this product is mentioned). In the same manner, the magistrate acquired cacao, which the Indians had to go into the coastal lowlands and trade for. Magistrates also sold the Indians mules, agricultural tools, and cards for wool production. All told, according to the president's report of 1738, the post generated profits of more than twelve thousand pesos per year. A former alcalde mayor testified in 1765 that magistrates could earn between eight and twenty thousand pesos annually, depending on their business skills and market conditions. To accomplish this level of profit, however, they had to invest between twelve and thirty-five thousand pesos to purchase cotton and cattle. They bought the cattle at the annual cattle fair at Laguna in the coastal province of Escuintla-Guazacapán, paying four pesos per head and then selling them at ten pesos. Some live-stock, however, died on the cattle drive and had to be written off as a loss, and as was always the case, the difference in price included the cost of credit. One alcalde mayor who failed to get adequate financial backing ended up making almost no money at all. If Indians died still owing money to the magistrate, village officials were held responsible, demonstrating again the crucial role of the indigenous governments.

Chimaltenango and Amatitanes-Sacatepéquez

The alcaldías mayores of Chimaltenango and Amatitanes-Sacatepé-quez were created in the 1750s in an effort to introduce more effective administration over the Valley of Guatemala, which formerly had been run by the city council of Santiago.[15] The creation of these posts deprived the city government of control of what was the most developed marketing system in Central America. The people in Chimaltenango—west of Santiago—were Cakchikel Mayas, but by the middle of the eighteenth century a large number of the people could speak Castilian. The same was true in Amatitanes, east of Santiago, where the people were Pokomam Mayas. In the valley, under the jurisdiction of the two new high magistracies, were seventy-five villages which in 1746 contained 21,665 tributaries, or about eighty-seven thousand Indians.

The new magistrates quickly replaced the city councilmen as the businessmen of the valley. They carried out repartimientos to sell the Indians hatchets, machetes, and other agricultural tools; hats; mules; and clothing. The latter is significant because it reveals the possible location of a market for some of the textiles produced in other highland provinces and acquired by alcaldes mayores through the repartimiento system. Some cloth sold there, however, could also have originated in China. The magistrates forced the Indians to pay part of their tribute in grain, which was then resold at a profit. The magistrates purchased raw cotton in the coastal lowland provinces and then required the native people of Chimaltenango and Amati-tanes to transport it to the highlands where it could be sold for tex-tile production elsewhere. Magistrates even organized a monopoly on the feathers—probably from the quetzal—that the Indians needed for their ceremonial festival dress. Feathers had already been com-mercialized by indigenous merchants from Verapaz and probably others as well;[16] alcaldes mayores probably learned of the commercial possibilities of the feathers from Indian entrepreneurs. However, the native people were apparently so busy with their own marketing activities that the magistrates did not carry out repartimientos of cotton or thread, which helps explain why these particular Indians, unlike most others in the highlands, were brought into the commer-cial system more as consumers than as producers of textiles.

Verapaz

In many of the highland provinces thus far discussed, the most important branch of the magistrates' business was the putting-out system for the production of cotton thread and textiles.[17] However, the highland people did not themselves produce the raw cotton necessary for this kind of repartimiento. A tropical or semitropical climate is required for cotton production. Yet the population of the coastal lowlands of Guatemala was small and insufficient to produce the large quantities of raw cotton required to keep the repartimiento system going. Production therefore had to come from elsewhere. The significance of the province of Verapaz, located in the northern highlands of Guatemala and stretching into the lowlands even fur-ther to the north, is precisely that it was one of the major suppliers of the cotton needed to keep the whole system functioning.

Verapaz was inhabited by K'iche', Poconchí, and Kekchí Mayas, as well as by a group of non-Maya Nahua, or Mexican, Indians who settled in the southeastern highlands of the province.[18] In 1746 its thirteen villages had a population of 8,413 tributaries, or about thirty-four thousand Indians. Non-Indians were few in number and included mostly mestizos and mulattoes. Although the southern part of Vera-paz is in the highlands, the river valleys in the area descend to lower altitudes than is the case elsewhere in Guatemala. As a result, the climate of these valleys is at times semitropical and thus appropriate for cotton production. Moreover, the northern villages were located in the southernmost part of the lowlands that stretched eventually into the tropical rainforest of the Petén. One of the most important cotton-producing areas was centered around the village of Cahabón (sixty kilometers east of Cobán), at an altitude of 250 meters and close to the edge of the lowlands. Another cotton area was San Agustín Lanquín, just west of Cahabón, at an altitude of 380 meters. The native people, then, lived in an environment embracing different ecological zones in close proximity to each other. A variety of resources were thus available for human use. Furthermore, there already existed a strong tradition of interregional trade organized in part by indigenous merchants.[19]

The magistrates of Verapaz took advantage of this varied ecology by carrying out repartimientos to acquire raw cotton in large quantities. They always worked through the village governments to advance cash to the Indians in August and September, when the planting season began, and the indigenous people repaid their debt the following May or June. The alcaldes mayores also advanced money to acquire maize, beans, achiote, chili peppers, and a little cacao. The ready supply of raw material also made it easy for the magistrates to "put out" cotton to be spun and thread to be woven. The weavers sometimes produced rough twine bags, which were sent to the Pacific coastal provinces for the bagging of cacao. As a result of all these businesses, the magistrates made good profits. The president's report of 1738 estimated the alcalde mayor's annual income to be eight thousand pesos, although the informants at the 1765–66 inquest complained of competition from the large number of commercially minded Indians. Many of them owned their own mules and transported both raw cotton and thread within the province as well as to the capital. They were also said to be transporting salt from the coastal province of Escuintla all the way into the northern highlands and lowlands. The Indians in fact shipped more thread to Santiago and other places than the people hired by the magistrates. No mention was made of the quantity of capital that had to be invested by the alcaldes mayores. Nor was there mention of a connection between tribute debts and repartimientos. The omission of any mention of credit could have been the result of the greater quantities of cash acquired by the Indians through their own marketing activities. With money available, the indigenous people would have been able to pay their tribute without relying on credit from the magistrate.

Chiquimula de la Sierra

The highland province of Chiquimula de la Sierra in modern-day eastern Guatemala was unlike any of the other highland areas thus far described.[20] The topography was similar to that of southern Verapaz, but Chiquimula's leeward position relative to surrounding mountains resulted in little rainfall for many parts of the province. The deep river valleys permitted cotton and sugar cultivation, but otherwise, agricultural potential was limited. This helps account for the substantial development of cattle ranching in this part of Guatemala.

The native population was made up mostly of Cholti and Pokomam Mayas, with an important group of Nahua speakers in the western part of the province. In 1746 its thirty villages contained 7,921 tributaries, or more than thirty-two thousand Indians. Some native people survived colonialism better than others. One group used its proximity to the Motagua River to participate in trade, legal and otherwise, on the Honduran coast. However, most of the Indians found themselves gradually overwhelmed by, and eventually working for, the large number of Spaniards, mestizos, and mulattoes who settled in the region to exploit the opportunities for ranching and sugarcane cultivation. Chiquimula province contained the largest group of non-Indians in Guatemala outside of the capital of Santiago. Since many of these people lived and worked on the numerous ranches and plantations, the population tended to be dispersed rather than concentrated in a few large villages. This settlement pattern differed considerably from that found in the central and western Guatemalan highlands.

Such a society provided the corregidores with few business opportunities. Some raw cotton was acquired through repartimientos, but the Indians could not be easily coerced into spinning and weaving. It is likely that such activities were directly related to the need for credit, and in this province, labor on haciendas provided people with enough cash to pay most of their tribute. Certainly the best "business" of the corregidores was the organization of a labor draft for the newly developing mines in the bordering province of Tegucigalpa. One corregidor of the province, as we saw in the previous chapter, was so successful at providing workers to the mines that the government granted him a rare reappointment to his position. Mine owners paid the magistrates a fee for each Indian worker provided. The socially destructive impact on the Indians of such long-distance labor migration may well be imagined. The president's report of 1738 estimated that the corregidor made approximately six thousand pesos annually from his businesses. This was about nine times more than his salary of 660 pesos.

Suchitepéquez

The province of Suchitepéquez, embracing half of the Pacific coast of Guatemala, was similar to Soconusco in that the environment was good for cacao but bad for humans.[21] However, some K'iche' and Tzutujil Mayas survived in the northern highlands of the province in sufficient numbers to make Suchitepéquez a very valuable post. In 1746 the province's twenty-five villages had 3,793 tributaries, or more than fifteen thousand Indians. In addition, a considerable number of non-Indians, mostly mulattoes, were settled in the province, especially in the lowlands. The climate was good for agriculture in general, for it was possible to bring in two harvests of maize per year. The indigenous people raised cotton virtually everywhere in the province, but only one-third of the villages produced cacao.

The business of the alcalde mayor consisted almost exclusively of repartimientos carried out to acquire cacao and cotton. The latter was either sold locally or shipped for sale to Santiago. Suchitepéquez thus was another of the cotton-producing provinces providing the raw material necessary to keep the repartimiento system going in the highlands. Demand for cotton was so great, in fact, that magistrates at times contracted non-Indians in order to acquire a future supply. This was one of the few places where repartimientos were made to anyone other than Indians. Another sign of the importance of cotton is the informants' mention of the use of force by magistrates in the collection of debts owed by the Indians. The cacao acquired through repartimientos to the Indians was sold in Santiago or exported to New Spain.

The 1738 report estimated that the alcalde mayor stood to gain more than ten thousand pesos annually from his business, which compared nicely to his salary of 1,158 pesos. Five-year gross revenues early in the century were said to reach anywhere between fifty and one hundred thousand pesos. Business on that scale required a total investment of more than sixteen thousand pesos. After the tribute reform of 1732 allowing the Indians to pay their tribute in money rather than in kind, magistrates were unable to force the indigenous people to pay in cacao, and this led to declining production of cacao and dwindling income for alcaldes mayores.[22] This draws attention once more to the frequent connection between repartimientos and tribute; when that connection was broken, repartimientos became more difficult to carry out. Moreover, according to the informants at the 1765–66 inquest, the magistrates were having little success in introducing the system of forced sales because the people were putting up strong resistance. If they were not in debt, it seems they could sometimes refuse to buy goods on credit from the magistrates. Here, then, we see that the indigenous people not only resisted the repartimiento system but at times were successful in their efforts. As time went on, the magistracy of Suchitepéquez became more and more undesirable from the point of view of prospective officeholders.

Escuintla-Guazacapán

The other half of the Pacific coast of Guatemala was covered by Escuintla-Guazacapán, and although some Nahua speakers and Xinca (non-Maya) people survived, the Indians were poor and difficult to exploit.[23] Its thirty settlements in 1746 included only 2,873 tributaries, or about eleven thousand Indians. Living in many of the villages were a considerable number of mulattoes. The province's main economic activities were cattle raising and production of cacao, cotton, sugar, and indigo. The province contained many small haciendas and even some small, Indian-owned sugar mills.

The repartimiento system functioned best in the presence of organized indigenous communities ruled by their own leaders, but in Escuintla the virtual nonexistence of these communities severely limited commercial opportunities for magistrates. Most Indians worked on nearby haciendas to earn the money needed to pay their tribute, and as a result they did not fall into the clutches of a money-lending alcalde mayor. The magistrates therefore tried to contract for the future delivery of cotton, but this brought in little money. One alcalde mayor tried to sell goods to the Indians, but the absence of strong village leaders made it difficult for him to collect on his debts. In fact, Indians resisted all efforts to introduce sales through repartimientos. One magistrate did succeed in "putting out" raw cotton for repayment in thread in three villages, but the quality of the product was said to be poor and hardly worth the effort. Those who held the office of alcalde mayor thus found it virtually impossible to make any money off of the post. The president's report of 1738 estimated that the alcalde mayor could make up to four thousand pesos by organizing various businesses, but none of the other informants agreed with that assessment. According to practically everyone, Escuintla was one of the worst posts in the kingdom; few wanted it, and still fewer made the mistake of buying it. The salary was a mere 331 pesos.

Sonsonate

Modern El Salvador comprises the two colonial alcaldías mayores of Sonsonate and San Salvador.[24] The former, bordered on the northwest by Escuintla, was much smaller than San Salvador, but it contained the important seacoast town of Acajutla, through which Sonsonate, San Salvador, and Guatemala all participated in commerce with other Pacific coast colonies as far south as Peru and as far north as Acapulco. Sonsonate contained twenty villages with a population in 1746 of 3,709 tributaries, or about fifteen thousand Indians. The native people were Nahua-speaking Pipils, although by the 1760s it was reported that most of them were *indios ladinos,* that is, they could speak Castilian. The province had a relatively large non-Indian population made up of a few Spanish families and a large number of mulattoes and people called *zambos* (of indigenous and African ancestry). Some of the Indians lived in concentrated settlements, especially in the center of the province around Izalcos and Sonsonate, but most people, especially the non-Indians, tended to live dispersed on numerous small private estates.

Sonsonate included both highlands and lowlands and consequently contained different ecological zones. Its varied terrain, plus the fertility of the soil, was a good basis for economic diversity. The native Pipils produced maize, cotton, and cacao, while non-Indians cultivated rice, indigo, and some sesame. Ethnicity, in short, was reflected in the structure of production. The alcalde mayor's main business was with the Indians, from whom he acquired raw cotton and cacao by carrying out repartimientos. Cacao was then exported to Santiago, while the cotton was "put out" in thirteen of the Indian villages to be spun into thread. By the middle of the century, as cacao production declined, the acquisition of thread became the magistrate's most lucrative business. He shipped most of it to Santiago for sale. Alcaldes mayores also engaged in the usual grain business, requiring tribute payments to be made in maize at artificially low rates and then reselling it at a profit. They bought up local production of rice (Sonsonate was one of the few provinces in America that produced that Old World grain), sugar, and indigo from the non-Indian producers, some of whom were advanced money in return for a lien on their crop. Here, we see again repartimientos involving the non-Indian population. Maize and rice were then shipped to Santiago and San Salvador for sale, while the indigo was exported to Peru. Magistrates managed to eat well while in office, for annually they apparently collected a hen from each tributary; this was thought to be worth perhaps six hundred pesos over five years. Finally, the alcalde mayor did a good business in meat, controlling a large part of sales to both Indians and non-Indians. It was reported that the magistrate could sell up to eight hundred calves per year. Efforts to introduce the forced sale of goods met with considerable resistance and were not successful. Once again, therefore, we see resistance on the part of the indigenous people to the sale of goods on credit.

According to the president's report of 1738, the high magistrate's annual income was about a thousand pesos, but this undoubtedly underestimated the total. Informants in 1765–66 guessed that the alcalde mayor's real annual income fluctuated between three and six thousand pesos, and came to between fifteen and sixteen thousand pesos in five years, but to accomplish that he had to invest at least ten thousand pesos. If he raised enough capital in advance, he could start making profits in his third year in office. The salary for high magistrates was six hundred pesos for most of the eighteenth century.

San Salvador

The province of San Salvador, occupying approximately three-quarters of modern El Salvador, bordered on the north with Honduras and on the east with Tegucigalpa and the Gulf of Fonseca.[25] In 1746 its 120 villages contained 6,552 tributaries, or more than twenty-six thousand Indians. As in Sonsonate, the native people were mostly Pipil, but some Indians of Lenca (non-Maya, non-Nahua) origin survived in the more isolated areas east of the Lempa River. In any case, by the 1760s practically all the Pipils were said to be indios ladinos, that is, Castilian-speaking. San Salvador also had a large non-Indian population, made up mostly of mulattoes and zambos. As was the case in other provinces with a large number of non-Indians, much of the population lived in a dispersed settlement pattern. Much of the province was in the highlands, but a considerable quantity of valuable agricultural land was found in the lower altitudes.

San Salvador's economy was based overwhelmingly on production of indigo for export to Spain via Honduras and Veracruz, and to Peru via Acajutla. The alcalde mayor's business, in turn, revolved around indigo. He loaned capital and provided goods to producers, practically all of whom were non-Indians, and in return he collected in kind, that is, in indigo. This means that a major part of his business involved the non-Indians. He also made considerable money using his political power to force the indigenous communities to provide laborers for the indigo producers, who paid the magistrates for each worker so provided. Alcaldes mayores in this province were successful in introducing the sale of goods, especially textiles manufactured elsewhere in Central America (*ropa de la tierra*) or even made in China, to the Indians. This enterprise worked in San Salvador because the native people spent much of their time working on the indigo plantations; controlling little of their own production, they needed to purchase most of the goods needed for survival. It was said, in fact, that the alcalde mayor did not have to force the Indians to purchase textiles; they were driven by need. Nevertheless, the magistrate still had to work through the village government officials, for otherwise he would have had trouble collecting the debts. One informant estimated the volume of the clothing business with the indigenous people at forty thousand pesos per year. Another source stated that the volume in five years was about a hundred fifty thousand pesos, but to carry out this business the alcalde mayor had to invest a hundred thousand pesos in capital. He thus stood to gain about fifty thousand pesos at the end of his term in office.

The province was becoming so agriculturally specialized that the magistrates also imported foodstuffs—maize from Nicaragua, cattle from Tegucigalpa and Nicaragua, and rice from Sonsonate—and controlled sales to the public. They also acquired rice from producers around San Vicente (about fifty kilometers east of the town of San Salvador). They imported European textiles to be sold on credit to the non-Indians; repayment was made in indigo. Most of the blue dye was taken overland to the Gulf of Honduras for export to Europe, but some made its way to Peru. As elsewhere, it was also reported that magistrates sometimes made money by authorizing illegal gambling; card games and dice seem to have been the most popular games of chance.

The alcalde mayor thus was perhaps the most important businessman in the province, dealing with Indians and non-Indians alike. During good years he stood to gain ten thousand pesos annually from his business, according to the president's report of 1738, while the salary varied between 827 and 1,000 pesos. Informants in 1765–66 agreed with the president's assessment, but also pointed out that the magistrate's business, dependent as it was on world trade, was risky, and that not all alcaldes mayores made fortunes in office. Frequent wars disrupted commerce, and as a result some magistrates ended up with little to show for their time in office.

Honduras

The governorship of Honduras included the four minor provinces of Gracias a Dios, San Pedro Sula, Comayagua, and Olancho.[26] In practice, however, it was called Honduras, Comayagua, or Comayagua-Honduras and was administered by a single governor. Some Maya people lived in the western areas bordering on Chiquimula, but for the most part, the Indians were Lenca, Jicaque, Paya, and Sumu people, culturally quite distinct from groups to the west. In fact, the border in Honduras between the Mayas and the non-Mayas was an important cultural frontier dividing Mesoamerican Indians from the circum-Caribbean peoples, who had been migrating north from South America for centuries.[27] The South American groups were invariably less organized, and therefore less exploitable, than Maya or Nahua people. In fact, they were so close to subsistence, and thus to extermination, that the Spaniards eventually gave up trying to extract much of a surplus from the native population of Honduras, which in any case was not very numerous.[28] In the 1740s Honduras included only 3,659 tributaries, or between fifteen and seventeen thousand Indians.[29] Also in the region were the Miskito Indians, who were a mixture of indigenous and African people. They were not under Spanish control and frequently allied themselves with the British, who carried out smuggling, attacked Spanish settlements and forts, and attempted to establish permanent settlements on the Mosquito Coast and to set up sugar and indigo plantations worked by African slaves. Their presence, evident in occasional raids into the Spanish-controlled region, made life uncertain for the subjects of the Spanish empire in both Honduras and Nicaragua.[30]

In these circumstances, governors would have found it virtually impossible to make anything beyond their salaries were it not for the opportunities presented by seaborne trade on the Gulf of Honduras. In fact, the post was somewhat lucrative, for the governor invariably made himself the leader of all illegal activities and engaged in smuggling.[31] He traded indigo and silver to the English in return for luxury goods in demand in Santiago and the other urban centers of Central America. He also participated in legal trade with the few Spanish ships stopping on the coast. A governor in the early eighteenth century attempted to carry out repartimientos to acquire cacao from the Indians, but apparently little came of this, and there is no further reference to this activity. Unfortunately, there is little information regarding the quantity of money to be made as governor, for the president made no attempt to estimate the official's income in his report of 1738, and no witnesses with knowledge of Honduras appeared at the inquest of 1765–66.

Tegucigalpa

Occupying the southern highlands of modern Honduras, the alcaldía mayor of Tegucigalpa, like neighboring Honduras, contained few Indians capable of producing a surplus that could be tapped by the colonial regime.[32] In 1757 the tributaries numbered only 1,046, or some four to five thousand people, settled in seventeen villages. Most of these Indians were Lenca people, with a small number of Chorotegas. The latter, like the Lenca, were a non-Nahua Mesoamerican people who had been pushed out of Soconusco by Nahua people in the Post-Classic era. They were settled on the Pacific coast around the Gulf of Fonseca. A large part of the population was made up of mulattoes and mestizos, who became more numerous as time went on and the indigenous population shrank still further. By the late eighteenth century, the non-Indian population made up more than 70 percent of the total.[33]

The economy of Tegucigalpa was based on stock raising and especially silver mining. This helps explain why sales of mercury (*azogues*), a government-monopolized metal used in silver amalgamation, accounted for as much as 8.4 percent of royal revenues in the entire Kingdom of Guatemala in the 1760s.[34] Needless to say, silver opened up all sorts of commercial opportunities for the alcalde mayor. Magistrates collected fees for providing mining entrepreneurs with Indians to work as mine laborers, and invested in silver mining "like any other merchant," according to informants. Their most important activity connected with this branch of the economy was the provision of the credit and goods necessary to carry out mining and to feed and clothe the workers. Debts were repaid, of course, in silver, at the rate of 51 reales per mark (227 grams), which the magistrates then sold to the mint at 61 reales to the mark. Alcaldes mayores also used their political power to control a large part of the meat markets in the mining camps and towns. They dominated the wholesale textile market, receiving cloth—manufactured in other parts of the kingdom or imported from China—from merchants in Santiago and distributing the goods to the stores in the mining camps.

All of the business of the magistrates of Tegucigalpa thus was with non-Indians. It was impossible to carry out any kind of repartimientos with the poor and relatively unorganized indigenous people, although it was reported in 1765 that the alcalde mayor was trying to introduce the practice. The results are unknown. The salary of the magistrate was four hundred pesos during most of the eighteenth century, but the president's report of 1738 estimated that the alcalde mayor stood to gain more than eight thousand pesos per year from his businesses. Informants in the 1760s, however, emphasized the risks involved in any economy based on mining, for people frequently defaulted on their debts. The high magistrate's income, dependent as it was on silver production, fluctuated widely from year to year.

Tegucigalpa, like San Salvador, was one of the crucial links of the commercial chain, tying magistrates from several provinces together in a network of trading relationships and vested interest. This province, along with San Salvador, and to a lesser extent, Sonsonate, produced the vital exports of raw materials shipped beyond Central America to Peru, Mexico, and Europe. In turn, San Salvador and Tegucigalpa served as the importers of the manufactured goods and foodstuffs produced in the other provinces. Much of the cotton textile manufacturing carried out in the highland provinces of overwhelmingly Indian population was to a certain extent a backward linkage of the export economies of the largely mestizo and mulatto provinces of modern-day El Salvador and Honduras. The commercial activities of the magistrates thus revolved overwhelmingly around interregional and international trade.

Sébaco-Chontales

Southeast of Tegucigalpa was the province of Sébaco-Chontales in the highlands of modern-day northern Nicaragua.[35] Here, however, the Central American mountain chain does not reach great heights, and consequently the inhabitants were in close proximity to tropical forests, climate, and disease. The Indians had less chance of survival than in the true highland provinces to the northwest. The native people were Sumu and Matagalpa people of circum-Caribbean, rather than Mesoamerican, origin. Their socioeconomic organization was less complex, and the people less exploitable. Eleven or twelve native settlements existed, which in the 1770s contained 1,375 tributaries. However, an especially large number of Indians were exempt from tribute, thereby making it difficult to estimate the population with any precision. A good guess would be between five and eight thousand Indians. A number of non-Indians, mostly mestizos and mulattoes, also lived in the province. These people lived in a dispersed manner and worked on the cattle ranches established to take advantage of the availability of land in an area of sparse indigenous population.

Corregidores found few commercial opportunities to exploit in Sébaco. No one at all purchased the post in the seventeenth century, and in the following century it could only be sold for four hundred pesos. At one time, the magistrates organized production of pitch and turpentine for the ships putting into Realejo, but once that port went into decline, demand for naval stores declined as well. By the 1760s the only business of the magistrates was the repartimiento to acquire some thread and textiles. However, the limited size of the native population meant few profits, and the exemption from tribute enjoyed by many villages deprived the corregidor of the opportunity to take advantage of Indian debts. The lack of an urban center of any size meant that there was no meat market to corner, and most non-Indians raised their own livestock. Consequently, corregidores were said to make only between one and two thousand pesos annually. It is likely that they made very little at all, for the post was sold quite infrequently. The salary was only about 250 pesos, which provided no incentive to anyone in search of a government job.

Sutiaba

The lowland province of Sutiaba, in the northwestern part of modern Nicaragua, was inhabited by Chorotega Indians and a related group called Maribio.[36] They were non-Nahua peoples who had been driven out of Soconusco and who then settled in this area in about 800 A.D. Their complex socioeconomic structure, characteristic of Mesoamerican people, easily distinguished them from the Matagalpa people to the north. The lowland climate and tropical diseases, however, undoubtedly hindered demographic expansion. The province contained only five native settlements, which in the 1760s contained 1,447 tributaries, or some six thousand, five hundred Indians. There was also a growing dispersed population of mulattoes and mestizos. These two groups could not easily be exploited, but the magistrates found ways to earn money using the Indians' talents.

Because cotton could be produced in this lowland province, one of the corregidor's major businesses was the repartimiento to acquire raw cotton, some of which was apparently exported via Realejo to San Salvador and possibly points north. Much of the product was also "put out" in the villages to be spun, and the availability of dyewood (*brasil*) allowed the women to produce a dyed purple thread—*hilo morado*—of great value. It was reported that in the middle of the century corregidores could acquire more than three and a half tons of this valuable thread every year. Magistrates also extended credit to the Indians for dyewood, which when available was exported to Peru. Still another business of the officials was the repartimiento to get the Indian women to produce thick cotton mats and heavy twine rope used to rig the ships operating on Lake Managua, Lake Nicaragua, and the Pacific.

All of these activities with the Indians were directly connected to the tributary system, for the cash provided by the magistrates went to pay tributaries' taxes. Informants therefore were supporters of the repartimiento system, and noted that production of the valuable thread declined significantly after the audiencia had issued an order making repartimientos voluntary. The fall in production, according to these informants, was because Indian women in all provinces were notoriously lazy and given to idleness; only involuntary repartimientos could make them productive. The only injustice, it was said, was in the low rates of pay in return for female labor. (If there was a connection between unwillingness to work and the low level of remuneration, it was apparently never seen by the defenders of the repartimiento.) Here, then, we see that the Indians' acceptance of credit in return for future delivery of goods was involuntary. Efforts to introduce repartimientos to sell goods failed, however, because the native people made most of their own clothing, except for some woolens made in Quezaltenango and purchased in the nearby stores of León. Corregidores made minor quantities of money by providing workers for haciendas and domestic servants for the Spanish residents of the city of León, the magistrates collecting a fee for each servant provided.

All of the commercial activities of the corregidores in Sutiaba were said to net four thousand pesos annually, according to the president in 1738. Informants in the 1760s recalled that the annual income of magistrates just a few years before had reached five to six thousand pesos. The magistrate's salary was only 250 pesos, but the province yielded good business profits throughout the eighteenth century. Sutiaba's small size, however, resulted in its incorporation into the corregimiento of Realejo in 1778.

Realejo

Located in the extreme northwestern part of modern Nicaragua, the province of Realejo consisted of the Pacific port by the same name and four Indian settlements.[37] The native people were Nicaraos, of Nahua origin, who had made their journey to this part of the world shortly after the Chorotegas had arrived in Sutiaba. Their numbers, however, were small, totaling only 458 tributaries, or some eighteen hundred to two thousand Indians. Like Sutiaba, Realejo was a lowland province, where indigenous people, whether Mesoamerican or not, found it difficult to thrive after the arrival of European diseases. On the other hand, the geographical conditions permitted cultivation of sugarcane, and consequently an industry based on the labor of African slaves emerged. Eventually a large part of the population was made up of non-Indians—mostly mulattoes, usually the descendants of slaves. The mulattoes frequently worked on sugar plantations and cattle ranches owned mostly by the Spanish citizens of nearby León.

A major business of the corregidor was control of the commerce between Realejo and San Salvador, across the Gulf of Fonseca. This trade included maize to be sold in San Salvador and raw cotton being shipped north to Guatemala. These trade goods were sometimes owned by the magistrate himself, for he carried out repartimientos to acquire both maize and cotton. Nevertheless, most cotton exports leaving Realejo were in fact produced in the next-door province of Nicaragua. Magistrates even ran a ferry service connecting Nicaragua with Conchagua, in San Salvador, across the Gulf of Fonseca. They also collected fees on every ship putting in to or departing from Realejo, but this income diminished as that port silted up and went into decline in the middle of the eighteenth century. By then, corregidores had succeeded in setting up a monopoly on cart traffic in the province, thereby depriving both Indians and non-Indians of an income-generating activity.

Another branch of business was the repartimiento for thread, but this was said to yield little profit because of the small number of Indians and the poor quality of the product. On the other hand, by the middle of the eighteenth century, magistrates had introduced repartimientos of textiles, mostly made in Guatemala, for sale to the Indians. They also sold cloth to the non-Indians, although not through repartimientos. The corregidor eventually monopolized this branch of commerce, driving out of business the numerous small Indian entrepreneurs who had peddled goods in the province before the magistrates got into the act. Finally, magistrates had begun to make a little money by providing the province's landed estates with Indian laborers. The president in 1738 made no attempt to quantify the income of the corregidor, whose salary was 537 pesos. However, informants in 1766 estimated that magistrates could make two thousand pesos per year despite the commercial decline of the port of Realejo.

Nicaragua

The gobernación of Nicaragua occupied most of the area around Lake Managua and Lake Nicaragua, as well as the Caribbean coast and two-thirds of the Pacific coast of modern Nicaragua.[38] The Indians of the western half of the province were mostly Chorotega, and a number of Nicarao villages were also present in relatively concentrated settlements, while the eastern seaboard was inhabited by Sumu and Rama people belonging to the circum-Caribbean cultures. The less complex socioeconomic structure of the eastern Indians made it difficult for the Spaniards to maintain control over the Caribbean coast, which served as an invasion route for the pirates and British who frequently went up the San Juan River and across Lake Nicaragua to attack Granada. The colonial regime was therefore based on the western, Mesoamerican Indians, whose thirty-four settlements in 1768–69 included 5,249 tributaries, or 21,000–23,600 Indians. A sizeable non-Indian population of Spaniards, mestizos, and mulattoes also resided in the province, which included the two Spanish cities of León and Granada and the smaller towns of Nueva Segovia and the Villa de Nicaragua (present-day Rivas). The warm climate and fertility of the soil allowed substantial production of maize, cotton, and sugarcane, and a little indigo.

In the long run, the Indians of Nicaragua, as a cultural group settled mostly in the lowlands, would not survive well. In the eighteenth century, however, they still offered commercial opportunity for the governors. The main business of the magistrates was raw cotton, which they acquired from the Indians through repartimientos. Some of the cotton was exported to San Salvador and Guatemala, but a large part was "put out" in the native villages to be spun, and then thread was allocated for the weaving of textiles, mats, and sails for the ships plying the lakes and the Pacific. Sisal twine extracted from the cabuya plant was also "put out" to make rigging. By the middle of the century the governors had set up a manufacturing operation in the village of Masaya, where men and women labored curing leather and producing textiles, mats, hats, hammocks, and rope. Finally, governors carried out the usual business of collecting tribute maize in kind and reselling it in the cities at a profit.

The president considered the governorship of Nicaragua to be worth little, but frequent inquests into the governors' activities revealed that in fact the post was somewhat lucrative. Because of the military importance of the position, the salary was two thousand pesos, one of the highest in the Kingdom of Guatemala. The governor's business will be discussed in more detail in chapter 5.

Nicaragua was thus an important part of Central America's interregional trading network. It exported little or nothing to Europe, some indigo to Peru, and a lot of cotton to Guatemala. It is possible that some of the province's cotton was even reexported from Guatemala to the textile industry in Chiapa. Nicaraguan cotton, once spun and woven, might thus have ended up as far north as New Spain, which imported textiles from Chiapa and other highland provinces in Guatemala. It is no mistake then that the repartimiento system found strong support among citizens and government officials in most of the corregimientos and gobernación of Nicaragua. The supporters claimed that it was the only way to guarantee that the Indians paid their tribute.

Nicoya

Nicoya was originally the southernmost outpost of Mesoamerican culture.[39] The province occupied the northwestern part of modern-day Costa Rica and was inhabited by Nicaraos in the north and Chorotegas in the south. However, tropical disease and Spanish colonialism resulted in severe depopulation, and by the middle of the eighteenth century, only one settlement, with fifty families, or at most 250 Indians, survived. Much of the land was then occupied by a small number of Spaniards who took advantage of the Indian population decline by establishing cattle ranches. It was reported that the lack of a labor supply made it impossible to produce indigo, which otherwise could have been produced in large quantities.

In these circumstances, magistrates would have had considerable difficulty in making money had it not been for the fortuitous proximity of the pearl-producing oysters found in the Gulf of Nicoya. The corregidor's main business was the organization of Indian labor teams to serve as pearl fishers. Profits were good enough to warrant payment of high salaries to the workers. In addition, magistrates carried out repartimientos to acquire a little cotton and thread from the Indians. They were not successful in introducing sales of cloth to the indigenous people. Corregidores also engaged in cattle ranching and produced some lard, which they shipped to Panama City for sale. All told, according to the president's report of 1738, the corregidor could earn about five thousand pesos per year, considerably better than his annual salary of a miserable 275 pesos.

Costa Rica

The province of Costa Rica, like Sébaco, was occupied entirely by circum-Caribbean people.[40] The Indian population, divided into small, distinct groups, was never large and diminished rapidly after the Spanish occupation. No tributary figures exist for 1746 or for most years in which tributaries were counted, but a count of 328 in 1803 meant a late-colonial indigenous population of only some fifteen hundred people. The real number was somewhat larger, however, for many Indians were so poor that they were not subject to tribute and thus were not counted. It is likely that the province had more indigenous people earlier in its history but that many of them blended in with the Spanish, African, mestizo, and mulatto population and thus disappeared as "Indians" from the records. The total population of Costa Rica was 24,022 in 1746.[41] The non-Indians thus greatly outnumbered the indigenous people in the middle of the eighteenth century, although no city reached any considerable size. The provincial capital of Cartago had a population of only 591 in 1682, although this figure rose to 7,491 in 1778.[42]

With such a small Indian population, and because non-Indians could not be subject to the repartimiento, governors of Costa Rica had few prospects for enriching themselves. They tried to make some money carrying out repartimientos for cotton and thread, but the small Indian population made this relatively insignificant. The only real commercial opportunity for governors was participation in smuggling, made possible by good maritime communications with Panama and with English and Dutch colonies. Nevertheless, all informants stressed that the governorship of Costa Rica yielded few profits, although it was strategically important because of the province's proximity to important trade routes. As a result, the president recommended in 1738 that the post always be given to a professional soldier, and in fact the salary of the governor—2,000 ducats (2,400 pesos) per year throughout the seventeenth and eighteenth centuries—was the highest of any provincial magistrate in the kingdom. Perhaps that made up for the lack of commercial opportunity.

II

By the middle of the eighteenth century, the business activities that magistrates carried out with Indians were known collectively as repartimientos. However, as the regional surveys demonstrate, governors, alcaldes mayores, and corregidores—regardless of their roles in government—were businessmen and as such they sought commercial benefit where they could find it. That is why they needed to raise significant investment capital, and when they failed to raise capital they also failed to prosper. Where there was a significant indigenous population with strong village government, it was possible to invest in repartimientos to acquire goods and sell merchandise because the Indian officials could effectively distribute the money, raw cotton, raw wool, thread, and articles of consumption and then collect the debts in kind. This made the provinces with large Indian populations—the highlands of Chiapa and Guatemala—the most valuable from the perspective of profits to be made.

Where a surplus-producing indigenous population was of insignificant size or nonexistent, on the other hand, magistrates had to find other ways to make money from their positions. This was not always possible, as was the case of Escuintla, Sébaco, and Costa Rica. Honduras and Tegucigalpa offered opportunities apart from the Indians because the former had smuggling possibilities and the latter contained a significant mining economy. In these cases, business with the non-Indians was paramount. Yet everywhere throughout the kingdom, magistrates tried to do business with the non-Indians and were limited only by the small quantity of such people in many provinces. The conclusion is inescapable: the colonial regime adapted to what it found in the way of people and physical environment. What could be done in one province was impossible elsewhere.

In the Kingdom of Guatemala, except for the twenty years between 1759 and 1779, all commercial activities by provincial magistrates were illegal. Nevertheless, the crown tolerated its officials' business as long as the Indians were not provoked into outright rebellion. As a result, for over a century magistrates were routinely charged with violating the law and then not only pardoned for the offense but even commended for their actions and recommended for future positions. Only a handful whose greed surpassed acceptable bounds were removed from office or subjected to serious fines.

The repartimiento system and commerce with the non-Indians can be understood as a form of tolerated corruption. However, as the above descriptions make clear, it was more than that. It was above all a commercial system integrating the provinces of the Kingdom of Guatemala. It tied regions of different ecological conditions into a network of trade based on regional specialization. Cotton was produced in the valleys and coastal lowlands, especially in Verapaz and Nicaragua, and transported to highland Guatemala and Chiapa to be made into thread and textiles. These trade goods were either exported to Mexico or shipped in large quantities to the mining camps of Tegucigalpa (highland Honduras), to the cities and villages of the indigo-producing province of San Salvador, and to the capital of Santiago, where large-scale merchant houses handled the magistrates' goods and arranged for the investment of capital that made the wheels of trade turn. Indigo—produced in part as a result of the capital invested by magistrates and their merchant partners—in turn was exported to Peru, Mexico, and Europe. Honduran silver went either to Europe or to Mexico, and from there is it likely that it joined the flow of precious metals crossing the Pacific and ending up in China. Cacao was also produced, sold locally, and exported to Spain and New Spain. Central America was thus tied, directly or indirectly, to the world economy. The magistrates, in short, in alliance with merchants, helped integrate the provinces into the kingdom and the kingdom into the global economy.[43]

At the same time, the repartimiento's involvement with the Indians became one of the most important branches of the peasant economy. Tribute, once the most important mechanism for channeling wealth away from the peasantry to support the colonial elites, in some cases became nothing but an adjunct to the magistrates' business. It is important to note that repartimientos of money or credit were usually carried out on Saint John's Day (June 24) and on Christmas; by no small coincidence, those dates happened to be the days when tribute payments were due. By the middle of the eighteenth century many Indians no longer paid their goods and money directly to their caciques, who then delivered them to the magistrates; rather, governors, alcaldes mayores, and corregidores had their business partners in Santiago pay the tribute to the treasury. The role of the caciques was that of debt collector as well as tax collector. The payment to the treasury was treated as a normal business expense of commercial companies that magistrates established with important merchants of the capital.[44] The royal government therefore benefited from the repartimiento because the extension of credit to the Indians enabled the latter to pay their tribute. Moreover, by overlapping with or even absorbing the tributary system, the repartimiento sometimes became the most important mechanism for extracting wealth from the peasants and for incorporating the Indians of Central America into the regional and world economies.

The commercial system run by the magistrates worked so well in part because it took advantage of an already existing division of labor by gender. Forced labor systems, after all, are not limited to the heavy tasks—usually carried out by males—of digging, hauling, planting, and harvesting. In the well-developed peasant economy of Central America, agriculture was the exclusive domain of Indian males, who produced not only the maize but also the wheat, cacao, wool, and cotton, that is, trade goods. The most valuable goods of all, however, quantitatively speaking, were textiles and thread, the products of the female sector of the domestic economy. Magistrates and visitors alike commented on the skillful women and girls who spun the cotton and wool and wove jackets, skirts, dresses, and cloth in general. The repartimiento in Central America was the means by which local government officials tapped the surplus labor of men, women, and children, that is, the entire peasant community.[45]

Spinning, weaving, and cultivation of cotton and cacao were traditional branches of the indigenous economy of Mesoamerica; in most places new productive processes were not needed. True, silver mining and large-scale indigo production were not traditional Indian activities, but they only affected the native people of Tegucigalpa, Chiquimula, and San Salvador. The disruption of the Indians was thus limited to a few places. For the most part, especially in the highlands of Chiapa and Guatemala, the indigenous people were left alone—as long as they produced the goods the Spaniards desired. Economic exploitation and commercialization, while disruptive in some contexts, were completely compatible with Indian traditions, and thus native culture had a better chance of adapting to colonialism, rather than collapsing because of the excessive demands of the colonists.[46] To this day, the Guatemalan and Chiapanecan highlands—which contained the most lucrative magistracies in the kingdom—are among the most Indian parts of Latin America.

Despite the commercial viability and profitability of the repartimiento, the Spanish government never reconciled itself to the participation of its officials in large-scale commercial activities. The local government officials frequently used their political power to prevent competing merchants from conducting business in the provinces under their jurisdiction. The system thus led to the establishment, in effect, of local monopolies and concomitant economic abuses. As a result, the magistrates inevitably represented themselves and their merchant partners better than they represented the interests of the king. As a visitor general to another part of America succinctly explained the problem, "It is not easy, or even possible, to improve the local government of the Provinces . . . as long as its Chief Officials or Corregidores are businessmen."[47]

Not all branches of government agreed with this negative assessment of the repartimiento system and of the magistrates' involvement in commerce. In 1764 the director of the royal treasury in Guatemala saw that the enterprises of the officials could be tapped in order to raise more revenue. He therefore recommended that the crown dispense with the fiction that posts were being awarded to worthy subjects who performed "monetary service," and proposed instead that gobernaciones, alcaldías mayores, and corregimientos be sold at public auction to the highest bidder. The proposal continued to circulate within the government and was only rejected by the Audiencia of Guatemala in 1780 and by the royal accounting office in Madrid in the following year.[48] Meanwhile, the audiencia itself was considering new ways to milk the magistracies, and in 1777 it proposed, as a measure to cut administrative costs, that the salaries of the alcaldes mayores and corregidores be reduced or eliminated altogether. This measure was thought to be feasible because, in the words of the audiencia, "these positions [are] not sought after for the assigned salary but because those who are rewarded with the offices make profits from business activities."[49] This time, the royal accounting office of the treasury in Madrid commented favorably on the proposal.[50] The system, then, had its defenders, because it was the means of maintaining Spanish control over Central America and of extracting revenues with a minimum of expenditure by the crown.

It should also be noted that although the activities of the magistrates were usually illegal, the men who carried out repartimientos undoubtedly did not feel themselves to be the evil villains denounced by Jorge Juan and Juan de Ulloa. Those two officials had described the system as a form of slavery, but that comparison is inaccurate with respect to Central America. Only a few of the magistrates would probably qualify as excessively greedy. As noted in the previous chapter, many of the alcaldes mayores, corregidores, and governors were old soldiers who had served their king for decades, had risked their lives in combat or on dangerous missions, and had sometimes suffered bodily harm. They believed themselves deserving of more than what the crown was able pay them in salaries.

Furthermore, service in most of the magistracies in the Kingdom of Guatemala was a hardship. These were places with little opportunity for the cultural interaction characteristic of southern European society, for most of the people were Indians who did not speak Spanish, and often the only Hispanic people with whom a magistrate could talk were the Catholic priests entrusted with the spiritual care of the indigenous people. Even the climate was hostile, for most officeholders came from places without the extreme humidity of the tropics and without the ubiquitous insects that make life difficult in humid climates. Many places were clearly unhealthy for humans. Most magistrates undoubtedly felt that they had been assigned to godforsaken places and had little chance of getting a second position, let alone a better one. Therefore they had to make enough money for retirement during the five years in office they had been allotted. It had been common since the first century of the Spanish empire for people with the highest concept of honor and born with high status to engage in lucrative but illegal business to make up for all of the unremunerated services that they had provided their king.[51] In their opinion and that of the magistrates in America, this was not corruption. It was justice.

Charles III and his advisors, however, saw the system's defects. The king reacted angrily to the recommendations of the audiencia and the accounting office to sell the magistracies.[52] The reformers in Spain instead moved to eliminate the repartimiento system. To do so, the crown had to violate one of the basic principles of royal government in America, namely, the policy of holding down both the size of the bureaucracy and the salaries of the bureaucrats. The reform program entailed the expansion of the bureaucracy through the introduction of the intendancy system, the reform of the magistracies, and the granting of offices for service or merit rather than for money. The costs of maintaining the old system, increasingly seen as corrupt, had finally come to outweigh the benefits.

CHAPTER 4

The Business of Politics
and the Politics of Business
in the Highlands

The Repartimiento in Huehuetenango, 1765–1786, or, A Tale of Two Juans

Because much of our knowledge about the repartimiento is based on documents resulting from political conflict within the bureaucracy, it would be useful and informative to approach this topic from a different point of view. One of the best sources would be either a magistrate involved in the repartimiento or a merchant involved in business dealings between government officials and the Indians. Although such sources are uncommon, the existence of a Spanish legal system handling civil, criminal, and commercial law inevitably permitted the survival of some documentation that was not just the product of partisan bureaucratic struggle. One such source fortunately combines the viewpoints of both a high magistrate—an alcalde mayor—and his merchant partner in highland Guatemala in the middle of the eighteenth century.[1] It includes not just the contract between the merchant and the magistrate but also the two partners' business accounts.

This chapter will employ that source and in the process analyze the repartimiento system from the point of view of its participants. This new perspective will not only manifest the realities of economic exchange between Indians and the outside world in the Spanish empire but also provide scholars with a better understanding of the complicated nature of commerce and government—the business of politics and the politics of business—in a region tied to the world economy through exports. Huehuetenango exported its textile products to other regions producing the precious metals that were a

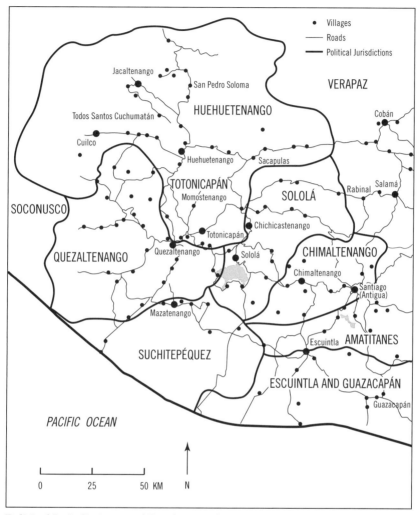

Political Jurisdictions and Roads in Eighteenth-Century Guatemala

driving force in the world economy in the era before the Industrial Revolution.

I

In 1771 Juan Bacaro, the former alcalde mayor of the district of Huehuetenango-Totonicapán (the northwestern highlands of modern-day

Guatemala), brought suit against his former business partner, Juan Montes de Oca, a merchant from the capital city of Santiago de Guatemala (modern-day Antigua). The lawsuit ended up in court and hence in the records, thus providing a great deal of documentation about the nature of business in late colonial Central America.

The historiography of local or regional commerce in colonial Spanish America is quite thin at the present time. Most of the research has concerned long-distance, and therefore very important, merchants.[2] An important exception is a work by Stanley J. Stein that has made an important contribution to our understanding of local commerce and mercantile activities in Mexico through the study of a small merchant in Cuautla-Amilpas, a mining-oriented region near Cuernavaca.[3] The value of a study of Huehuetenango in highland Guatemala lies in the "clientele" of the alcalde mayor and merchant and in the local economic environment. Whereas the merchant in Cuautla-Amilpas dealt almost entirely with non-Indians, the merchant and the magistrate in Huehuetenango carried out business almost entirely with K'iche' and Mam Maya Indians in an economy completely devoid of mineral wealth and even of natural resources. Colonialism fostered economic relationships that differed from place to place because of local conditions, as Spaniards shaped the nature of commercial exchange in order to serve their particular ends and Indians defended themselves as best they could.

The state always has some effect on economic activity, but in colonial societies, political power is frequently a crucial factor in the functioning of the economy. This is made clear in the case of the commercial agreement reached between the newly appointed alcalde mayor Juan Bacaro and his new business partner Juan Montes de Oca. Bacaro, a Spaniard from Andalusia, had come to America to serve in the military, and while in Mexico he had married well. His marriage in 1755 to Doña María Ignacia Cabrera, daughter of a prominent merchant from Mexico City, had helped provide him with capital, for her dowry included ten thousand pesos as well as jewelry and clothing worth another two thousand pesos. Bacaro in turn provided his wife with two thousand more pesos in cash as her *arras* (a customary fund to provide for the wife).[4] He was in Spain, not America, at the time he was appointed to the office in Guatemala. This was probably because it was easier to get appointed to a position if the applicant was in Spain rather than in America. (Sometimes the Council of the Indies appointed people not in Spain but specifically noted that it was "despite" the applicant being in America.) But as an outsider in Guatemala, Bacaro needed access to the marketing skills, lines of communication, and personal connections—in short, the local knowledge—that only a resident merchant would have. Since the annual salary of the position was only 331 pesos, Bacaro was not going to get rich on his government pay. Like all the other alcaldes mayores, he took up the post because of the prospect of economic gain resulting from repartimientos.

It was for that purpose that Juan Bacaro joined Juan Montes de Oca in forming a commercial company on July 24, 1765. The contract's major provisions ran as follows:

(1) Montes de Oca, the merchant, would find the guarantors (*fiadores*) that the law required Bacaro to have in order to guarantee the payment of tribute to the royal treasury.

(2) Bacaro agreed to invest his financial assets—in fact, most of his wife's dowry—making his total cash investment eight thousand pesos. However, his right as alcalde mayor to carry out business in his jurisdiction—the repartimiento—was counted as being worth another twelve thousand pesos, raising his total investment on paper to twenty thousand. Montes de Oca, in turn, would invest fourteen thousand up front, but after that Montes de Oca would be responsible for investing the capital necessary to keep the business going. Their business was described as consisting of "cotton, tools, mules, cattle, wheat, wool, and tiles."

(3) Montes de Oca, in Santiago, was to provide Bacaro with all the necessary goods to sell in the jurisdiction of Huehuetenango, to take charge of the business accounts, and to provide Bacaro with updated reports on those accounts.

(4) Montes de Oca was supposed to distribute the thread acquired in Huehuetenango through the repartimiento only to weavers (*texedores*) of "good credit" in Santiago, who then would repay their debts in woven cloth.

(5) To ensure that Bacaro would not set up competing operations that would harm their joint business, the alcalde mayor agreed to carry out no business activity in Huehuetenango other than that of the company. On the other hand, his salary as high magistrate—his 331 pesos paid to him annually by the royal treasury—would remain separate from the operations of the company.

(6) The high magistrate and the merchant agreed that upon completion of the former's term in office, revenues would be distributed according to a schedule of priorities. First, Bacaro would receive twelve thousand pesos, "the value of the alcaldía mayor" as recognized in the earlier paragraph. Second, the administrative fee Bacaro paid to get his title of office would be returned to him. Third, all capital invested by Bacaro and Montes de Oca would be recovered. Fourth, the two associates would be reimbursed for the cost of the "gifts that are customarily given to His Lordship the Lord President Captain General of the Kingdom and to the lord judges of the Royal Audiencia on their birthdays and on Easter." Fifth, the salaries of the people who carried out clerical work for them would be paid. Finally, whatever money was left would be split evenly between the two business associates.[5]

What is important to note in this contract is the inclusion of twelve thousand fictitious pesos on Bacaro's part, the evaluation of his right to carry out the repartimiento. Besides serving as a means to increase Bacaro's share of the profits—had he put up no capital he could not expect to share in the profits to this extent—in effect, this meant that the office itself was treated as a franchise, the right to do business in Huehuetenango. As Bacaro later explained the system, the principal asset he brought to the company was "the permission, granted to Alcaldes Mayores by law and municipal custom, in those Provinces, to carry out commerce in the villages and district with the ability to put out [repartir] to the Indians on credit certain portions of items and consumer goods used by the natives."[6]

Of course, Montes de Oca, not to mention other merchants, had the right to conduct business in the area. Bacaro himself could even have tried his hand at it without being the magistrate. So what was Bacaro actually contributing to the company by being the alcalde mayor, and why was the merchant willing to give Bacaro such a large share of the profits? After all, the alcalde mayor was going to be allowed to take twelve thousand pesos in cash right off the top of revenues, even though his cash investment was much less than that of Montes de Oca. Why, in other words, was the alcalde mayor's right to carry out business considered so valuable when, technically, any private citizen had the right to do the same?

The answer is to be found in the fundamental difference between a private merchant and a merchant-magistrate: the former had nothing more than economic suasion to force payment of debt. The cost of default would be perhaps harassment and ultimately the denial of future business to the person who defaulted. However, since most of the Indians were poor and not worth the expense of a lawsuit, little else could have happened, and the merchant would have had to accept unpaid debts as losses. ("When you ain't got nothing, you got nothing to lose," wrote the chief justice of the U.S. Supreme Court recently, citing Bob Dylan.) A magistrate—in this case Juan Bacaro— had options not available to a merchant. He could use the full powers of his office, including the power to arrest debtors and even flog them, to compel payment of debt. Moreover, he had the power to detain and whip the village leaders, who were almost always the people who took responsibility for distributing among the villagers whatever was sold through the repartimiento and then collecting the goods being used to repay the debts.

On the other hand, the magistrate had no power at all over people beyond the borders of his alcaldía mayor and thus could do nothing if the above-mentioned weavers in Santiago reneged on their debts. That is why the merchant was supposed to distribute the thread only to those of "good credit." If they defaulted, civil proceedings against them would follow, but they could not be as easily coerced to pay up as the Indians back in Huehuetenango. The chances for loss therefore were greater when it came to non-Indians, as many in the capital were.

In effect, what an alcalde mayor had that a merchant did not was political capital with recognized commercial value. Political power, not simply market forces, was an integral and essential part of business between government officials and Indians in the highlands of Guatemala. If strong commercial institutions had existed, and if the rule of law had extended to the village level, the magistrate would have been responsible for enforcing the laws that required Indians to pay their debts to private merchants. The reality was otherwise, and the alcalde mayor only collected the debts owed to him. Thus the weak institutional structure favored the person holding the power of the state. This is why merchants were willing to assign real commercial value to political capital, which in effect became a financial asset.

Of course, market forces were by no means absent from business operations. The value of the franchise varied from place to place in the Spanish empire, depending on the perception of commercial gain. The post that Juan Bacaro had received, the alcaldía mayor of Huehuetenango, was recognized as one of the most valuable magistracies in Central America. During the period from 1675 to 1750, when posts as alcalde mayor were usually sold, it was one of the most expensive magistracies in all of Spanish America, the purchase price rising to five thousand, eight hundred pesos by the 1740s.[7] As we saw in chapter 2, Huehuetenango was the fifth most expensive alcaldía mayor in the entire Spanish empire in the first half of the eighteenth century.[8]

The twenty-two thousand pesos in cash that the merchant and the magistrate invested in Huehuetenango were eventually supplemented by capital that Montes de Oca borrowed from the heirs of a recently deceased merchant named Francisco Benítez. The deceased's son-in-law, José Melchor de Ugalde, who had previously worked as an assistant to the alcalde mayor of Sonsonate, became involved in the partnership's business activities, though on a minor scale.[9]

Montes de Oca eventually spent 67,000 pesos to acquire the merchandise to sell to the Indians and to cover all the other expenses. The company produced revenues totaling between 90,000 and 101,000 pesos in four and a half years of the company's existence.[10] This was not an enormous sum, of course, but it does demonstrate that Huehuetenango could hardly be considered commercially isolated. Unfortunately, the circumstances of the company's abrupt dissolution, a dispute between the two men, makes it difficult to estimate profits accurately, for Montes de Oca, in charge of the accounts, probably understated the real revenues from sales in order to short-change Bacaro. The latter eventually claimed that net profits totaled over twenty-eight thousand pesos. Nevertheless, it is clear that business expenses ate up a substantial part of revenues. This is an important point, for critics of the repartimiento system at the time never took into account the cost of doing business and thus they grossly inflated real profits being made. The reality seems to have been that profits, after expenses had been deducted from revenues and after capital investment been recovered, were good but not spectacular.

To operate a business of this magnitude and, as we shall see, geographical reach, Bacaro and Montes de Oca had to employ several locally based agents who received commissions of either 3 or 6 percent of the sale price. The most important of these were Domingo Antonio Anido, who worked in the capital, Santiago, and received goods coming in from the province (Totonicapán), and Felipe Manrique de Guzmán, who lived in the province. Manrique de Guzmán was the former alcalde mayor of the province, and his participation in the enterprise with Bacaro demonstrates the new magistrate's reliance on people with local knowledge. At least three other men, Manuel Pinillos, Diego del Barco, and Carlos José Guillén, also worked for the company as agents handling special goods, and Pinillos, who was also involved in the shipping of indigo from El Salvador to Spain, once came to Bacaro's rescue with a loan to be repaid in indigo. Still other agents handled the sale of wheat shipped to the capital or to Ciudad Real in Chiapa. Consequently, although during his term Juan Bacaro may have been the only salaried government official in the high magistracy of Huehuetenango, he could not operate without people whose income was not in the form of a government salary. Rather, they were paid out of the revenues being generated by the company. Local knowledge was thus rewarded.

Although revenues were probably understated in the suit, both sides agreed on the nature of the business. The single most important item of commerce was thread, usually cotton but sometimes wool, spun by Maya women in their houses and then either woven into cloth by the same women using their traditional backstrap looms or shipped to the capital of Santiago to be made into textiles by weavers there. Second in importance was cloth, especially cotton cloth. At the same time, the acquisition of raw cotton and wool to be spun was a cost of business that the company had to defray. Wool was available in Huehuetenango itself, for the highland province was one of the most important centers of the sheep-raising industry in Central America. Two types of wool, black and white, appear in the accounts. The most common was white, which in 1772 sold for three pesos per arroba (25 pounds), while the black sold for four pesos.[11] The all-important cotton, however, could not be grown in the chilly, mountainous environment of Huehuetenango. Therefore the business partners had to arrange to buy it in the Pacific coastal province of San Antonio Suchitepéquez, where the alcalde mayor of that magistracy made raw cotton one of his major items of business.[12] After acquiring it from the Indians of his province, the magistrate of Suchitepéquez sold it to the alcaldes mayores of other districts for their business operations.

In practice, therefore, the repartimiento system in Huehuetenango was a putting-out system organized for the purpose of acquiring textiles. The Indian population received money, credit, or the raw materials to spin thread, weave textiles, and raise sheep for wool. Meanwhile, people in the coastal lowlands to the south received money or credit in return for the raw cotton needed for the repartimientos in the highlands. The business activities of one magistrate, therefore, depended to a great extent on those of another. The commercial activities of the magistrates thus stimulated the economic integration of the coast and highlands, that is, areas of different ecological conditions and commercial opportunities.

The business accounts provide information that illuminates why the repartimiento system was controversial and so often criticized by reformers. Juan Bacaro advanced money or credit to the Indians so they could pay their tribute. The indigenous people repaid most of the debt in the thread that they spun, which was evaluated at two reales per pound, in the case of most thread (coarse, called *hilo grueso*) or four reales in the case of the higher-quality kind (*hilo fino*), which came exclusively from the villages of Chiquimula, San Cristóbal, and Aguacaliente. A sample of merchandise sold in 1772 was made up of 57 percent coarse thread and 43 percent fine thread.[13] Normally the debt had to be paid off in six months, although in practice the Indians sometimes fell into arrears and the thread ended up being delivered late. The accounts reveal that the alcalde mayor's business agent sold the coarse thread to textile manufacturers at the price of six reales per pound, while the fine thread went for eight reales.[14] Gross revenues after six months therefore were either 200 percent or 100 percent of investment. If the difference between what the Indians were paid and the eventual price of the goods on the market was in fact disguised interest on a loan, then the rate of interest charged was either 200 percent or 100 percent—for a six-month loan. This of course looks like gross exploitation and helps explains why the repartimiento was an important issue in bureaucratic politics. On the other hand, as noted, reformers rarely took the costs of doing business into account, and therefore judgments made by distant bureaucrats were misleading because they overestimated profits by leaving out losses and the costs of doing business.

Although the alcalde mayor of Huehuetenango carried out repartimientos primarily to acquire thread and cloth, he advanced money and credit to the Indians to purchase other goods as well. Most of these were of minor importance, such as lambs, candles, honey, and hams (the latter always mentioned as among the "gifts" given to high-ranking government officials). Of greater significance was wheat, to be taken to cities to be made into bread.[15] The non-Indian population tended to live in those cities, and of course, because of their European cultural heritage, they wanted to eat bread like Europeans. This branch of the business took on considerable importance in 1769–70 because a locust plague, after destroying most of the indigo crop in San Salvador, ended up causing famine in various places in Central America as well as in Chiapa and Yucatan. It even caused crop failure in parts of Huehuetenango, and the Indians of several villages were granted two years of tribute relief as a result.[16] The shortage of food opened up opportunities, and Juan Bacaro shipped wheat produced in Huehuetenango to Santiago as well as to Ciudad Real.[17] Normally, the high cost of transportation made this unprofitable. The profits became a major bone of contention between the two partners because the shipments to Chiapa took place just as the partnership was breaking up. Nevertheless, the activities of the merchant and the magistrate, by stimulating commercial exchange between different regions, demonstrate again that economic integration was an important effect of the collaboration between business and government in the eighteenth century.

For the most part, then, the repartimientos of the magistrate of Huehuetenango consisted of grants of money, credit, or raw materials in return for repayment in kind at a later date. However, Bacaro and Montes de Oca also sold goods to the Indians. Some of these were directly related to textile production, such as cards and looms for making crude sacks. The most important sales to the native people, however, were in the form of livestock, namely, mules, calves (to be raised), and cows and bulls (for meat provided at village fiestas). Mules apparently were used exclusively as pack animals to transport goods into and out of the district of Huehuetenango, for the highland mountainous terrain was rarely appropriate for plows and plow teams, and the roads were much too narrow for wheeled vehicles. The special nature of Indian demand seems to have been understood as well, for the magistrate also imported quetzal feathers, used in Maya ritual clothing, and sold them to the native people. Agricultural implements like hoes and machetes also figured prominently among the goods sold to the Indians.[18] The magistrate also handled imports exclusively for the small number of Spanish priests and colonists in the area: cacao for chocolate, tobacco, sugar, gunpowder, shoes, writing paper, and even on one occasion a flute.[19]

The commercial networks of the company of Bacaro and Montes de Oca were extensive. Most of the livestock sold to the Indians apparently came from other regions of Guatemala, while the iron tools were imported from Puebla (New Spain).[20] Most of the goods made in Huehuetenango were shipped to Santiago, where they were sold. As a result, at that point we lose track of them. However, other sources reveal that cotton textiles were normally shipped from the capital to the textile-importing regions of Tegucigalpa (a silver-mining camp) and San Salvador (the leading producer of indigo, which in the eighteenth century was the most important export from Central America to the world economy). Demand for cotton textiles in San Salvador was so great that eventually that province became a main importer of cloth shipped all the way from China on the Nao de Manila.[21]

In Santiago itself, the thread was provided to people in the city identified as "texedores" (weavers) or *nagüeros* (makers of *naguas*, that is, petticoats), who were involved in a putting-out system with merchants like Montes de Oca.[22] Thread was also sold to a small number of non-Indians who were evidently textile manufacturers or hat makers (who purchased only woolen thread, less plentiful than cotton). One batch of cotton thread—more than two and a half tons (5,165 pounds)—sold in the capital in 1772 was bought by eleven different individuals, two of them women. None was identified as an Indian. At the time, Santiago had approximately 210 textile producers, although it is impossible to determine the scale of operations of these industrialists.[23] The sales by Montes de Oca reveal that the scale of purchases varied, which was reflected in the value of the thread purchased. Manuel Martínez bought 59 percent of the thread, based on value, but 87 percent of the fine thread. A distant second was Doña Dominga Morga, with 17 percent of the thread, based on value, and 7 percent of the fine thread. Another woman, Rosalía Gálvez, took away the rest of the high-quality thread. Because Martínez was not referred to as "Don Manuel," he must not have been of the colonial elite. The "Doña" before Morga's name means that she might have been a person of some social importance, and certainly demonstrates that she was of significantly higher social status than the other woman. The other buyers were clearly small operators.[24]

Some of the Guatemalan-made textiles, including some from Huehuetenango, were sent to Oaxaca, at which point we once again lose track of them. However, since Oaxaca itself was a major exporter of cotton textiles and would not have been importing them from Guatemala for local use, it is virtually certain that the cloth of Huehuetenango was purchased by the Mexico City merchants who acquired textiles in Oaxaca to ship to the mining region of northern New Spain.[25] These inexpensive textiles thus served to tie Guatemala into Mexico's export economy as a backward linkage of the mining economy. Wheat, as already noted, went either to Santiago or to Chiapa. Meanwhile, because liquidity was always a business problem in colonial Spanish America, Montes de Oca traded with clients in San Salvador to acquire indigo, which was frequently accepted in lieu of cash even by the agents of the royal treasury.[26] The exportable nature of indigo allowed Montes de Oca to carry out commerce with associates in Cádiz. This in turn got him involved as an investor in a slave-trading company working the African coast.[27] Business and government thus worked together in Central America, not just to effect the economic integration of the region's provinces, but also to tie the region into the world economy as an exporter of indigo (San Salvador) and silver (Tegucigalpa).

The close relationship between business and government is reflected in the accounts Montes de Oca kept of his business dealings with Juan Bacaro. The records are incomplete but do reveal an important feature: the single most important outlay of company funds was for the payment of tribute. This had to be delivered to the royal treasury twice a year, on June 24 (the Feast of Saint John) and on Christmas. The quantity of money handed over to Real Hacienda varied. In the records kept during the first two years (1766–67) of the company, the four payments made to the treasury were as follows:

June 1766	4,545 pesos 5 reales
Christmas 1766	6,024 pesos 6 1/2 reales
June 1767	4,542 pesos 3 reales
Christmas 1767	6,562 pesos 1 real[28]

The four-year total was 21,674 pesos 7 1/2 reales. Unfortunately, confusion in record-keeping—in which years were mixed up—makes it impossible to determine the proportion of total outlays represented by tribute payments to the treasury. The annual average of tribute paid by Montes de Oca for Bacaro was 10,837 pesos 3 1/4 reales. In the four and a half years of Bacaro's tenure in office, he would thus have had to pay a total of some 48,768 pesos. That would have represented somewhere close to half of the company's total revenues of probably over a hundred thousand pesos.

The Spanish crown assessed tribute on a per-capita basis, although it is unlikely that the year-to-year fluctuations in payments meant that someone was taking into account short-term fluctuations in the number of tributaries. As was seen in a previous chapter, tribute counts were infrequent. The value of goods varied, of course, depending on market conditions, and thus a more likely explanation for the differences from one year to the next, as seen in the extract above, is the changing assessment of the value of what was being paid in kind. The value of tribute paid in kind on the Feast of Saint John was less than that paid on Christmas.

The inclusion of tribute payments in the company's accounts demonstrates the close connection between the alcalde mayor's business with the Indians and his official duty as the person responsible for collecting tribute. It was presumably easier to combine the business and tribute records than for either the magistrate or the merchant to keep them separate. Business and government thus worked hand-in-glove and were virtually inseparable. The result, however, was that tribute came to be considered as simply a cost of doing business, that is, a payment to the king of his share of the profits. Once again, it should be noted that private merchants operating in Huehuetenango would not have had this expense, but they also would not have had the ability that the magistrate and his partner had to compel repayment of debt. That Bacaro and Montes de Oca chose to operate in this way demonstrates the advantage a merchant-magistrate had over a private businessman or woman. That explains why people like Montes de Oca formed business partnerships with people like Bacaro. Colonialism, in short, counted for a lot in highland Guatemalan commerce and was an important force mediating relations between the indigenous population and the world around them.

The second most important outlay of funds by the company was the payment of taxes on goods it shipped out of the alcaldía mayor and sold in the capital. In 1766–67, the only years for which accurate records were kept, the company paid 981 pesos 3 1/2 reales in sales taxes (*alcabalas*) and 438 pesos in customs duties (*derechos de aduana*).[29] Duties were charged not just on goods imported from outside the kingdom but also on goods shipped from one province to another. Thus, in two years the company paid the sizeable sum of 1,419 pesos 3 1/2 reales in taxes and duties. All told, if alcabalas and derechos de aduana were paid at this rate for the full four and one-half years of the company's existence, taxes and duties would have totaled approximately 3,194 pesos.

Bearing in mind that gross revenues over four and a half years totaled some hundred thousand pesos and that Juan Bacaro estimated profits to have been twenty-eight thousand, then clearly the government's share of business revenues derived from commercial taxes was not large. On the other hand, the repartimiento also aided in the collection of more than forty-eight thousand pesos in tribute, and therefore it can be concluded that the business activity of the magistrate and his merchant partner—the overlap of business and government—was very beneficial to the royal treasury. Furthermore, although derechos de aduana were a minor expense to be deducted from gross revenues, they were enough to encourage Montes de Oca to hire a guide to get around the customs agents, for no more payments were mentioned until, as we shall see, Bacaro paid them when he no longer had the help of his business partner.

The other costs incurred by the company of Bacaro and Montes de Oca were overwhelmingly of three kinds: (1) transportation of goods between Santiago and Huehuetenango (in both directions), between Huehuetenango and Chiapa, and within the district of Huehuetenango-Totonicapán; (2) the purchase of livestock to sell to the Indians; and (3) the cost of buying cotton in the coastal province of San Antonio Suchitepéquez. All goods moved on the backs of mules, for there were virtually no roads for wheeled vehicles. Each mule regularly carried a load of about 250 pounds. The lading cost per mule was 12 reales (1 peso 4 reales) from Totonicapán to the capital, 18 reales (2 pesos 2 reales) from Huehuetenango to the capital, and 24 reales (3 pesos) from Huehuetenango to Ciudad Real.[30] Three decades later, in the 1790s, it took fifteen days for the mail to be delivered to the new Guatemala City from Totonicapán and forty days from Ciudad Real,[31] and though the trip was slightly shorter in the 1760s, the need to feed both mule drivers and beasts of burden for weeks would have contributed significantly to the cost of transportation. At times the mule trains were virtual caravans, for during the food shortage of 1769–1770, two hundred mules carried the wheat from the province to the capital, while fifty transported the grain to Chiapa.[32]

Unfortunately, the accounts only permit an analysis of freight charges as a proportion of gross revenues in the case of wheat: these accounted for 27 percent of the value of the grain shipped to the capital and 35 percent of that sent to Ciudad Real.[33] These numbers, however, are derived from the sale of wheat during time of scarcity, when grain prices were double or triple what was considered normal. During a year without a severe food shortage, freight rates were probably prohibitively high to Chiapa, and very high indeed to the capital. On the other hand, thread and textiles had a higher value per pound than wheat, even during a food shortage, and therefore freight charges for them, while high, would not have amounted to 27 percent.

The only other expenditures mentioned were usually minor: sacks (to wrap up the thread, clothing, and wheat), the cost of labor for wrapping those goods (not inconsiderable in the case of tons of thread), rental of a market stall to sell the wheat, an occasional interpreter for dealing with the Mayas, the delivery of mail, and the purchase of an account book. Minor losses occurred because of the theft of goods from a warehouse and when the Indian mule drivers stole a mule-load of wheat. Moreover, some of the lard purchased went bad before it could be sold.[34] However, the accounts also include a particular expense demonstrating the close relationship between business and government in colonial Spanish America: contributions to government officials. As already mentioned, Bacaro and Montes de Oca had to provide "gifts" to the president–captain general and to the judges of the audiencia on their birthdays and Easter (Easter being much more important than Christmas for most Christians at this time in history).[35] These, however, were minor.

On one occasion, as noted above, there was mention of another expense: Bacaro's payment of customs duties "because of the lack of a guide."[36] A guide apparently could find a way around the tax collection posts (garitas). However, once Montes de Oca had stopped cooperating with Bacaro, the latter could not easily find a way around taxes and ended up paying both customs and sales taxes.[37] That seems to have been one of the advantages that an alcalde mayor had by working with a local businessman with local knowledge. Once the tie was cut, Bacaro was on his own.

The colonial state, nevertheless, was not always a reliable participant in a system in which royal officials served as both magistrates and businessmen. Colonial policies sometimes changed. After receiving numerous recommendations to legalize repartimientos, the Spanish crown decided to do just that, and in 1751 it issued an order to that effect. Then, in 1759, the Audiencia of Guatemala backtracked a bit

and put restrictions on the alcaldes mayores by specifically prohibiting repartimientos for the purpose of acquiring thread and
cloth. Then, in 1779, with the reformers and opponents of the system
dominant for the moment in Madrid, the audiencia reversed itself
altogether and once again prohibited all business activities by government officials. This did not, however, mean a return to the pre-1751
situation when the laws were ignored, for the court, with considerable prodding from Charles III himself, actually began to enforce
the laws.[38]

Technically, therefore, some of Bacaro's activities, including the
most lucrative—the acquisition of thread and cloth—were illegal in
the 1760s, the time when he held office. Nevertheless, the laws were
not yet being enforced, and therefore the alcalde mayor of Huehuetenango had every reason to believe that he could act with impunity.
He therefore took a step that eventually contributed to his downfall.
Having discovered that the priests of his jurisdiction habitually carried
out their own business activities with the Indians and made special,
and illegal, demands for labor, Bacaro intervened to "protect" the
indigenous people by prohibiting the business activities carried out
by members of the Church. One suspects that he did this not as a
humanitarian but because he believed the priests' loss would be his
gain. He undoubtedly hoped to make more money for himself by
eliminating such competition. He may also have tried to increase
profits by increasing the quantity of goods demanded from the Indians
or by shortchanging them. This, however, is not certain, for all alcaldes mayores were accused of doing that, and therefore the accusations to this effect against Bacaro were certainly, to a great extent,
partisan in nature. What is certain is that the priests became his enemies
and soon denounced him before the ecclesiastical court and eventually
before the audiencia for exacting unpaid forced labor, for carrying
out illegal repartimientos for thread and textiles, and for forcing the
Indians to accept repartimientos against their will.[39] It is unlikely that
the priests, who had already been exploiting the Indians, were shocked
to discover that the magistrate was exploiting them, too.

To make matters worse, a new archbishop, Pedro Cortés y Larraz,
then appeared on the scene carrying out his mandatory episcopal

visitation. When Cortés y Larraz showed up in the Huehuetenango-Totonicapán area, the local priests complained vociferously against Bacaro, and when the archbishop returned to Santiago he brought formal charges against the alcalde mayor.[40] This proved to be of great significance, for Cortés y Larraz was a most determined archbishop who pursued his political goals more vigorously, and effectively, than most of his bland predecessors. He was the kind of prelate who frequently came into conflict with presidents, and therefore he was more than willing to take on an alcalde mayor. The coincidence of a new and bothersome archbishop with Juan Bacaro's time in office proved fatal to the business of government in Huehuetenango.

Juan Bacaro thus had succeeded in creating powerful enemies. Denounced and accused of having forced the Indians of his district to accept repartimientos, Bacaro did not deny the charge; he openly admitted having compelled the indigenous people to accept repartimientos of credit, money, and goods. In fact, he claimed that all magistrates were compelled to use force to ensure the Indians' participation in business. The supporters of the repartimiento usually made no bones about the involuntary nature of the system. Nevertheless, to be on the safe side, Bacaro got the fiscal of the audiencia to issue a ruling to the effect that the court's decision of March 24, 1759, had specifically legalized coercion to force the Indians to accept the repartimientos of their alcaldes mayores.[41]

This, it should be noted, is the "smoking gun" that proves that coercion was sometimes used to compel the Indians not just to pay their debts but also to participate in the repartimiento. To be sure, because of the connection between tribute debts and loans of money by the alcalde mayor, in many cases no coercion was necessary to begin the process, and it was needed only when it came time to collect the debt in kind. Yet, at other times, especially when it came to the forced sale of goods, but also when magistrates wanted to contract the Indians for certain products of their labor, the alcaldes mayores sometimes had to use force to get them to participate in repartimientos. Such compulsion had been in effect for some time but was legalized only in the 1759 ruling. In short, Bacaro demonstrated that his use of the coercive powers of his office was perfectly legal and widely practiced. It is important to draw attention to this point, for it belies the attempt to argue that the repartimiento system was free from coercion. That may have been true elsewhere, but in highland Guatemala, the court clarified that the magistrates were legally permitted to use the powers of their office to compel the acceptance of credit, money, and goods and then to use force to ensure the payment of debt. From the insider's point of view, that was the whole point of buying the office in the first place, and it helps explain why these commercial dealings affecting relations between the Indians and the outside world had fallen under the control of government magistrates rather than private merchants.

Nevertheless, Bacaro was now in trouble because of the bad luck of having a meddlesome archbishop show up in the kingdom. Shortly thereafter, the ecclesiastical court, seeking to defend the position of the clergy, fined the magistrate five hundred pesos for his alleged mistreatment of the priests, while the archbishop pushed for civil or criminal penalties as well.[42] Both Bacaro and Montes de Oca feared that the audiencia would give in to the pressure of a churchman whose political power was hard to ignore. They of course tried to stay on the good side of the powerful people in government by continuing to provide gifts to the president and the judges of the audiencia.[43] Nevertheless, throughout most of 1770, they scrambled to complete their business transactions and get the money into the hands of Montes de Oca or transferred to Oaxaca (under the jurisdiction of the Audiencia of Mexico) before Bacaro's property could be impounded.[44] José Melchor de Ugalde, the husband of one of the heirs to the Benítez estate—the source of some of Montes de Oca's investment capital—helped effect one transfer.[45] Both Bacaro and Montes de Oca were influenced by the fate of Bernabé de la Torre Trassierra, a former alcalde mayor of San Salvador, who in 1760 had been removed from office, fined, and his property impounded after falling afoul of powerful people. It had taken a direct order from the king to restore his property.[46] The memory of that event was obviously still very much alive ten years later. Montes de Oca complained to Bacaro that they, too, had powerful enemies, including the president of the audiencia, the attorney general, and one of the attorney general's prosecutors; the latter was said to want to impound everything to the point that not even the kitchen pots would be left.[47]

To avoid a catastrophe, Montes de Oca advised Bacaro to remove the company's merchandise in Huehuetenango and hide it on a nearby hacienda. This was to be done "so that this way they won't get a single real from us" in case the order to impound the property was given. He also told his business partner to guard his letters carefully to prevent them from falling into the wrong hands.[48] Meanwhile, the Indians, probably encouraged by the priests, were causing them problems, and Montes de Oca commented that the business was "going to the devil." Nevertheless, he informed Bacaro that their lawyer had assured him that everything they had done with respect to the repartimientos with the Indians was legal, and that the chances were good that all charges against Bacaro would be postponed until his residencia, the trial that all magistrates faced after leaving office. Residencias, everyone knew, were usually whitewashes. Montes de Oca also suggested that the alcalde mayor was taking too long to hide the merchandise; he should get the goods out of the province "without wasting time, which is extremely short." In fact, he warned ominously, if the business ended up badly it would be Bacaro's fault.[49]

Before they could finish up, however, the blow fell: the court ordered Bacaro's property impounded, and shortly after, he was removed from office, having served four years and two months rather than the usual five years. Formal charges were brought against him for allegedly provoking a rebellion in an Indian village in 1768. Eventually he would be exonerated of that charge, and in 1774 the fiscal of the Council of the Indies would report that the Audiencia of Guatemala, by ordering Bacaro's removal from office, had acted in a biased manner against the magistrate, and that the fine imposed on him should be canceled and the money returned.[50] In the context of the time (when Spain was ruled by a king who was determined to reduce the power of the Church in America), this was a rebuke to the court for buckling under the pressure of the archbishop and thereby permitting ecclesiastical meddling in politics. The audiencia had failed to defend a royal official in the performance of his duties.

In the meantime, however, Bacaro was in deep trouble, and this is what provoked the breakdown of the relationship between Juan Bacaro and Juan Montes de Oca. That personal relationship had started off well and had been further strengthened by ritual co-parenthood: they called each other *compadre*, meaning that one of the men was godfather of the other's child. (Two of their local agents were also compadres of each other, suggesting that business relationships were frequently strengthened by ritual kinship ties.) But Montes de Oca, by his own admission, had not been able to put up enough capital to make the company flourish.[51] Bacaro, meanwhile, had balked at carrying out his partner's orders to hide their merchandise from the government, probably because he feared the consequences of going along with a practice that was so obviously illegal. Then, fearing that his business associate's problems would drag him down, Montes de Oca informed Bacaro on January 25, 1771, that he had decided not to pay the tribute due the royal treasury for June and December 1770. Bacaro in turn had to sell off some assets quickly and borrow money in order to make the June payment and part of that of December.[52]

The alcalde mayor therefore decided to liquidate the company and ordered the sale of the remaining stock. Montes de Oca did the same, but sold the goods at what Bacaro considered to be below-market prices. A preliminary settling of accounts took place on May 16, 1771, followed by the final account made on September 9, 1771.[53] Nevertheless, even after that, Montes de Oca continually raised issues that according to Bacaro had been dealt with and that his partner had already accepted as final. In fact, the liquidation of the enterprise had opened up a Pandora's box of issues that led Bacaro and Montes de Oca into a lengthy lawsuit. The merchant argued that the alcalde mayor did not deserve full restitution of the twenty thousand pesos he had put into the company—including the twelve thousand in political capital, that is—because he had not served out his full term, and that the quantity returned to Bacaro should be prorated.[54] The alcalde mayor suspected that his partner was shortchanging him by selling the goods at prices higher than what he was reporting and pocketing the difference. Montes de Oca charged Bacaro with trying to hide some sales of wheat sold during the food shortage of 1769–70. The alcalde mayor, however, pointed out that the wheat sales had taken place only after Montes de Oca had specifically granted him the power to carry out that business on his own. Nevertheless, because Bacaro had made significant profits from the sale of wheat, Montes de Oca, who had not anticipated the famine that had resulted in much higher wheat prices, tried to claim that he deserved a share.[55]

Charges and countercharges multiplied. Bacaro claimed that Montes de Oca had tried to write off as unrecoverable debts for the thread given to the weavers in Santiago, when in fact he probably collected the money and pocketed it secretly.[56] Montes de Oca in turn asserted that either just before or after the breakup of the partnership, Bacaro on his own had been involved in the purchase of cacao "on the coast" (presumably in the jurisdiction of San Antonio Suchitepéquez on the Pacific coast) and had sold it in the highlands. Among the purchasers were the Dominicans in Huehuetenango. He had also acquired some indigo—produced only in San Salvador or Nicaragua—and had supposedly shipped it to Spain on his own account.[57] Furthermore, it was alleged that Bacaro's wife had been carrying out the production of petticoats in Huehuetenango, although it is difficult to determine whether she did this as a businesswoman in her own right—she was after all the daughter of a merchant—or as a front for her husband (who, it will be remembered, had agreed not to engage in any business other than that of the company).[58] It is likely that neither business partner was a paragon of virtue.

The dispute between the alcalde mayor and his former business associate got nasty. Bacaro frequently used the word "malicious" to describe his partner and provided the government with Montes de Oca's letters counseling him to hide their merchandise so it could not be impounded. He did this, he said, to "vindicate his honor," pointing out that "if I had let myself be seduced by his depraved advice, there would not have been one cent [maravedí] impounded." He also noted Montes de Oca's scheme to lie to the prosecutors regarding their accounts, concluding that his partner "took up the task of fabricating an account based on fantasy and that was entirely fictitious," thereby demonstrating "the irreligious twisting of the conscience" of the man. Montes de Oca, wrote Bacaro, was "ready to perjure himself without the slightest scruple, and determined to get me to do the same."[59] Montes de Oca's charges against Bacaro were in a similar vein, although he lacked the kind of evidence that Bacaro had to support his case. The prosecutor noted that the dispute would probably take a long time to settle, "for the case has reached the point that they are revealing confidential information" about each other.[60]

The suit brought by Juan Bacaro against Juan Montes de Oca dragged on for more than sixteen years. In 1786, Bacaro complained to the king about how slow the wheels of justice were turning, but the fiscal of the Council of the Indies could only respond that such delays were normal when powerful commercial interests were involved. Shortly after that, Bacaro died and was replaced as plaintiff by his widow, Doña María Ignacia Cabrera, whose dowry had been invested in the company back in 1765. Finally, in 1787 the courts decided the case in favor of Bacaro, but Montes de Oca responded by declaring bankruptcy. Bacaro's widow thus ended up in a suit against the heirs of Francisco Benítez, whose estate, it will be remembered, had provided capital to Montes de Oca to finance his investment in the company.[61] The fate of that suit—as well as that of the widow— is unknown.

II

If politics was the basis of the alcalde mayor's economic power in Huehuetenango, it was also politics that brought him down. Nevertheless, the documents resulting from Juan Bacaro's lawsuit against Juan Montes de Oca provide insight into the nature of commerce and the political economy of the Kingdom of Guatemala in the mid-eighteenth century. The history of places like Huehuetenango is frequently treated using terms such as "backward" or "commercially isolated." This was clearly not the case. Huehuetenango was brought into the world economy primarily as an industrial producer. Its traditional technology and structure of production were used by the colonial regime to acquire goods for shipment either to consumers elsewhere (in the case of textiles) or to industry elsewhere or in Huehuetenango itself (in the case of thread).

This case study of the activities of a magistrate and a merchant— the repartimiento—reveals that real profits were undoubtedly lower than the critics of the system charged. There were costs of operation that had to be deducted from gross revenues before yielding net profits. Tribute payments to the crown, sales taxes, and internal customs duties ate up more than half of gross revenues. On the other hand, the amount of money paid to the royal treasury by the alcalde mayor and his merchant partner demonstrates that the government had a good fiscal reason for ignoring the illegal nature of the repartimiento system. The business activities of the magistrates and their associates clearly aided in the payment of tribute and in the volume of commercial taxes. Any reform would upset the applecart—as the defenders of the system correctly pointed out.

Also important was the cost of transporting goods into, out of, and through a mountainous terrain completely lacking in navigable rivers, good-quality roads, or, of course, railroads. Everything had to be transported on the backs of mules. This was an effective but costly means of transportation. The mules and muleteers had to eat and rest during a journey of several days, and this contributed to expenses. The result was that only relatively valuable goods—thread, textiles, raw cotton, raw wool, cacao, indigo—could be transported some distance and sold at a profit. Food products like wheat or maize could be profitably transported long distances only during food shortages, when prices were well above normal. This happened in 1770, allowing Bacaro to sell wheat as far away as Chiapa. Normally, this did not happen. On the other hand, the market in Santiago was within reach, and thus the alcalde mayor did contract the Indians for wheat to sell in the capital. Regional markets thus were to a certain extent protected by the poor communications network resulting from geographic and technological factors. Only the high-value goods connected the provinces to the outside world.

It is also worth noting that despite the fame Huehuetenango's repartimiento had for dealing with thread and textiles, the sale of cattle for meat was an important branch of the business of the magistrate and his merchant partner. The latter had to buy cattle either locally or from other provinces and then arrange for the animals to be herded to Huehuetenango. As noted, this was a significant expense. The consumers were to a certain extent the non-indigenous population of the province, but as the size of that population was quite small, the primary consumers were the Indians. This represents a significant cultural change, for cattle were not native to America. The indigenous people, of course, were too poor to eat meat regularly, but beef had become an important food served at festivals and thus several times a year the alcalde mayor had the opportunity to sell cattle. The Indians, in short, had accepted something of the dominant culture.

On the other hand, there is no evidence that the indigenous people consumed any of the wheat they produced. All that the magistrate acquired was shipped to markets for consumption by the non-Indian population. The alcalde mayor succeeded in getting the indigenous people to produce it by advancing them credit—by paying their tribute—and collecting the debt in wheat. He did not need to force them with the whip to accept the deal, since they knew they had to pay tribute. If the debt was not paid, there was the possibility of punishment, but in most cases that was probably unnecessary. There was no mention of such punishment in the documents, although there was mention of resistance to the alcalde mayor's efforts to increase cloth production. Thus the Indians could be compelled to produce wheat—but not to eat it. This was evidence of cultural resistance to change. Meat could be accepted, but it was, after all, a complement to the basic diet. Maize was different: it *was* the basic diet, and since it was believed that human beings were made of maize, it defined who the indigenous people were in their own minds. To be an Indian, one had to eat maize.

Another major expense of the alcalde mayor and his associate was the purchase of cotton from other provinces. Cotton was a high-value good and thus could be profitably transported from the lowlands, such as Suchitepéquez and perhaps even Nicaragua, or the mid-altitude provinces like Verapaz, to the highlands, where it was "put out" to the indigenous people for spinning into thread and weaving. Consequently, the alcaldes mayores carried out the economic integration of their provinces and tied the people of their jurisdictions into the world economy. As will be recalled, Bacaro's associate Montes de Oca used his capital obtained from the business to invest in slave-trading in Africa through a company in Cádiz.

Finally, the activities of the alcalde mayor of Huehuetenango reveal that magistrates played a significant role in stimulating the local economy. The indigenous people would have been incorporated into the world economy anyway because of their need to pay tribute. But the magistrate used the obligation to his own advantage, paying the money on their behalf to get the Indians indebted to him. A significant part of tribute, in turn, was paid in kind, in the form of thread and cloth. These were sold to acquire the cash that had to be delivered to the royal treasury. The alcalde mayor also got the indigenous people in debt by selling them cattle for their fiestas, calves and sheep to raise, and mules used in the transportation business. Then he used his political power to get the people to produce more of what he, not they, wanted. The result was production of wheat and larger quantities of thread and cloth. Magistrates therefore played a significant role as local entrepreneurs in a world in which private merchants would have been much less successful because of their inability to compel the indigenous people to pay their debts.

To carry out business, the alcalde mayor depended on other individuals as business associates, employees, and customers. The alcalde mayor may have been the lowest-ranking salaried member of the royal bureaucracy outside of the capital, but as a businessman he had people with whom he did business and whom he employed to do his work. He provided numerous weavers, petticoat makers, and hatters with the woolen thread needed for their work. He sold thread to the businessmen—and women—in the capital who organized the manufacture of woolen textiles. He employed permanent agents in Santiago and Totonicapán, who received commissions on their sales. He also dealt with at least three others to handle special goods, one of whom dealt with the indigo coming from San Salvador. Still other agents took commissions from the sale of wheat in the capital and in Ciudad Real. Many muleteers—normally a profession monopolized by Indians—numerous enough at times to move in veritable caravans, earned money transporting the magistrate's goods. He apparently hired someone to guide the mule trains in order to circumvent the tax-collecting stations. He even provided food for the tables of the judges and president of the audiencia.

Without the magistrate and his partner, economic activity would have been carried out, but at a diminished level. This is why the repartimiento system had its supporters. Defenders of the status quo did not simply deny that the system was exploitative. They argued that the repartimiento was a form of commercial stimulus—what they called *habilitación* (capital investment)—that helped move the wheels of trade, resulted in increased levels of production, and produced the revenues that good government depended on. Leaving out the issue of exploitation, these supporters of the repartimiento were largely correct in their assessment.

All of this was accomplished, however, with help. The alcalde mayor relied completely on the village governments, without which goods could not be collected for repayment of debts and the distribution of cattle and cotton could not be carried out.[62] These village leaders cooperated because in return they received the unwritten but understood promise that their power and position in society would be recognized by Spanish authority and that significant village political autonomy would continue to be respected. They also went along, to a point, with the magistrate's demands because in return they received the also unwritten but understood promise that the level of exploitation by the Spanish authorities would be limited and therefore tolerable. Colonialism, in short, was based on a moral polity, in which indigenous political power was respected, and a moral economy, in which the economic demands of the Spaniards were not unlimited. When an alcalde mayor went beyond those political or economic limits, he was asking for trouble.[63] And when he made important enemies, as Juan Bacaro did, he could suffer severe consequences.

At the same time, merchants like Juan Montes de Oca would have been much less successful had they not made deals with magistrates like Juan Bacaro. As President–Captain General José de Araujo explained to the king in 1749, it was "necessary that commerce be accompanied by authority, because without sales being carried out in return for repayment in kind rather than in cash over a six- to twelve-month period or paid for in labor, the private merchant would not be able to sell because he lacks the authority to collect."[64] It was the royal official, the alcalde mayor, who provided the political power—the "muscle," so to speak (or "authority," as Captain General Araujo politely put it) that made the system work. In short, even when Indian acceptance of repartimientos was not coerced, when it came to paying their debts to the magistrates, the potential use of force was always there. It was for this reason that business and government worked together in Spanish America to control economic exchange between the indigenous people and the wider world.

CHAPTER 5

Government and Business in the Lowlands

Nicaragua, 1730–1790

Whereas in the highlands of Huehuetenango the royal government's goals of good government and tribute collection—facilitated by the repartimiento system—contradicted each other, in Nicaragua good government would come into conflict with what in modern times is referred to as national security. Huehuetenango, the highest province in the kingdom, was inland and virtually invulnerable to foreign invasion. Nicaragua, however, was not only vulnerable but had been attacked by pirates and English military forces several times in its history. This external threat made for an institutional difference between Huehuetenango and Nicaragua: the former was ruled by an alcalde mayor, the latter by a governor invested with more military power. Alcaldes mayores were usually former military officers. Governors were usually active military officers with some experience in command. A Nicaragua permanently in the hands of the English would have been a significant threat to the Spanish empire, and therefore Spanish rulers believed they had to continue to hold on to it.

I

Nicaragua was significantly different from the highland Guatemalan provinces.[1] First, its non-Indian population was significantly larger, which meant that tribute collection from the indigenous people did not have the priority it had elsewhere.

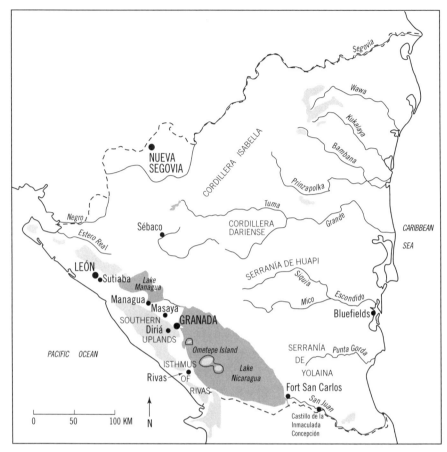

Eighteenth-Century Nicaragua

Second, the Indian population was ethnically unrelated to the Mayas of the highlands. Those living in the more populated western part of the province were mostly Chorotegas, culturally unrelated to the Mayas to the north and even to the Nicaraos, a Nahua people who occupied the Pacific coast of modern Nicaragua (to the west of the Chorotega-dominant region). Those in the thinly populated, lowland east were circum-Caribbean people who were hard to control and exploit because their economy was at the subsistence level. This meant that it was difficult for the Spaniards to occupy the entire east coast and the eastern half of the province effectively.[2] On the other hand, the Chorotegas of the swath of land between Lake Nicaragua and Lake Managua did not resist the cultural onslaught of colonialism as well as the Mayas of the highlands.[3] By the 1790s all of the village leaders in the area spoke Spanish, which allowed colonial officials to gain access to those villages. In the Maya area, however, the indigenous people rarely spoke the language of their colonial masters, and this allowed them to construct a linguistic wall protecting them from the Spanish and at times making it difficult for the colonial officials to find out what was happening among the Indians.[4]

Third, the mountainous parts of Nicaragua are not high in altitude compared with those of Guatemala, and most people lived in the lowlands or in areas within relatively easy access to the lowlands. The lowland climate favored not just traditional products like indigo and cacao but also sugarcane. As a result, haciendas were more numerous than in the highlands, and the owners brought in Africans to work as slaves. Eventually a large, free mulatto population emerged, and some areas ended up with few Indians. On the other hand, the generally warm or hot climate, combined with the fertility of the soil, allowed the Indians to get in two maize harvests per year. The first was usually the best, but the second—called the *postrera*—permitted the growth of a population that would otherwise have been relatively insignificant.

Finally, to resist foreign invasion, the Spanish government built forts and maintained garrisons in strategic locations. Most important was the Castillo de la Inmaculata Concepción, located near the point where the San Juan River begins to flow to the Caribbean Sea from Lake Nicaragua.[5] The government also maintained a small flotilla of ships to patrol the lake. Military expenditures thus helped stimulate the economy somewhat, but at the same time, the need to provide the soldiers with rations led the government to exempt the Indians from the provision allowing tribute to be paid in money. In Nicaragua, they were required to pay part of their tribute in maize, beans, and cabuya (a plant producing a sisal fiber used to make cable, rope, mats, and hammocks). The question eventually came up of what the Indians should pay in case of a crop failure and a shortage of maize and beans. When crop failure actually occurred, the governor found himself on the horns of a dilemma.

II

In 1779 Spain once again went to war with Great Britain. The last time this had happened, during the Seven Years' War, the British had sent a force up the San Juan River and carried out an unsuccessful attack on the fort of the Inmaculata Concepción.[6] This time, however, the international situation was more favorable to the Spanish empire than ever before in eighteenth-century conflicts with the British. Not only did Great Britain lack an ally on the European continent to force France to divide its military forces, but at the same time, most of the British colonies in North America were in armed rebellion against their imperial ruler. This forced the British to commit a significant quantity of their resources to crushing the rebellion and preventing one in Canada, thereby leaving fewer resources for other fronts. This helps explain why the Spanish, for once, were on the winning side of a war, and they ended up repossessing Florida, the Banda Oriental (Uruguay), Menorca (one of the Balearic Islands in the Mediterranean) and much of coastal Honduras after the 1783 treaty signed at Versailles.

Nevertheless, naval power during the war gave the British the opportunity to strike far from home, and the English bulldog had considerable bite even when confronted by a host of European enemies. In anticipation of an attack, the Spanish government took steps to strengthen its military presence in Nicaragua. The new president–captain general, Matías de Gálvez, brother of the Spanish minister of the Indies, sent reinforcements to Lieutenant Colonel Manuel de Quiroga, governor of the province, and to Lieutenant Juan de Ayssa, commandant of the fort on the San Juan River.[7]

Meanwhile, the British struck. In February 1780, the British governor of Jamaica, John Dalling, launched an expedition with orders to go up the San Juan River, attack and capture the Castillo de la Inmaculata Concepción, and cross Lake Nicaragua to attack the city of Granada. It was hoped that this would be the beginning of the British capture of all of Central America. Some seven hundred soldiers commanded by Captain John Polson, assisted by several hundred black, mulatto, and Miskito Indian volunteers recruited in eastern Nicaragua, were to make the attack. Transported by naval forces commanded by twenty-one-year-old Horatio Nelson, the British sailed up the river and attacked the Inmaculata Concepción on April 13, 1780. Lieutenant Ayssa defended the fort with some 150 regulars and eighty-six local volunteers, who held out as long as they could. The rainy season then began on April 20, and tropical disease soon decimated the invaders. Nelson and others had to be invalided out, victims of malaria. Meanwhile, Captain General Gálvez, recently returned from a triumphal campaign that had culminated in the recapture of Fort Omoa on the Honduran coast, sent a relief expedition to Nicaragua. That force proved to be too weak to interfere with the British siege, and so the Spanish troops of the relief column instead began the construction of a wooden stockade higher up on the San Juan to block any further enemy advance. Eventually this became Fort San Carlos.

The Inmaculata Concepción was a large stone fortress strong enough to withstand storming, but it had a fatal flaw: the lack of a source of water inside the fort. Once the invaders had cut the garrison off from the river, the end was inevitable. Ayssa surrendered on April 29, but the surviving British force was now diminished in strength and too sickly to proceed with the attack on Granada. Reinforcements numbering 450 men arrived on the British side, but the local volunteers deserted. The British forces then were too few in number even to hold on to what had been captured, and therefore on October 8, Polson ordered his engineers to blow up the fort and he and his men departed back downriver. The expedition was seen at the time as one of the biggest British failures of the war.[8]

When Governor Quiroga died in office, he was replaced in 1782 by Brigadier José de Estachería.[9] The new governor was an experienced soldier who had just served as Gálvez's second-in-command on the campaign that had recaptured Omoa, and Estachería had been appointed to command that fortress once it was back in Spanish hands. During the war, he had been promoted from lieutenant colonel to the rank of a general officer. Gálvez apparently had complete confidence in Brigadier Estachería. When the new governor took up his post later that year, the war was still in progress, and although the Inmaculata Concepción had to be abandoned, the new fort of San Carlos at the source of the San Juan River had to be strengthened and the garrison provisioned. There existed the real threat that the

British would return—as they would do in the Río de la Plata region in 1806–1808—and they were still holding on to some settlements in Mosquitia, on the Nicaraguan Caribbean coast at the mouth of the San Juan. Estachería therefore cooperated with Bernardo de Gálvez, the governor of Louisiana, who happened to be the son of the president and captain general of Guatemala. The younger Gálvez arrived with military forces and drove the British out of most of the Caribbean islands, and he was preparing to invade Jamaica, the final stronghold of the British Empire in the Caribbean.

Moreover, the new governor had to act decisively to secure the strategic site of the fort at the confluence of the San Juan River and Lake Nicaragua. He did so. In the second half of 1782, drought caused crop failure and food shortage. The crop failure was not universal, for the people in the areas at slightly higher altitudes managed to bring in their harvest. But the maize shortage was severe enough to make it impossible for many Indians to pay their tribute in maize from their own harvest.

Brigadier Estachería was in a dilemma. If he forced the indigenous people to pay their tribute in maize, they might go hungry and certainly would have to try to buy it on the market at higher than normal prices. If he pursued this course, he risked being accused of cruelty and extortion during his residencia. On the other hand, if he let the Indians off the hook, he would end up without enough food for the garrison. Without food, the soldiers would certainly desert, and the forts would be left undefended. The British might show up at any moment. Estachería made what must have been a difficult choice: he decided that the Indians must pay their tribute in maize even if it meant they would have to travel to more distant villages to purchase the grain. At the same time, to pay for his own expenses, he continued the long-established custom of carrying out repartimientos. This was precisely at the time that the Spanish government issued strict prohibitions against that practice, and Estachería was surely aware of the crown's decision to prohibit its officials from carrying out repartimientos.

In the short run, this did not affect Estachería or his career. In fact, whatever he had done as governor of Nicaragua must have been seen favorably by President–Captain General Gálvez, because the latter recommended Estachería to succeed him upon his elevation to the coveted position of viceroy of New Spain.[10] The crown accepted this recommendation and appointed Estachería to succeed Gálvez as president–captain general of Guatemala. (His term was for eight years, although in 1789 he asked to be relieved and stepped down after six years in office.)[11] Meanwhile, Juan de Ayssa's actions as commander of the Castillo de la Inmaculata Concepción were also approved by his superiors, for he had held out as long as humanly possible. Ayssa was promoted to colonel and named to replace Estachería as governor of Nicaragua. Shortly thereafter, Ayssa was appointed to be the province's first intendant.

It is likely that the promotion of Estachería to the presidency went through in part because the outgoing president and new viceroy of New Spain who recommended him was the brother of José de Gálvez, minister of the Indies. It is unlikely, however, that Estachería was a relative of the notoriously nepotism-prone Gálvez family, for José de Gálvez was from Málaga and Estachería was from Aragon. The most likely explanations for Estachería's promotion, therefore, are competence and either friendship or political alliance with the Gálvez family. It was probably a combination of all of these. Nevertheless, once death removed Matías de Gálvez from the scene in 1785, followed by the death of his son Bernardo de Gálvez in 1786, and the death of José de Gálvez himself in 1787, the former brigadier who had commanded Nicaragua during dangerous times became politically vulnerable.

In the meantime, fate looked kindly on Estachería. Shortly after his arrival in Guatemala City, as was the tradition, a magnificent banquet was held in his honor. Among other food purchased for the event were 475 pounds of sugar, as well as large quantities of almonds, raisins, flour, cloves, cinnamon, milk, and 60 pesos' worth of eggs for cakes and sweets; and 3 pesos' worth of marzipan and 31 pesos for other candies; olives, coffee, lentils, chickpeas, and vinegar; turtles (perhaps for soup); rice, various kinds of shellfish worth 45 pesos, and 5 pesos' worth of saffron (probably for paella). What was probably the first course included two hundred servings of fried fish and fifty pounds of baked fish (worth 57 pesos and 12 pesos respectively). Later courses included veal; 22 pesos' worth of ham; two pairs of pigeons; twenty-four tongues (presumably of beef); sausages, which along with salt and chile cost 8 pesos; nine dozen chickens, two hens, and two pullets; six turkeys; six lambs; and six suckling pigs. Accompanying the dinner were pineapple, watermelon, and other unidentified fruits, as well as 9 pesos' worth of bread. Beverages included two barrels of wine and fifty bottles of *rosolí* (a festive liqueur made with rose petals). To give grandeur to the scene, a background screen worth 8 pesos was built, and presented to the president was a bouquet of flowers worth 29 pesos plus 4 1/2 pesos for the florist who made it. Additional expenses included 4 1/2 pesos for candles; paper and letters sent by post (invitations?); 19 pesos for ceramic dishes made in Totonicapán; outlays for nails, baskets, braziers, firewood, charcoal, knives, and spoons; and finally, 9 pesos for the chefs, 112 pesos for the sous-chefs, 8 pesos for the captain of the waiters, and 38 pesos 3 1/2 reales for the Indians who carried the goods to the banquet. The total cost came to 1,318 pesos 5 reales.[12]

To modern eyes, all this seems excessive, even scandalous considering the poverty of Guatemala. But contemporaries saw things differently. Guatemala was, relatively speaking, not as poor or "backward" then as now, and such a banquet was an effective display of majesty, designed to manifest the power and might of the person ruling in the king's name in America. Such displays created a sense of the awesomeness of power. As a result, a president inspired not only awe but also fear. That fear helps explain the reluctance of some individuals to come forward and denounce a person in power.

III

In 1784 the Ministry of the Indies, headed by José de Gálvez, received an anonymous letter, dated November 1 of the previous year, from people in Nicaragua.[13] The author or authors claimed to speak in the name of the "Province of Nicaragua." They asserted that José de Estachería, who was then serving as president and captain general of the entire Kingdom of Guatemala, had abused his power when he was governor of Nicaragua. It was said that he collected part of the Indians' tribute in kind, as was the custom, but that he did so at a time when a crop failure had made maize scarce and thus very expensive. A fanega of the grain usually sold for between four and five reales, depending on whether it was of the first harvest or the second. Yet the shortage allowed Estachería's agent, Don Manuel de Cea, to sell the grain collected from the Indians at thirty-six reales per fanega, that is, at eight or nine times the usual price. The indigenous people were also required to pay tribute in cabuya, which normally sold for four reales per arroba (twenty-five pounds); Cea resold it for twelve reales, that is, three times the usual price. Finally, to make even more money, Estachería and his agent were said to have set up a manufacturing plant in the Casa Real (a building for government use) in the village of Masaya, where Indian women were being forced to spin thread from raw cotton and Indian men were put to work making hats, curing leather, and making chairs, mats, and baskets. Many of the products of the enterprise were being sold to the Spanish, mulatto, mestizo, and even Indian population of the province at prices that were 400 or 500 percent higher than what they had cost the governor to make.

The authors then stated that their allegations could be verified if the government were to carry out an inquest and question the royal officials of the provinces, the curate of Managua, the Spanish *vecinos* (non-Indians) of the villages including the village of Masaya, and the Indians themselves. What made the complaint of these citizens rare compared to that of most anonymous letters is that the authors provided the names and residences of twenty-five Spaniards in Nicaragua who were said to be able to prove their allegations. It is of course possible that some of the authors of the letter were among those twenty-five Spaniards named, all of whom were from the part of the province under the jurisdiction of the city of Granada, which was the area closest to Lake Nicaragua and therefore most vulnerable to attacks by the English.

The authors closed their denunciation of the man who at the moment was the president and captain general of the kingdom with an explanation for the anonymous nature of their letter. The president was a man of great power, and since the provincial governors and corregidores were involved in the same kinds of activities as those that they were denouncing, no legal authority could help them. "The justified fear of violence that could be experienced by the wretched citizens of this Province impels them to pray that Your Majesty deem it suitable to absolve them from putting their signatures" on the document. People in power really did instill fear in their subjects.

The fiscal of the Consejo de Indias reported on the letter on July 22, 1784. First, he cited the Laws of the Indies specifying that the government would not respond to anonymous accusations. But he also noted that the authors would have had good reasons for refusing to identify themselves, and that they also provided the means of verifying their allegations (by providing the names of people who would support their accusations against the president). Then, noting that laws existed to deal with "regular and common cases," whereas the current case "should be categorized as extraordinary and of another kind," he gave his opinion: the newly appointed bishop should be given a copy of the letter and told to investigate the matter "with all reserve and caution."[14]

The matter went before the Council of the Indies one week later. That body did not accept the suggestion of the fiscal, but instead agreed to pass the matter on, using top secret channels—the *vía reservada*—to the minister of the Indies, José de Gálvez.[15] There is no record of what happened next. In government affairs, of course, many decisions are not put into writing, and this seems to have been one of them. What is clear is that nothing was done. If indeed President Estachería was a protégé of the Gálvez party, this is what we would expect to happen. The decision seems to have been either to ignore the matter or to wait until Estachería had filled out his term in office before acting. What is certain is that nothing was done until after the death of José de Gálvez.

Meanwhile, back in the Kingdom of Guatemala, the power of the Gálvez clan and associates was being manifested. In an unprecedented move, the crown announced in 1783 that former president–captain general Matías de Gálvez, recently promoted to viceroy of New Spain, had performed in such an outstanding manner during the last war that he would be exempt from the traditional residencia, the trial for conduct in office. This meant that citizens would not be invited before a judge to make complaints or criticisms of the former president, although they were still allowed to sue Gálvez for redress of grievance. As far as is known, no one did.[16] His exemption from the residencia must have instilled more than just respect in the people of the kingdom.

In Nicaragua, the city leaders of Granada took steps to protect themselves from the possible wrath of President Estachería over the anonymous letter denouncing him. They probably had found out about the letter, and indeed some may have participated in writing it. Most of the people and villages mentioned in the letter were in the Granada region of Nicaragua. The leaders must have suspected that by now Estachería had found out about the matter, and they feared the consequences. Therefore, on April 25, 1785, the cabildo of Granada wrote a letter to the king, pointing out that governors in Nicaragua frequently abused their authority by establishing business activities involving the Casa Real in Masaya, where tribute goods were delivered and the governor's manufacturing enterprises were located. Governors traditionally benefited by collecting the payments in kind and reselling them at higher prices than their official evalua-tion. They also put the Indians to work by carrying out repartimientos: cotton given to the women to be spun into thread, and money or credit advanced to the men for repayment in wax and cabuya fiber. People were put to work in the Casa Real curing leather, making hats from palm thatch, mats from straw, hammocks and rope from cabuya fiber, and cloth from cotton thread.

The leading citizens of Granada, however, rather than denouncing the sitting president of the audiencia and captain general, instead proclaimed that José de Estachería had refrained from such activities while governor of Nicaragua. On the contrary, they argued, he had taken considerable care to see that the indigenous people were not exploited, and when the price of maize rose sharply as a result of the crop failure, Estachería had seen to it that the royal tribute collected in maize was sold to the needy not at an extraordinarily high market price but at only one-third of that. Indeed, he had acted without finan-cial interest at a level "never seen" before in Nicaragua, and he had not engaged in the usual business activities and repartimientos. For this, they were very grateful to former president–captain general Matías de Gálvez, who had appointed Estachería as their governor in order to root out the above-mentioned abuses. Instead of denouncing their former governor, therefore, they denounced their current governor, Juan de Ayssa, for engaging in all of the above-mentioned abuses.

Having thus, they hoped, ingratiated themselves with the Gálvez clan, the cabildo then requested that the crown entrust the city government with tribute collection and endow it, as in the distant past, with jurisdiction over a hinterland with a radius of thirty leagues. In this way, they assured the king, the governor would not be able to carry out his illegal business activities and tribute would be more fairly collected, especially if the Indians were allowed to pay all of their tribute—except for that needed to provision the fort—in money.[17] The crown, however, rejected both petitions in 1789, observing that the Royal Ordinances of Intendancies of 1786 and the establishment of the intendancy in Nicaragua in 1787 would provide for a more reliable method of tribute collection and administration of justice.[18] The first appointed intendant was none other than the sitting governor, Juan de Ayssa, who now held the post of governor-intendant.

This was the background for the residencia of former governor José de Estachería. It was carried out in 1786, when he was the sitting president–captain general. The judge was none other than Juan de Ayssa, Estachería's successor as governor and the very man whom the cabildo of Granada had denounced for carrying out repartimientos. The old practice of having the incoming official be the one to judge the outgoing was still operative. In the past, this usually meant a whitewash: the repartimientos of the former official were revealed, but the judge ruled that those business activities had always been accepted practice in the kingdom and that without them tribute could not have been collected. The residencia ruling would then exonerate the outgoing official, praise him for his service to the king, and recommend him for future or even higher offices. The judge, of course, expected the same treatment when his time came.

The Estachería residencia, however, was different. Repartimientos had been vociferously and vehemently prohibited of all government officials, and "severe" punishment for engaging in them prescribed. Everyone seemed to know that *this* time the crown was serious. Residencia judges were required to read aloud to the public the proclamations prohibiting repartimientos. Ayssa did as he was instructed, and he must have concluded that it was no longer safe to carry out a whitewash. Therefore he carried out a cover-up. Citizens from all over the province testified, but no major infractions on Estachería's part were found. The people from Granada, undoubtedly aware of the way the political wind was blowing, reiterated their cabildo's claim that the former governor had not engaged in the usual business activities, now illegal, of previous governors. Ayssa found Estachería to be a fine servant of the king and his performance as governor exemplary.[19] The sitting president was in the clear—for a while.

Then, in 1787 the powerful minster of the Indies, José de Gálvez, died, and the following year Charles III also passed away. Already in 1788, perhaps even before the death of the king, the case of Estachería resurfaced in Spain. A royal order of August 3 of that year, presented to the Consejo de Indias by the new minister of the Indies, Antonio Valdés, took cognizance of the reported abuses in Nicaragua and ordered that tribute could be paid in money or in kind, depending on the wishes of the Indians. Moreover, President Estachería's conduct as governor of Nicaragua would be investigated as part of the residencia that would investigate his performance as president.[20]

Shortly thereafter, at the end of 1789, Estachería decided to step down as president two years before his term was up. There is no record of why he took this decision. As noted, many political decisions are not put into writing. It is of course possible that the former governor of Nicaragua and sitting president of the audiencia believed that the realignment of politics following the death of José de Gálvez and Charles III made it wise for him to withdraw, especially since he was now faced not only with the usual residencia for his term as president but also with a special inquest into his activities as governor of Nicaragua.

Another political decision made for which there is no documentation was the selection of the person who would carry out both the residencia and the special inquest. The choice fell on Licenciado Josef Ortiz, formerly an oidor of the Audiencia of Guatemala and since 1785 the governor-intendant of the new Intendancy of San Salvador.[21] Because Ortiz had served as a high-court judge (oidor) during the first two years or so of Estachería's presidency, he would have known the outgoing president quite well. Ortiz stepped down from his position as intendant in 1789 to carry out the residencia and special inquest.

We would like to know, of course, if relations between the two men were friendly, cordial, or hostile. The documents, once again, are silent on the subject. However, the two officials probably got along quite well prior to this time, for the president had entrusted the oidor with important business. In 1784 Estachería had appointed Ortiz to carry out an inquest into the need for labor in El Salvador's indigo industry, and as a result Ortiz had drawn up new rules for the regulation of drafts of Indian laborers to be provided to the producers. The president approved these rules.[22] In 1785 Estachería had appointed Ortiz to take charge of the part of San Salvador where a new and promising deposit of silver had been discovered. This is what eventually led to Ortiz's appointment as the first intendant of San Salvador.[23] One suspects, therefore, that unless the two had had a falling-out at a later time, Ortiz was not hostile to Estachería when he was appointed to investigate his former superior.

It is also known that Ortiz as intendant had written reports that were critical of the activities of the previous alcaldes mayores of San Salvador.[24] He therefore may have had the reputation of being honest or at least of being a member of the reformist group that wanted to eliminate the repartimiento system. He had also recently submitted a series of reports regarding the substantial progress that his province was making during his tenure in office.[25] These may also have impressed his superiors. In any case, a real cédula of November 20, 1789, named Ortiz to carry out the special inquest in Nicaragua, and another royal order three days later appointed him to be judge of the residencia of former president Estachería. Shortly thereafter, Ortiz got sick and almost died. Upon recovery from his illness, he left for Nicaragua and in May 1790 arrived to carry out the special inquest into Estachería's alleged abuses as governor of the province.

IV

When Brigadier José de Estachería became governor of Nicaragua in 1782, he was not just taking up a political post. He was taking a position within a long-standing system of relationships between the indigenous population and the colonial state that he represented.

No one can be sure how far back in history those relationships went. In the archives in Spain the first detailed inquest into the governor's repartimientos and other business activities dates only from the 1730s, by which time certain practices had come into existence that persisted until the time of Estachería. It is likely that these commercial operations had originated some years before that, but it is only in the residencia of Maestre de Campo Bartolomé González Fitoria,[26] governor from 1731 to 1736, that enough details were provided to allow us to compare the business of an earlier governor with that of Governor Estachería almost fifty years later.[27]

In both the 1730s and 1790s the province's political jurisdictions consisted of four areas within the western part of Nicaragua, each centered on a primary city or town: León in the northwest; Nueva Segovia in the northeast; Granada in the center; and the Villa de Nicaragua, also known as Rivas, in the southeast. The rest of the modern country of Nicaragua was either under the jurisdiction of the corregidores of Sébaco-Chontales and Realejo (which had absorbed the former corregimiento of Sutiaba in 1778) or was beyond Spanish control. The latter was true of most of the eastern one-third of modern Nicaragua.

Governors ruled over those four political entities and developed business activities in Granada but not in the other three. This was probably for three reasons. First, the indigenous population in León, Nueva Segovia, and the Villa de Nicaragua was relatively sparse and therefore unlikely to be as commercially useful as that found in the area stretching from the city of Granada to the northwest as far as what was then the large village of Managua (later the national capital). Here was the large and important village of Masaya, which had already emerged as an important site for artisanal activity. Its population in 1776 was composed of twelve hundred Indians, two hundred mulattoes, eight hundred mestizos and twenty-five Spaniards.[28] Also in the area was Managua, the second-largest indigenous settlement in Nicaragua after Masaya. As noted, the whole region was populated mostly by Chorotega people, with smaller numbers of Nicaraos in a few locations. During the inquest it was revealed that this region contained some 3,486 Indian tributaries, which would have meant an indigenous population of approximately sixteen thousand. Comparable data from 1782–83 are unavailable for the other three jurisdictions, but comparing these figures with earlier and later data from the others, it is clear that the Granada jurisdiction must have contained between 40 and 60 percent of the indigenous population of the entire province of Nicaragua. It is no wonder that the governors' activities were concentrated there.

Second, as noted, Granada was on the west bank of Lake Nicaragua and therefore was exposed to attacks by pirates or British invaders. The governor therefore had to be present in the area, even though the offices of the royal treasury and the diocesan see were located safely to the northwest in León. Moreover, the Granada area was the base used for provisioning the patrol boats on the lake and the Castillo de la Inmaculata Concepción on the other side of Lake Nicaragua slightly downriver from the source of the San Juan River. Therefore the whole political jurisdiction of Granada, stretching to Managua, was the hinterland that fed and provisioned not only the city but also the military garrison and water-borne forces guarding the province from invasion. It was for this reason that the governors of Nicaragua got deeply involved in the economy of the Granada region.

Finally, because governors had to pay so much attention to the Granada region, they had been entrusted with political powers that they did not have in the other three jurisdictions. Normally, the alcaldes of a Spanish city in America had direct jurisdiction as judges of first instance over all the king's subjects, including Indians, within a wide area. Where a royal executive officer was present, however, the power of judge of first instance was exercised by that royal official. In Nicaragua this meant that whereas the city alcaldes of León, Nueva Segovia, and the Villa de Nicaragua acted as magistrates with judicial power over the Indians, those of Granada did not. Those powers were exercised by the governor. Everywhere in Spanish America, cities in this situation struggled, often for centuries, against governors like those in Nicaragua, but usually they lost those political battles. This helps explain why most of the complaints against the governors of Nicaragua tended to come from the city leaders of Granada. Indeed, as we have seen, the first letter denouncing Estachería for his illegal business activities came from someone or some people of Granada. It was part and parcel of a long-standing struggle for power.

Nevertheless, the crown usually rejected the complaints, with what it considered to be good reason. In 1767, for example, the fiscal of the audiencia pointed out that it was necessary for the governor rather than Granada's alcaldes to have jurisdiction over the Indians, for not only was his presence necessary to defend the fort across the lake, but also "since the city alcaldes are mostly *hacendados*, and those who are not are relatives of people who own haciendas, they would allocate [the Indians] in forced labor drafts at the expense of their liberty and in offense of the laws, and would carry out other abuses, as has been experienced elsewhere."[29] This helps explain how the city alcaldes of León, Nueva Segovia, and the Villa de Nicaragua were undoubtedly treating the Indians in their areas, and why the city elite of Granada wanted to do the same—and would have done if the governor had not stood in its way.

Consequently, it was with the indigenous people of the Granada jurisdiction that governors of Nicaragua carried out business. Comparing the activities of González Fitoria in the 1730s with those of Estachería in the 1780s, what is notable at first glance, as is demonstrated in table 5.1, is that all of the business and repartimientos of the earlier period continued into the era of Estachería.[30] Quantities are not available for the earlier period, but by the 1780s the governor was providing the Indians annually with 565 arrobas (22.6 tons) of raw cotton and contracting them through advance payments for the future delivery of over 279 arrobas (3.5 tons) of thread. The thread was of three categories: thick (*grueso* or *gordo*), middleweight (*mediano*), and fine (*fino* or *delgado*). Most of the thread delivered was of the thick variety, which the sources identify as being used for the making of canvas for sails. This demonstrates the direct link between the governor's economic activities and defense of the province, for the sails were used on the ships patrolling the lake and provisioning the fort on the other side.

Practically all the remaining thread was of the fine variety referred to as *hilo de caracol* or *hilo morado* (purple), which was dyed with an extract from sea snails (not dyewood as in Sutiaba). This was for export beyond the province and was unconnected to the needs of the military. Nothing is known of the use for the very small quantity of middle-weight thread, but the purple or fine product was

Table 5.1

VILLAGES IN THE JURISDICTION OF GRANADA:
REPARTIMIENTOS, 1782–83 (IN ARROBAS, OR 25-POUND UNITS)

	Tributaries	Cotton	Thread	Wax	Twine
Morinbo (Masaya)[1]	544	48	12	15	70
Diriega (Masaya)	273	7	5	—	20
Guillen (Masaya)	261	7	5	—	20
San Sebastian (Masaya)	226	7	5	—	20
Nindiní	309	40	10	10	—
Santa Catarina Namotiva	182	30	7 1/2	6	—
Niquinohomo	216	36	9	9	—
San Juan Namotiva	73	30	7 1/2	5	—
San Jorge de Nicaragua	—	—	20 lbs. (morado)	—	—
Diriá	116	82	21 (grueso) 4 lbs. (morado)	7	—
Diriomo	256	60	15 (grueso)	12	—
Jalata	52	21	5 1/4 (grueso)	6	12
Masatepet	279	72	18 (mediano) 6 lbs. (morado)	8	—
Nandasmo	34	12	3 (fino)	4	—
Diriambo	122	48	delgado?	10	10
Jinotepet	90	35	8.75 (delgado) 6 lbs. (morado)	7	20
Managua[2]	453	30	7 1/2 (grueso) 4 lbs. (morado)	24	—

Source: AGI, Guatemala 577, expediente 1, Testimonio de los Autos de Pesquisa Ynstruidos por el Señor Don Josef Ortiz de la Peña, fols. 21–97 (1790).
Note: Unless otherwise stated, the kind of thread was not identified in the source.
[1]Masaya was composed of four parcialidades: Morinbo, Diriega, Guillen, San Sebastian.
[2]Managua was composed of four parcialidades: Managua, Tepalmeca, Matagalpa, Cuastepec.

sold in distant markets for a profit. In this case the repartimiento was unconnected to the defense of the province; it was carried out to provide more income for the governor, whose salary of two thousand pesos was considered by many officials to be too small, given a governor's needs and responsibilities.[31]

There is no record of where Estachería acquired the raw cotton needed for all this spinning and weaving. However, since Nicaragua itself was a producer and exporter of cotton, it is likely that the cotton was purchased from local hacendados, who would have benefited from the stimulus provided to the economy by government defense spending, especially if the governor could be induced to provide the landowners with Indian laborers at a low rate of pay. This was probably done by some previous governors of Nicaragua, for some of the Indians who testified at the Estachería inquest stated that they were grateful to the former governor because he had liberated them from forced labor on haciendas.[32] The work of spinning the thread was carried out, in Nicaragua as everywhere else in the Kingdom of Guatemala, by women, invariably identified in the documents as "las yndias."

Another repartimiento activity of the governors in both the 1730s and the 1780s was allocation of money for the future delivery of sisal fiber from the cabuya plant. Once again, data from the González Fitoria repartimiento are lacking, but Estachería's operations netted him 344 arrobas, or something over four tons, of the fiber, which was used, among other things, to make rope and cable, that is, the tackle needed by ships on the lake. Once again, then, we see the connection between the governor's repartimiento and the genuine needs of the province's defense establishment. On the other hand, not all of the sisal was used to provide for the ships, and the supply allowed the governor to make even more money which he dedicated to manufacturing.

There were three significant differences between González Fitoria's business activities and those of Estachería. First, whereas in the 1730s, repartimientos were carried out in only six villages and in two of the four *parcialidades* (subdivisions) of Masaya, by the 1780s, the system had been extended to seven more villages and to all four of Masaya's parcialidades. In other words, the reach of the system got wider, extending to fourteen villages, including all parts of the largest settlement in the province. More Indians were involved in business with the governor.

Second, a new item was acquired through the repartimiento. This was local wax, called *cera criolla*, of which Estachería managed to collect 246 arrobas, that is, something over three tons. Thirteen of the fourteen villages received repartimientos for wax, compared with none in the 1730s. The use of this wax is unknown. There is no mention of any exports, so it was likely used locally. Part of the wax could have been used to provision the fort with candles and some could likewise have been used for the ships, so again there could have been a connection between the governor's repartimiento and maintenance of the defense establishment. But it is also probable that some of the wax was sold locally, for there was a demand for wax candles used in churches.

Third, sometime between the 1730s and the 1780s an entirely new business, focused on manufacturing, was opened up by the governors. It was centered on Masaya, the largest village in the area and the center of artisanal production. Masaya had taken on considerable importance for the governors not only because of its size but also because of its location right in the middle of the jurisdiction, roughly halfway between Granada and Managua. The chief executives of Nicaragua lived there part of the year to be able to make quick visits to or inspections of Granada and León. Masaya also served as a convenient place for the collection of tribute, and governors appointed a so-called lieutenant to live there permanently to supervise the incoming flow of tribute goods. (Later the crown objected to the use of the title of lieutenant for that position, so that at the time of Estachería the governor's agent was called a *factor*—that is, someone in charge of a trading post.) They also built a thatched-roof house in the village to serve as the collection point and storage facility.

Then, sometime in the 1760s, Governor Domingo Cabello ordered the construction of a more solid structure in Masaya. This was known locally as the Casa Real (royal house). It served not only as a warehouse but also as a manufacturing plant. This was brought to the attention of the crown in 1767 by Gerónimo de la Vega y Lacayo, who had just been appointed to serve as alcalde mayor of Tegucigalpa and had previously been the judge hearing the residencia of Melchor Vidal, former governor of Nicaragua. De la Vega reported that Indians in the Casa Real were being put to work for the governor, weaving canvas cloth, extracting sisal fiber from the raw leaves of the cabuya, and making hammocks, sacks, mats, mattresses, straw hats, and wooden chairs and washbasins. Governors also made a great deal of money by collecting tribute in kind that was evaluated at below market prices and then reselling it for a great deal more money.[33]

The fiscal of the audiencia responded to De la Vega's letter in 1769 by ordering an inquest. The citizens of Granada and the Indians of the surrounding villages did not support De la Vega's allegations that the repartimientos were abusive. Neither did the vecinos and Indian leaders of Managua, Masaya, or the other villages. No attempt was made to hide the fact that the governor was carrying out repartimientos and other business dealings with the Indians that required them to deliver goods at below-market prices. Even the Indians said that the system benefited them, for it guaranteed that they would be able to sell whatever cotton thread or sisal product they made, without the difficulty of finding a buyer. Even the practice of evaluating tribute goods at below-market prices found defenders, for it was pointed out that sometimes a good harvest lowered prices below the official evaluations, yet the governor still evaluated the goods at a rate that was in fact more than what they were worth on the market. All witnesses also agreed that the Indians did not need to be coerced to accept payments for their goods in advance, and that the governor's agent did not whip them or punish them in any way. The governor's manufacturing business in the Casa Real was said to be simply a way to provide employment for people while relieving them of any worry about selling their goods.[34] In short, the repartimiento and other businesses were whitewashed, and De la Vega was fined a thousand pesos for having forced the government to pay for an expensive inquest.

The inquest into Estachería's business dealings by Residencia Judge Ortiz revealed that the manufacturing concern located in Masaya was expanding into new areas. Not only were all of the activities mentioned in the complaint by De la Vega still going on, but the manufacturing of furniture had grown substantially, and in addition most

villages were being required to have their local stonemasons manufacture grinding stones (some of them two-handled, for grinding
chocolate) and other goods for sale. Most interesting, perhaps, were
the new activities in the Casa Real, which the Indians of Masaya
reported was built with their unremunerated labor and at their own
cost during the governorship of Domingo Cabello; they had also
covered the expenses for repairs to the structure since that time.[35]
Whereas spinning thread and weaving cloth were normally the work
of Indian women who labored in their thatched-roof huts—truly a
cottage industry—in Estachería's time some Indian women were put
to work permanently in the Casa Real spinning thread and making
textiles. In addition, specialists in dyeing thread—people called *teñidores*
—were also found to be working in the building, making the material
needed to weave what by local standards were fairly fancy, colored
textiles. The business had also expanded to include the tanning of
calfskin and deerhide.

    All these industrial workers were reported to be earning less than
what they could have earned doing the same things for private individuals. This, of course, helps explain the advantage the governor
had over any private entrepreneurs who might have wanted to
establish cotton-producing obrajes (mills) in Nicaragua like those in
Puebla.[36] On the other hand, it is by no means certain that a large,
privately owned textile industry could have been founded in Nicaragua at the time. Entrepreneurs had no power to compel people to
work in factories for wages, and had they carried out their own
putting-out system in the villages, they would have had difficulty
in forcing the Indians to deliver the goods they had been contracted
to produce. Moreover, village government officials would have felt
no need to collect those debts. There is no mention of any such competing private textile sector in the province at the time, which strongly
suggests that it was the power of the governor—fundamentally political power—that brought the industry into existence and provided it
with the underpaid labor necessary for its continuation. There is no
evidence for the existence yet of a labor market outside of the governor's putting-out system—which arguably was not based on wages
at all because money was paid in advance to get the laborers in debt

and force them to pay off the debt in goods. It is unlikely, therefore, that the activities of Nicaragua's governors hindered the emergence of a factory-based textile industry. Indeed, after the termination of the repartimiento system, no such industry emerged until long after the province's independence from Spain.

Residencia Judge Ortiz dutifully noted all of these now-illegal business activities in which the former governor had been involved. What upset him the most, however, was the use—formerly widespread throughout the Kingdom of Guatemala—of the tributary system for private gain. This activity had diminished elsewhere after the 1740s because the crown had issued an order allowing the Indians to pay their tribute in money if they should so choose. But, as we have seen, the government had exempted Nicaragua from this order because of the need to provision the fort with maize, beans, and hens. Every year, Estachería's government provided the fort across the lake with 650 fanegas of maize, as was required, but he collected no less than 4,764 fanegas from the indigenous people. The military in fact only consumed some 14 percent of the tribute maize; the rest was sold on the market. Yet the Indians were credited with the grain at the rate of four reales per fanega, while the market price was sometimes two or three times that because of the bad harvest in the second half of 1782. This yielded good profits for the governor, although Ortiz admitted that he could not precisely calculate how much money Estachería earned from the sales.

Ortiz eventually brought nine charges against the former governor. In his opinion, the most serious was the second one: that during a grain shortage, the governor had allowed his factor, Manuel de Cea, to require the Indians to pay their tribute in kind. The judge admitted that Estachería may not have been aware of this, for anyone knowingly responsible for such a policy would be "completely lacking in the feelings of humanity." But it was clear in Ortiz's mind that Cea had committed a "scandalous impiety" by refusing to allow the indigenous people to pay their tribute in money during the grain shortage, and as a result many villages had sent people to other parts of the province in search of maize, which of course was sold to them at high prices. Estachería was also charged with carrying out repartimientos and other business activities with the indigenous people despite strict legal prohibition from doing so. The governor, wrote Ortiz, could not have been ignorant of the illegal nature of his actions.[37]

It is important to note that the evidence gathered during the inquest of former governor Estachería included both negative and positive reports. Many villagers testified that during the grain shortage they had asked to be allowed to pay their tribute in money only to be turned down by Cea, thus forcing them to buy the maize far from their villages, sometimes as far away as León. Many complained that their tribute maize and sisal were being evaluated at less than what they were worth, and that the money they were paid for spinning thread and extracting sisal fiber was not as much as what they could have earned working for someone other than the governor. The Indians of Masaya complained that they were threatened with being whipped if they tried to accept work for someone other than the governor's agent. They were also required to provide the Casa Real with firewood, milk, extra food, fish, grooms for the horses, stableboys to feed the horses, a cook, and several women to grind corn. Some of the artisans reported that Cea required them to work even on religious holidays.[38] Many of the surrounding villages were required to provide the Casa Real with guards to protect the goods being produced and stored inside.

In addition to Masaya, other villages also had special complaints. The village leaders of Niquinohomo and San Juan Namotiva stated that the wax repartimiento was burdensome to them because their villages did not normally produce wax and therefore they had to buy it on the market.[39] The leaders of San Jorge de Nicaragua complained that to produce the purple thread contracted by the governor they had to travel all the way to a fishing village called Murciélago in the neighboring province of Nicoya.[40] The Indians of Masatepet reported that the governor had carried out what was apparently a new type of repartimiento, requiring them to deliver ninety bed mats (*petates cameros*).[41] The village leaders of Managua complained that the governor had forced them to deliver fish every Friday and during Lent, for which they were paid nothing.[42]

On the other hand, not all Indians suffered the loss of their crops, and the village of Duriomo, at a higher altitude than the other villages, even had enough maize to sell to those that needed it.[43] The Indians of Diriá also reported that they had more than enough grain during the shortage and that they had sold their surplus to other villages.[44] The people from the village of Masatepet and Nandasmo could not pay all of their maize tribute during the grain shortage, but Cea allowed them to pay their debt in money.[45] The villagers of Managua reported that when they could not pay all of their tribute maize and had to buy some in the León area, the governor's agent counted what they delivered as worth twice the normal amount, thus effectively lowering the amount owed.[46] No one complained about having to be whipped in order to accept the repartimientos, and in fact the villagers all agreed that Estachería had simply done what all governors had done. The repartimiento, in other words, seems to have been viewed as a burden that the Indians had to bear, rather than a vicious abuse inflicted on them by heartless government officials.

Some village leaders went out of their way to praise the former governor. The Indian leaders of Niquinohomo stated that "they were living in a very thankful condition because in [Estachería's] time he liberated them from the forced labor drafts [for the haciendas] that before and after they have suffered."[47] Those of San Juan Namotiva testified that Estachería carried out no abuses against them with the repartimientos, and that "they must confess" that the former governor "in everything else treated them charitably, and liberated them from forced labor on the haciendas, which has always caused them injury because they usually lose time for their own labor, and they suffer bad treatment and are badly paid by the hacendados."[48] These were the same villages that had complained that the governor's wax repartimiento had forced them to buy wax on the market because their own people did not produce it.

When Ortiz returned to the new capital of Guatemala City later in 1790, he carried out the residencia of the former president.[49] No major charges were brought against Estachería for the time he served as captain general and president of the audiencia, but he was charged with nine offenses committed during the time he was governor of Nicaragua: (1) he forced the Indians to pay tribute in kind at rates below the market value of the goods, (2) he forced the Indians to pay their tribute in kind during the grain shortage, (3) he carried out repartimientos for wax and sisal using evaluations that were half their real value, (4) he carried out repartimientos for thread at one-quarter of its real value, (5) he carried out repartimientos for manufactured goods (chairs, hammocks, sacks, leather, and so on) in Masaya, (6) he prevented the Indian artisans from getting better deals from private merchants, (7) he forced the Indians to make rope, (8) he used government property (the Casa Real) for his private business, and (9) he required the Indians of several villages to provide him with free food.

The former governor's defense counsel argued that Estachería had been unaware that his factor, Manuel de Cea, had been collecting tribute in maize during the shortage. No attempt was made, however, to deny the repartimientos and other business activities. These were admitted, and defended on the grounds that they were necessary to ensure the payment of tribute, and that for as long as anyone could remember all governors had carried out those activities. That defense had usually worked in the past and so was used again.

The evidence provided by the Indians in Nicaragua helped Estachería escape from the second charge, which the judge had declared to be the most serious. All the witnesses stated that the person who rejected, or in a few cases accepted, their requests to pay in money rather than in kind had been Manuel de Cea, not Governor Estachería. Moreover, no one had died as a result of the policy. The Indians who could not pay their tribute from their own harvest had been able to buy it elsewhere. This meant they had been forced to go off in search of maize in other villages or even as far away as León, and that this tedious and expensive task was paid for by the Indians themselves, thereby relieving the governor's agent of the need to search out the maize himself. The cost had been shifted to the Indians, who paid for it with their time and labor. This, then, was a policy of exploitation, not of forced starvation. The charge against Estachería was dropped.

Whatever the intentions of the judge, however, he could hardly overlook the repartimientos that had been carried out in contravention of the law and contrary to the explicit new rules laid down in 1782, when repartimientos had been banned and residencia judges had been instructed to punish offenders. Ortiz followed his instructions, and since Estachería was found guilty of eight of the charges, the judge fined him fifteen hundred pesos. This punishment was not nearly as severe as that inflicted on past presidents who had notoriously flouted the law (as we have seen in chapter 2). Nevertheless, since the governor's salary had been only two thousand pesos per year, the fine was not a mere slap on the wrist. The crown really was serious about eliminating the repartimiento system. Brigadier José de Estachería was made to pay the price. The old defense of the system—that it had always been done and that it was necessary to ensure the payment of tribute—was no longer acceptable.

V

The repartimiento in lowland Nicaragua was perhaps surprisingly similar to that of highland regions like Huehuetenango. First, it depended on the cooperation and participation of the indigenous village governments, for without them the system could not function. The village leaders were responsible not only for tribute collection but also for accepting the money or credit provided by the governor or the alcalde mayor and then for collecting the goods from the Indians. These arrangements were always directly related to the tribute system, for the number of tributaries was used to calculate the quantities of goods to be contracted. These leaders thus played a crucial role in the colonial regime, even in areas like Nicaragua where indigenous culture was weaker than in the highlands. This weakness was demonstrated in part by the widespread knowledge of Spanish among those leaders: in none of the villages questioned during the inquests of the 1730s or in that of 1790 did the "indios principales," as they were called, need an interpreter to communicate in Spanish. All of them were described as ladinos, that is, Spanish-speaking. In the highlands, on the other hand, these leaders always needed—or claimed to need—an interpreter. However, wherever Indian leaders and government were too weak to control the indigenous population or extract a surplus from them, the colonial regime could not effectively function. That was the case along the east coast of Nicaragua, which was occupied by non-Mesoamerican people largely at the subsistence level.

Second, the repartimiento systems in Huehuetenango and Nicaragua were virtually the same in that they were fundamentally a kind of putting-out system. In both regions, the single most important branch of the government official's business was the contracting for thread and cloth to be spun and woven by the Indians. This was true even in lowland Nicaragua. Whereas the markets for highland goods were to be found in cities, mining camps, and indigo-producing regions, the market for lowland cloth was first and foremost the military, which demanded large quantities of sailcloth, which would have had to be imported, at great expense, had it not been for the production of the Indians. The fancy, colored thread was also important and found markets in the same places as that produced in the highlands. The putting-out system, organized through the mechanism of colonialism, thus was an essential economic activity maintaining the colonial regime.

Third, in both the highlands and the lowlands, government officials profited from the tributary system by forcing the Indians to pay in goods that were deliberately undervalued. Those goods were then resold at much higher prices. This business had declined in the highlands after the tributary reform of the 1730s had allowed the indigenous people to pay either in money or in kind, but even then, Juan Bacaro, the alcalde mayor of Huehuetenango, had profited by shipping scarce foodstuffs from his jurisdiction all the way to Chiapa. In Nicaragua, where Indians were still required to pay part of their tribute in kind, governors González Fitoria and Estachería profited by undervaluing the tributary maize, beans, and sisal fiber that they collected and then reselling those goods at higher prices. Thus the nature of colonialism, based as it was on tribute, naturally led to levels of exploitation that Josef Ortiz, residencia judge in the case of Estachería, categorized as "exorbitant." Similar criticisms were often made of the highland alcaldes mayores.

Fourth, in both the highlands and the lowlands, government officials adapted to local resources and people, and did their best to profit from what they found. In the highlands and the lowlands, the Indians already had a developed cotton textile industry, which was retained in the tribute system and then exploited by the government officials through repartimientos. In Nicaragua, the indigenous people had already developed uses for the cabuya plant and its sisal fiber, a branch of production not only retained in the tribute system but also, like cotton thread and textiles, acquired by the governors through the repartimiento. The same was true of wax. Already-existing structures of production were the basis of the system.

Finally, in both the highlands and the lowlands little violence or overt coercion was used to force the Indians to participate in the repartimiento system. This was because it was directly linked to tribute, part of which was frequently paid with the credit being advanced by the government officials. Over and over again, the Indian leaders testified that this was how it was always done in Huehuetenango and Nicaragua. The result was that repayment of the debt to the alcalde mayor or governor was indistinguishable from tribute collection, and in fact was carried out by the very same indigenous who received the cash or credit that was paid in advance for the future delivery of goods. Payment of tribute, of course, was never voluntary, and therefore neither was the repartimiento. The coercion needed to collect repartimiento debts was the same as that used to collect taxes. The coercive nature of the repartimiento therefore was revealed only when participation became voluntary. When that happened, the Indians in both the highlands and lowlands refused to participate—as the supporters of the repartimiento system had always predicted. This proves that the system was to a certain extent coercive.

The differences that existed between the highland and the lowland repartimientos were due in part to geographic factors, which determined what products could and could not be profitably exploited. In the highlands, sheep raising was possible and eventually led to a putting-out system for the spinning of woolen thread. This was impossible in the lowlands of Nicaragua. On the other hand, the highland Indian demand for meat allowed the alcalde mayor of Huehuetenango to profit by monopolizing the provisioning of the meat market in the villages. This was not possible in Nicaragua, which was a major cattle-raising region. Moreover, it was impossible for anyone to monopolize local meat markets in Nicaragua, especially when the lowland villages, unlike those in the highlands, contained large numbers of mestizos, mulattoes, and Spaniards who could not be treated the way Indians were treated. The indigenous people therefore were subject to forms of exploitation that no one else had to endure.

On the other hand, political factors also contributed to the differences between the highland and lowland regions. Had there been no need to maintain a fort on the San Juan River to protect against foreign invasion, then the level of demand for indigenous products— like sailcloth and provisions for the garrison—would have been significantly lower, and colonialism would have been considerably less profitable to the governors of Nicaragua. To be sure, the region would have had economic development, for it is clear that by the second half of the eighteenth century, a considerable number of haciendas had emerged and were producing not just cattle but also cacao, sugar, and indigo.[50] Some of these items were exported to markets outside Nicaragua and as far away as Peru. Nevertheless, the military presence provided substantial economic stimulus that would have been absent without a foreign threat. Economic activity would therefore have been carried out at a somewhat lower level.

In a sense, then, the very nature of Spanish colonialism, which in Central America was based on the indigenous economy, led naturally to the repartimiento system, given that the Spanish government was unwilling or unable to pay its bureaucrats what the latter felt they needed to survive and prosper. This is why the repartimiento system was ubiquitous in the Spanish empire, existing not just in nearby Mexico but also rather distant Peru and Bolivia and in the very distant Philippines.[51] Corruption is usually guaranteed in such circumstances, and the nature of the Spanish colonial regime practically guaranteed that its officials would act in virtually identical ways despite thousands of miles of distance between them.

VI

Just as politics had brought down Alcalde Mayor Juan Bacaro in Huehuetenango, so too was José de Estachería undone by political factors beyond his control. The decision to end the repartimiento system, made by Charles III in consultation with his colonial advisor,

José de Gálvez, was a serious effort to root out perceived government corruption in America. The new policy was largely enforced, even against someone who had apparently been a protégé of the Gálvez group.

Nevertheless, politics was continually changing and sometimes resulted in the bending of the rules. This is clearly revealed by the fate of Juan de Ayssa, who had replaced Estachería in Nicaragua as governor. As will be recalled, Ayssa had been the judge of the first residencia of Estachería and had carried out a cover-up of the activities of the previous ruler. Nothing bad had been revealed, and nothing dangerous had been reported. Ayssa did not suffer any consequences for the perpetration of the cover-up. On the contrary, in 1786 he was appointed to be Nicaragua's first intendant, a very prestigious position, a post he held until 1794. Upon assuming the governorship in Nicaragua, he continued to carry out the very same repartimientos and business activities as his predecessor. When Judge Josef Ortiz arrived in Nicaragua to carry out the inquest into Estachería's activities as governor, he discovered this and ordered Ayssa to cease his activities. Ortiz included this information in the report he submitted at the time of Estachería's residencia.[52] Yet at Ayssa's residencia, four years after that of Estachería, none of this was reported.[53] He could easily have been charged with carrying out repartimientos between 1783 and 1790, but for some reason he was not. He was found to be a good servant of His Majesty and was declared fit to hold future offices. Clearly, even in the more honest environment that reigned after the Gálvez reforms and the elimination of most of the business activities of government officials, justice was sometimes selective.

Yet Brigadier José de Estachería, while punished, was not disgraced as two earlier presidents had been. In Aragon he eventually came to be considered a local boy made good, and in his hometown of Blancas, near Teruel, the main street is named Calle José de Estachería.

CHAPTER 6

IMPERIAL REFORM AND POLITICAL CONFLICT IN THE EIGHTEENTH CENTURY

Looking back on the course of imperial reform in Central America during the previous three and a half decades, the fiscal of the Council of the Indies noted with satisfaction in 1796 that the infamously corrupt corregimientos and alcaldías mayores had taken on a "different aspect." On the one hand the establishment of intendancies in Chiapas, Comayagua-Honduras, El Salvador, and Nicaragua, and on the other the reform of the magistracies in Guatemala, had created a different political and administrative world in which corruption was greatly diminished. Although the salaries of corregidores and alcaldes mayores had not been raised significantly, other measures taken had made it easier for the magistrates to avoid the necessity of carrying out extensive business with the Indians. Indeed, they were no longer permitted to do so, for the crown no longer tolerated the notorious repartimiento system.[1] Fourteen years later, after even further reforms, President–Captain General Antonio González Saravia prayed that there would never be a return to the old system when government positions were "desired only because of the mean spirit of business and monopoly."[2]

This apparent success in diminishing corruption in government is even more notable because this reform took place—in what is now Guatemala—without the establishment of the intendancy. In most of Spanish America, administrative reform in the age of Charles III and Charles IV revolved around the intendancy, the subject of a large part of the enormous historiography regarding the Bourbon

Reforms. Not all of America, however, experienced that institution. Two regions that did not were the units comprising the modern-day countries of Colombia and Guatemala.[3] How, without the intendancy, was it possible to reform the magistracies and turn the magistrates into honest officials who furthered the king's, rather than their own, interests? What impact did this reform have on politics, economy, and society? Specifically, did the attack on corruption contribute in any way to the outbreak of the Independence movement? These are some of the questions that this chapter will address with respect to the Kingdom of Guatemala.

I

The impulse to root out corruption in Spanish colonial government and achieve justice through the rule of law did not begin with Charles III.[4] At no time, after all, were the sale of offices and the concomitant corruption seen as anything but a necessary evil, given the lack of resources to pay adequate salaries to officials who therefore had to resort to illegal business activities to support themselves. Moreover, even in very adverse circumstances, the government tried to remedy egregious abuses and never officially gave up on the principle of good government, especially the administration of justice.

The commitment to justice in principle but not in practice was revealed in the controversy over the magistrates' treatment of the Indians of the Kingdom of Guatemala in the 1740s. The abuses associated with the repartimiento system were once more being investigated, this time by the fiscal of the audiencia, Diego Holgado de Guzmán, who had received complaints from Indians in Sololá, Soconusco, and Nicaragua. When the fiscal tried to investigate, he found that there were no funds to pay for a formal legal inquiry, which would have required the dispatch of an attorney on the audiencia staff to the province to carry out a full investigation. Moreover, he discovered that the custom in the kingdom was for such inquests to be carried out—if they were carried out at all—by magistrates of a neighboring province. This lowered considerably the legal costs, but as Holgado de Guzmán pointed out, this meant that magistrates without formal training in the law were being called on to investigate the same illegal acts that they all were involved in. The result, as was to be expected, was a whitewash. The fiscal tried to convince the crown to establish a Tribunal de Indios—a special court to protect the interests of Indians against the Spanish colonists—as in the Viceroyalties of New Spain and Peru, but he failed because the financial cost was judged to be too high for a poor region like Guatemala. Meanwhile, the audiencia ordered that all complaints against magistrates be left for their residencias, which were conducted after they had left office. However, as Holgado de Guzmán pointed out, residencias seldom produced justice; among other reasons, because the Indians were afraid to tell the truth at the hearings and were usually coerced into committing perjury.[5]

All the information was passed on to the government in Spain. The king, Ferdinand VI, responded with a real cédula in which he criticized the president and the audiencia for failing to pursue justice in a case of such "manifest transgression of the laws." He further stated that their handling of the case was worthy of "a severe reprimand."[6] Yet commitment to principle and implementation of policy are two different things. In the end, the crown failed to establish a Tribunal de Indios. Diego Holgado de Guzmán was rewarded for his concern over the Indians by being promoted to the highly sought-after position of fiscal of the Audiencia of Lima. Certainly in Guatemala, injustices committed at the expense of the Indians continued.

At all times, royal officials in Guatemala and Spain were perfectly aware of the abuses perpetrated by the magistrates and of the failure of residencias to produce justice. True, on occasion, residencia judges punished royal officials in America for their actions. In 1725, as we have seen in chapter 2, former President–Captain General Francisco Rodríguez de Rivas was fined eighty thousand pesos, denied future office, and exiled from America for five years for a variety of offenses, including having demanded cash payments from would-be interim magistrates in return for their appointments and for having carried out illegal business deals, some of which involved trade between Guatemala and Peru.[7] Similarly, in 1748 former President–Captain General Tomás de Rivera Santa Cruz, after having been suspended from office, was fined eighty thousand pesos and had some of his property in Mexico impounded as punishment for accepting bribes, permitting gambling, selling positions in the Church, interfering with the provisioning of the capital city with meat, and many other offenses. In addition, he was declared unfit for future office.[8] Yet these were important cases of notoriously abusive officials, and their residencias were carried out by audiencia judges who would have looked bad if they had not imposed substantial punishment.

More typical was the residencia of Francisco Antonio de Granda and Nicolás Mencos, former alcaldes mayores of Huehuetenango, in 1749. The position had originally been bought in 1737 by Felipe Manrrique de Guzmán for five thousand pesos with the right to appoint a successor if he chose not to continue in office. Manrrique de Guzmán, who at the time of the purchase was a *regidor* (city councilman) of the capital of Santiago, stepped down in 1741 to become the assistant to the alcalde mayor of Sololá, in which position he was one of those denounced for abuses by Fiscal Diego Holgado de Guzmán in 1743. When he gave up his position as alcalde mayor of Huehuetenango in 1741, Manrrique de Guzmán appointed Granda as his replacement, and when the latter died in office, the original purchaser appointed Mencos to replace Granda. Normally the next person appointed to serve the following five-year term as alcalde mayor would have carried out the residencies of Manrrique de Guzmán, Granda (subject to trial despite being deceased), and Mencos. However, in this case, the incoming alcalde mayor, Diego de Arrollave y Beteta, was the brother-in-law of both Granda and Mencos (he was married to Granda's sister and his own sister was Mencos' wife). To avoid so obvious a conflict of interest, the audiencia appointed as residencia judge Manuel de Plazaola, who less than three years later would become an alcalde mayor and serve as the magistrate of Chimaltenango for ten years (and who would be embarrassed by a rebellion by the Indians of Tecpán).[9] Also investigated at the residencia was Juan José Bocanegra, who had served as the assistant of Granda and Mencos and had been accused of abuses in Totonicapán by Fiscal Diego Holgado de Guzmán. Because the Indians of Totonicapán had complained about Bocanegra in an inquest into his abuses, Judge Plazaola ordered them to appear and testify. This time the Indians retracted their earlier testimony and denied all abuses. On the other hand, many Spaniards, several of whom were former or future alcaldes mayores, and some priests, including Franciscans, testified in behalf of the magistrates and vouched for their good character. Judge Plazaola found all the accused men to be innocent and commended them for being good servants of His Majesty.[10]

Since practically all residencies resulted in the pardoning, exoneration, or even commendation of the magistrates, these trials clearly failed to check the abuses perpetrated by government officials. In fact, as the audiencia noted in 1767, the judges who conducted the residencies were usually untrained in the law and unaided by legal councilors. What they learned at the trial was not the law but the art of the whitewash, thereby preparing themselves for when their own turn came to be tried and exonerated in still another cover-up. Residencias, the audiencia realized, served the residencia judges and even the officials being tried, but did not serve the cause of justice.[11] A similar assessment was made in the same year by the bishop of Nicaragua, who made complaints against the corregidor of Sutiaba.[12]

The commitment to good government in principle but not in practice was evident throughout the eighteenth century. The new Bourbon monarchy committed itself to reform, and from the reign of Philip V on, it tried to encourage honesty in government by terminating the practice of selling the offices of corregidor, alcalde mayor, and oidor throughout the empire. Yet every time war broke out, the crown resumed the sale of offices to raise desperately needed cash.[13] What was needed, then, was a monarch who would not backslide, one who would stick to a consistent policy of reform.

The king who would not backslide was Charles III, who came to power in 1759 during very adverse international conditions. By his first year as king, the war between Great Britain and France had begun to turn against the latter as the British conquered Canada and occupied many French colonies in the Caribbean. Soon British arrogance and aggression against Spanish interests were so great that Charles thought it necessary to go to war even though his only potential ally, France, had already been beaten. This led to disaster, for the British were given the opportunity to turn on their second, and weaker, enemy. They captured both Havana and Manila—two strategic sites crucial for the Spanish empire's survival—and to get those two vital seaports back, Charles had to give up Florida at the peace table. But he learned how weak Spain was relative to Great Britain and that British aggression, unless checked by power, might end up taking possession of the entire Spanish empire.

Reform was necessary to save the empire. The notoriously corrupt government in America had to be made honest in order to increase its efficiency, to serve the king's interests rather than those of local elites, and to provide the monetary resources necessary to strengthen the Spanish army and navy. These were the goals of what were known in history as the Bourbon Reforms.

II

Charles III and his chief advisors never prepared a detailed plan of reform that would allow us to get an overall picture of what he intended to do and how he intended to do it. We can therefore discern his plan only by considering the details of what emerged as government policy, and then try to understand the principles behind those policies.

The first change in policy toward Central America took place in 1760, when the king raised the salary of the president–captain general from five thousand silver ducats (six thousand pesos) to eight thousand pesos per year.[14] Although pay raises were likely to make it more possible for officeholders to be honest, this measure was not the beginning of a general policy to raise the salaries of other officials. Indeed, in 1764 the king denied a request from the audiencia to increase the salaries of the judges. In 1769 he denied two more such requests.[15] Rather, the pay raise for the president–captain general was more likely a measure taken when war with Great Britain was on the horizon and the king wanted to provide the chief military officer of the kingdom with greater personal income, such officials being expected to use some of the income for good causes like improving the equipment of the militia. At the time, therefore, the pay raise was certainly not seen as a change in direction of policy.

A truly new direction of policy emerged during the Seven Years' War. As already mentioned, Charles III, unlike all of his Bourbon

predecessors, refused to resume the sale of offices.[16] This decision
had an extremely important consequence: it meant that a newly
appointed officeholder was no longer allowed to name his own
replacement. The naming of replacements had been standard practice
for decades for all posts that had been purchased. It was convenient
for those buying offices, for it allowed them to transfer the post to a
third party (in return, one suspects, for monetary compensation).
Those in Spain who did not want to go to America thus got a quick
reward for buying or being appointed to a magistracy. Also, the
practice allowed people who would normally be considered unsuitable for office because of conflict of interest to acquire a post anyway.
Presumably many of those appointed acted as fronts for others with
more resources to milk an office for all it was worth. Finally, the
practice had allowed people to pass their office on to relatives or
business associates in case they died in office before recouping their
payment. The crown's policy therefore was an innovation. It disrupted previous practices that had served to protect the investments
of previous officeholders who had bought their positions.

Still another change, small by itself but significant when put into
context, was a new policy introduced in 1774 that affected the cost of
taking office as magistrate. Prior to that year, all government employees
were required to pay what was known as the *media anata*—a half-
year's salary—in advance of taking office. Although the sums involved
usually were only between 175 and 550 pesos, which had been insignificant for those purchasing their posts for thousands of pesos, it
was a significant expense for the relatively poor soldiers appointed
to positions as rewards for past service. It had required them to borrow
money from mercantile interests that expected something in return
once the magistrates had assumed office. But a real cédula of May 26,
1774, permitted a magistrate to pay the media anata *after* taking office
by having it deducted partially from his salary each year in office.[17]
In short, it became a withholding tax. At a minimum, this measure
helped lessen the magistrates' dependence on merchants and thus
allowed them more freedom to be honest.

In 1780 the government turned to the problem of residencias, which,
as we have seen, did not serve the interests of justice or the state by
failing to punish magistrates for malfeasance in office. It was still

frequently the practice in the 1770s for incoming alcaldes mayores to serve as judges of the residencias of their predecessors. However, new procedures that went into effect in the next decade brought about a change. After 1780, the government began to appoint military officers who were not incoming magistrates to carry out residencias. As a result, the judge no longer was forced to participate in a whitewash or cover-up in hopes of receiving the same treatment from his successor.[18]

The Spanish crown presumably hoped that residencies thereafter would produce justice. Needless to say, this did not always take place. In some cases the audiencia, when allowed to do so, continued the old practice of naming the incoming official to carry out the trial of his predecessor. This tended to produce the same result as in the past. As we saw in the previous chapter, this is what happened in 1784 when the outgoing governor of Nicaragua, José de Estachería, was exonerated by the residencia judge, the incoming governor Juan de Ayssa. Estachería went on to serve as president–captain general. However, once Minister of the Indies José de Gálvez died, a former audiencia judge was appointed to carry out the residencia of Estachería's tenure as president and to conduct an inquest into his activities in Nicaragua as governor. The new inquest revealed what the former residencia judge had covered up, namely, the former governor's repartimientos. Estachería was found guilty and was eventually fined 1,500 pesos.[19] Thus, although justice was not denied, it was delayed.

Included in the new procedures of 1780 for residencias were special instructions regarding the repartimientos, which had provided most of the magistrates with the larger part of their income. The Audiencia of Guatemala, as we have seen, had legalized these business activities of the alcaldes mayores, corregidores, and governors in 1751 only to ban them again in 1779. The new procedures included instructions for the residencia judges to recognize that repartimientos were absolutely and positively prohibited, and that magistrates who carried them out should be punished. This disposition against the repartimiento was further strengthened by a royal order of June 27, 1782, prohibiting alcaldes mayores, corregidores, and governors from carrying out those business dealings.[20] Furthermore, the new residencia procedures reaffirmed earlier rulings that all Indians were to be given the freedom to pay their tribute in cash or kind, thereby diminishing the leverage that magistrates had over the indigenous people. Formerly the royal officials had been allowed to force payment in money when the supply of goods was plentiful and prices therefore were low. Thereafter Indians supposedly could pay in kind when their production made it advantageous to them to do so. On the other hand, because the crown officials had concluded that Indian village governments frequently misused their community funds (*bienes de comunidad*), magistrates were given greater powers to supervise those funds, although they were to be held accountable for their actions during their residencias.[21]

Unfortunately, as we have seen, the new procedures did not have the desired effect. In Nicaragua all that happened as a result of the new prohibitions against the repartimiento was that the governor covered up his business dealings, whereas in the past he would have openly admitted them and then been exonerated because the judge would declare the repartimientos to be necessary and widely practiced. Similarly, the new powers to supervise the Indian community funds could clearly result in abuse by the magistrates unless they were checked by honest residencias. The latter may have become more common after 1780, but this was by no means assured.

Although these reform measures undoubtedly had a cumulative effect, they did not address the crux of the problem: magistrates were badly paid, so badly paid, in fact, that all of them had to break the law and engage in business activities to make ends meet. It was for this reason that again and again during residencias, the judges—almost always the incoming magistrate—had found the officials guilty of carrying out repartimientos and then exonerated them. This was, it was alleged, because illegal business was necessary to provide magistrates with income, because everyone did it, because it was the custom "since time immemorial," and because it was necessary as the means of getting the "lazy Indians" to pay their taxes. Those were exactly the reasons why in 1774 in Mexico, Viceroy Bucareli opposed the establishment of the intendancy system: it failed to address the problem of providing income for the subordinate officials on whom the intendant would have to rely to make the system work.[22]

III

As long as no program to solve the problem was forthcoming from the king, colonial officials had every reason to suspect, or perhaps hope, that Charles III would eventually become a backslider like his predecessor and back away from meaningful reform. Without a clear program from Spain, local officials therefore went ahead with their own plans. One of these, proposed as early as 1751 and still circulating in the 1770s, was to legalize repartimientos, thereby providing income for the magistrates without the need for them to break the law or to raise taxes. In fact, repartimientos had been temporarily legalized after 1751, and in 1759 the audiencia had ruled that magistrates could legally use coercion to force the Indians to accept the repartimiento and could use force to collect debts from the Indians.[23] Since it was the repartimiento system that made the posts profitable to officeholders, it was therefore logical to consider eliminating altogether the salaries paid to the magistrates. This is in part what the comptroller general (*contador de cuentas*) of the royal treasury recommended in a report of 1764. As an economizing measure, he argued, the 12,852 pesos paid to nineteen magistrates could be used for other purposes and the officeholders would receive no salary. This would work, he thought, because the magistrates took the posts not for the low salaries they were paid but for the profits from the repartimiento. Furthermore, even more money could be added to the treasury if the posts were sold not at prices agreed upon in advance, as was then the practice, but rather at public auction. The positions in government would thus go to the highest bidder, and tribute payments would be assured because the royal officials charged with their collection would be men of means who could be made to pay if the Indians failed to do so.[24]

The response of Felipe Romana, fiscal of the audiencia, to what even for the Spanish imperial bureaucracy was a bizarre proposal, was to order an inquest into the repartimientos carried out by the magistrates. This investigation revealed that most of the allegations regarding the money to be made as a magistrate were true, although it was also pointed out that all royal officials ran risks and could not be certain of acquiring wealth. Market conditions could change abruptly, especially because of the outbreak of war, which seriously interrupted peacetime commercial patterns. The business acumen of the officials varied. Finally, political factors beyond their control could cause grave problems (as has been shown in the case of Juan Bacaro in Huehuetenango). As a result, not all officials got rich.[25] The same proposal to abolish salaries and sell the posts at public auction continued to circulate for decades, even though the accounting department (*contaduría*) of the royal treasury had reported negatively on the plan in 1774.[26] So too, in 1780 and again in 1781, did the audiencia, which expressed its outrage by noting that since the magistrates exercised the powers of both administration and justice, selling the magistracies at public auction would be "opposed to all good government and in no way lead to a clear conscience."[27]

Yet the audiencia's outrage, like that of *Casablanca*'s Captain Renault, who was "shocked, shocked" to discover that there was gambling going on in the casino that let him win at roulette, was feigned. The outrage was in fact quite new, the result of a political reprimand from the king. For only three years earlier, that august body of judges had submitted a plan that recommended cutting the magistrates' salaries in half or eliminating them altogether in order to pay for the needed expansion of the audiencia's staff. When it made this proposal, the audiencia pointed out that the pay cut would not adversely affect the magistrates because "these positions were not sought after for the assigned salary" but for the profits to be made from the business activities that had been formerly illegal but were now legal. Fiscal Romana, in turn, upon reflection, had suggested only that the proposed pay cuts not apply in the case of incumbents.[28]

The audiencia's suggestion to cut or eliminate the salaries provoked a furious reaction in Spain. The king got angry, for officials with inadequate salaries or with none at all would surely be corrupt. The king's anger was communicated by the fiscal of the Council of the Indies to the audiencia, the judges of which were informed that it was bad policy and contrary to the wishes of the king to appoint people to posts without assigning them salaries.[29] The same fiscal responded in the same year to a suggestion from the accounting department to assign no salary to the governor of Nicaragua, pointing out again that "it is completely foreign to the sovereign intentions of His Majesty to create, select, and appoint a Minister with no income or fixed salary." Such a practice would mean the sanctioning of arbitrary impositions and would be "a slippery beginning for bribery [*cohecho*] and dirty dealing [*baraterías*]."[30] No wonder that the audiencia of Guatemala was soon spouting platitudes about good government and honest justice.

IV

While the royal government in Spain dithered over the issue of how to pay its officials proper salaries, it also found it difficult to change its way of thinking about the magistracies in America. The posts were seen as rewards for payment or for service, not as the local or regional level of a modern bureaucracy. As long as the posts were considered rewards, the purpose of making appointments would be to thank the many worthy people by rewarding as many of them as possible. This goal was furthered by the standing policy of appointing magistrates for five-year terms with little chance of reappointment or promotion or being named to another governmental position. As a result, there was rapid turnover among officeholders: each time a magistrate finished his term in office, another worthy person replaced him, thereby maximizing the number of people who received their reward. If an alcalde mayor, corregidor, or governor were to be reappointed or given an additional office, one less person could be rewarded.

Many people, in the crown's opinion, deserved rewards for their services, and the existing system worked well in filling the posts with people who had served the king. But it did so at considerable cost. With little prospect of being given another post or of reappointment to the one he was holding, and with no reward for honesty or good government, each magistrate had to make the most of what was usually his one and only opportunity. He had to make as much money as he could as fast as possible, without any consideration of the long-term effects such activities would have. In short, he would engage in whatever lucrative enterprises he could, despite their illegality, and would use repartimientos for all they were worth—at the expense of the well-being of the Indians.

Those in the worst position as magistrates were those given interim appointments by the president to fill vacancies. Sometimes such men could serve at the chief executive's pleasure for a few years, until the magistrate appointed by the king to the usual five-year term showed up. But in 1758 the crown decided to limit the terms of interim appointments to only two years. President Pedro de Salazar responded by arguing that the new policy was a bad idea. He pointed out that without future prospects, "it is most natural that the person appointed [for no more than two years] become deeply enmeshed, to the detriment of those under his power, in attempts to extract from them as much juice as he can from the post during the time he serves, since he has no hope of governing for more than two years."[31] But in fact those appointed for full five-year terms were in the same boat, with the difference that they had three additional years to accomplish their goals.

That the government viewed the magistracies as rewards was revealed whenever the issue of reappointment came up. This happened often after 1759, because in 1752 two new alcaldías mayores—Chimaltenango and Amatitlán-Sacatepéquez—had been created, and in order to ensure their survival in the face of the extremely strong opposition of Santiago's city council, the crown in 1759 had reappointed both of the first magistrates who held these posts. Reappointment of the two was made in Spain on the same day, thereby demonstrating that their cases were linked.[32] Moreover, the government continued to reappoint the two magistrates holding the new alcaldías mayores of Chimaltenango and Amatitlán-Sacatepéquez, and eventually Estanislao Croquer, the alcalde mayor of the latter, ended up holding on to the position for twenty years.[33]

Of course, there had always been exceptions to the policy of appointing people to magistracies only once. As noted in chapter 2, during the final century-and-a-half of the colonial regime, one out of every four magistrates succeeded in getting more than one appointment. However, only one in twenty got more than two appointments, and hence few people really could make a career of holding posts in the bureaucracy. Probably even fewer considered it.

Since precedent can become tradition, the reappointment of the alcaldes mayores of Chimaltenango and Amatitán-Sacatepéquez encouraged other magistrates to appeal more often for reappointment or for new posts. In 1760 Vicente de Toledo y Vivero, the incumbent alcalde mayor of Tegucigalpa, requested that he either be reappointed or given the post of San Salvador or Chiapa. Since the latter two were more lucrative than Tegucigalpa, the granting of the request would in effect have been a promotion. But the government did not respond favorably to the idea, and in any case both San Salvador and Chiapa had already been granted to other worthy people. But Toledo y Vivero's service before his arrival in America had been substantial, for he was a veteran of the wars of the 1730s and had been a prisoner of war. Therefore the crown informed him that he would be put on the waiting list for an equivalent post in New Spain.[34]

Even when occasionally granting a request for a post from someone who had already had one, the government continued to see the magistracies as rewards. As noted in chapter 2, in 1769 José González Rancaño, the alcalde mayor of Sololá, who had already served previously as the corregidor of Chiquimula and as governor of Nicaragua, requested an extension of his term in office or, in lieu of that, a pension of five hundred pesos for each of his four daughters. In Spain the accounting office noted that while the solicitant had served His Majesty well, especially in military matters, he had not done something so spectacular as to justify a pension. Moreover, it was noted, González Rancaño had already been given several good posts, including "various lucrative positions." Posts like this, the contaduría official emphasized, should be shared out among the numerous deserving candidates, rather than monopolized by a favored few. But because of his military service in pacifying the Indians in Verapaz and driving the Miskito Indians back to the Caribbean coast of Nicaragua, the Consejo de Indias decided to consider him for still another post. King Charles agreed and saw to it that González Rancaño was given once again the corregimiento of Chiquimula.[35] His career in the bureaucracy thus had been circuitous. His final post was not a promotion, but neither was it a demotion. It was just a reward, and as such it capped what at the time was considered an extraordinarily successful career.

An equally important exception to the rule occurred in 1771, when Fernando Martínez de Pisón, the alcalde mayor of Texcoco (New Spain) was named governor of Soconusco.[36] This was a promotion of sorts, for governors held important military powers that alcaldes mayores did not. Perhaps more important, however, was that Soconusco, unlike the other three gobernaciones in the Kingdom of Guatemala, was a very lucrative position. Moreover, shortly after this, in the 1780s, governors of Veracruz (New Spain) and Nicaragua moved up to become presidents–captain generals in the Kingdom of Guatemala, and the president–captain general of Guatemala even moved up to become viceroy of New Spain.[37] The latter promotion was not really subject to the normal rules, however, for the president in question, Matías de Gálvez, was the brother of Minister of the Indies José de Gálvez; the operating principle presumably was nepotism. Nevertheless, if lower-ranking alcaldes mayores could be seen as moving up to the rank of governor and governors could move up to be president–captain general, this would constitute a hierarchy or ladder-system of promotion, a characteristic of modern bureaucracies.

Nevertheless, although most petitions for reappointment or reassignment were turned down, the increasing number of requests for exceptions to the rule suggests that a gradual change of perception may have been occurring in Spain and in Guatemala. Two years after González Rancaño's request for reappointment, reassignment, or a pension for his daughters, Juan de Oliver, the magistrate of the newly founded alcaldía mayor of Tuxtla (which had been separated from the alcaldía mayor of Chiapa in 1770) requested reappointment to his position, arguing that his post, like those of Chimaltenango and Amatitlán-Sacatepéquez, was new and therefore needed continuity that could be accomplished by keeping the first official named to the position in place for more than the usual five years. The fiscal of the Council of the Indies objected to the petition, arguing that to grant still another request for reappointment would open the floodgates to further, similar petitions. Moreover, Oliver had yet to go through his residencia. Finally, the fiscal noted, the extensions in the cases of Chimaltenango and Amatitlán-Sacatepéquez had been granted to ensure continuity in the completion of important public works begun by the first incumbents.

Nevertheless, the fiscal did not follow blindly the old policy and reject the petition out of hand. Rather, while he recommended against reappointment, the fiscal suggested putting Oliver on the list of people being considered for other posts. However, the Cámara of the Council of the Indies, which actually made the appointments to office with the supervision of the king, once again violated the old practice and granted Oliver a two-year extension to his term of office.[38] Clearly, precedents were becoming more common, and if this kept up they might become a tradition. Before the century was over, this would result in the emergence of a modern view of offices as the lower echelons of a bureaucratic chain-of-command.

V

Meanwhile, still another change was taking place. Before the reign of Charles III, every time the crown stopped selling offices during peacetime, the tendency was to give the posts to military veterans who just happened to be European Spaniards. American Spaniards (creoles) would in turn make a resurgence as officeholders during wartime when the positions were once more put up for sale. But under Charles III the sale of magistracies stopped definitively and was not resumed in wartime, thereby depriving the American Spaniards of a comeback as officeholders. Certainly by the 1770s most of the magistrates being appointed were Europeans.[39] If this process continued for long, practically all the magistrates would be Europeans and the Americans would be denied the opportunity to exercise power.

It is likely that this was not a coincidence but rather a conscious, albeit unstated, policy. It is clear that in the Kingdom of Guatemala there was intense conflict between European and American Spaniards, and that this produced as well as exacerbated political tensions. The conflict over control of the Valley of Guatemala, personified in the conflictive institutions of the audiencia, representing the Europeans, and the city council of Santiago, representing the creoles—a conflict going back into the late seventeenth century and resurrected with the creation of two new alcaldías mayores in 1752—has already been mentioned.[40] But in fact conflict between the two groups was a basic feature of Guatemalan politics in the last half of the eighteenth century.

The conflict reared its ugly head in a variety of circumstances. For example, when an Indian rebellion took place against the alcalde mayor of Sololá in 1762, the magistrate pointed out that as a European Spaniard he had been confronted by opposition from the American Spaniards at every turn, for the latter, sometimes occupying important positions in government, routinely favored their compatriots. This was especially true, he stated, if a good (that is, European) servant of His Majesty tried to protect the Indians from the creoles.[41] Similarly, when the curate of a parish in the jurisdiction of Chiquimula complained that the corregidores of the province were corrupt and inept, he added that the magistrates got away with their abuses by cooperating with the Indian village governments, for the indigenous officials always got into conflict with an honest European-born priest.[42]

Certainly one of the most vicious attacks by one group on the other was a report by the Audiencia of Guatemala in 1765 defending its actions in setting up the new alcaldías mayores in the Valley of Guatemala. Not only did it state that the actions of the regidores were motivated by personal greed—the council members' desire to control the repartimientos in the valley and also profit from the corrupt mechanisms for administering the provisioning of the city with meat. The audiencia went further, named the names of many Americans who in the judges' opinion hated Europeans, and made a detailed criticism of each and every regidor. It even alleged that the few Europeans on the city council had vested interests that caused them to side with the Americans in every dispute. One such man even owned "a wretched store," and it was not uncommon for Europeans of lowly background, "finding themselves clever in commerce and trade, and [knowing how] to sell goods according to the style of the country, to end up lucky and get the opportunity to marry a rich woman, the daughter of another similar person, by which means, it is notorious, they become men [of importance]." When Europeans like this got onto the city council, they supported the American side because it was in their interest to do so. Yet despite all their illegal activities, the audiencia alleged, nothing could be done against the councilmen, for as members of the colonial militia they enjoyed the *fuero militar* (special privileges, including exemption from civil jurisdiction when mobilized).[43]

Because conflict between creoles and peninsulars in the Church was notorious since the early colonial period in other parts of America,[44] it is not surprising to find it in Central America. As early as 1573 the city council of Santiago found it necessary to request that the crown facilitate the appointment of "sons of citizens of this city" to important benefices.[45] The council members would not have made that request if they had felt that native sons were receiving their fair share. In the seventeenth century, the Dominicans were required to introduce the annual alternation between creoles and peninsulars in power—a system called the *alternativa*—to ensure that the American-born were not excluded from the important posts within the order, and in 1652 the city council thanked the king for institutionalizing that procedure.[46] But internal conflicts in the Dominican and Franciscan orders continued and became acute in the late colonial period. In a 1792 letter to the crown, creole Franciscans complained that the European-born friars discriminated against them, including allegations that they were frequently of illegitimate birth or of mixed-race ancestry. They also claimed that the *alternativa* had broken down. A closer examination, however, revealed that most of the signatures on the letter were forged, and that the system of alternating power was functioning as it should. The crown, concluding the whole affair to be the work of a handful of malcontents, chose to do nothing about the complaint. The very existence of the letter, however, demonstrates the existence of bad feelings within the ranks of the orders and of ruthlessness on the part of some aggrieved priests.[47]

Despite the numerous instances of conflict between the American-born and the European-born friars, it is important to note that until 1810 or so, the two groups were not always at each other's throats and on many occasions worked together against perceived threats against them both. This was revealed by the unanticipated discord that broke out within the Dominican Order at the end of the eighteenth century. The policy of transferring control of parishes from the religious orders to secular priests had picked up momentum after 1750 and resulted in a sharp decline in the number of creoles who chose to be friars, that is, regular priests. To staff the parishes still in their hands, the Dominicans and Franciscans had felt compelled to ask for friars from Spain. These were forthcoming, but they were different from those of previous centuries, for the Bourbon period witnessed the entrance of people from the lands of the Crown of Aragon into large-scale evangelical activity in America.[48] Aragonese and especially Catalan friars began to cross the ocean, and many went to Guatemala. This meant the European-born priests were no longer united by culture.

Thus the arrival of a group of mostly Catalan Dominicans in 1791 soon provoked disorder. In 1794 Fray Juan Infante, the provincial, or superior, of the Dominicans and a native of La Mancha, reported to the king that the newcomers "came imbued with ideas very foreign to those of humility and religious poverty." Rather, they had "a dominating spirit and had a desire for material possessions. They imagined, of course, that they had come to take charge of everything and possess everything." The provincial reported that some of the friars compared the Catalans to "French revolutionaries."[49] The cause of the discord was history: although Dominicans were all the same by training, the internal arrangement of convents based on the Castilian model but modified in America differed from that in place in the Crown of Aragon. Consequently, the Catalans expected to take power despite the *alternativa* procedures, and this was very displeasing to the "creoles and Castilians." Fray Infante therefore requested that in the future the government should see that only priests from Castile be sent to Guatemala.[50]

The Castilian-born archbishop, Juan Félix de Villegas, looked into the matter and took sides in the affair. He blamed everything on the people from the lands of the Crown of Aragon, who were not only younger than the others but possessed conflictive personalities and wanted to assume important positions immediately. This caused the friars who were already in Guatemala to band together, and the resulting conflict was not between the American-born and the European-born "but between Castilians and Americans united on one side and the Catalans, Aragonese, Valencians and Mallorcans on the other."[51] President José Domas y Valle also sided with the Castilians and creoles, whom he reported to be good men, and asserted that the others were dominated by a spirit of acrimony.[52] The Council of the Indies simply warned the Dominicans to improve their behavior and discipline, for "otherwise His Majesty will take executive measures."[53] Officials in Spain thus refused to take sides, but in America it was clear that when it came to Catalans, Castilians sided with creoles in defense of what they perceived to be their common interests.

Thus it was possible, given the nature of the threat, for Castilians and Americans to band together. In the political realm, Castilian and American members of the cabildo of the capital sometimes cooperated to defend their economic interests, for merchants were dominant on the council and their interests frequently conflicted with those of the audiencia judges and president. The latter usually opposed the interests of the merchants by wanting to cut down on smuggling.[54] But such cooperation was rare, and conflicts between European and American Spaniards were generally bitter and long-standing. The crown was certainly aware of the discord. Moreover, the officials who served as the head of the Ministry of the Indies during most of the reign of Charles III, Julián de Arriaga and José de Gálvez, had served in America and knew of these conflicts firsthand. However, rather than attempt conciliation and mediation by appointing Americans to positions, the crown chose to side with the Europeans and preferred them, rather than Americans, as magistrates. There were some exceptions, but well into the reign of Charles III, most people serving as corregidores, alcaldes mayors, and governors in Central America were European Spaniards. All of those appointed as intendants were Europeans.

The crown undoubtedly justified its policy as part of a broader program to get better men to serve in office in America. Indeed, in 1774 Viceroy Bucareli in New Spain had argued strenuously against the establishment of the intendancy system by asserting that "the evil is not in the system or method of government that the Laws prescribe, but in the quality of the officeholders."[55] The assumption behind appointing only Europeans was that they were better for the job, presumably because they did not have family ties with the people of the kingdom and because they had not been corrupted by growing up in America.

At least, they did not have family ties at the time of their appointment to office. Some later developed such ties after being in America for some time, as is demonstrated by the case of Manuel de Plazaola, a European Spaniard whose appointment in the 1750s as alcalde mayor of Chimaltenango greatly antagonized the American-born elite. He later married into local society, had a son who became the alcalde mayor of Chimaltenango, and had a granddaughter who was the descendant not just of the Plazaolas but also, on her mother's side, of another alcalde mayor and of oidores of the audiencia.[56] Manuel Antonio Treixanes Pereira, Knight of Santiago, the European Spaniard who succeeded Plazaola as alcalde mayor of Chimaltenango and later went on to serve the royal treasury as the accountant in charge of the revenues of the sales tax, also integrated well into American society—so well in fact that he came to own an hacienda worth more than fifty thousand pesos and even requested permission from the king to found an entail.[57]

Nevertheless, Charles III and his ministers undoubtedly believed that they really were appointing better men to office. For not only were most of the appointed officials European Spaniards—more and more of them had university decrees and were trained lawyers. This happened as early as 1764, when Licenciado Fernando Gómez de Andrade y Medina, a lawyer working for the audiencia of Quito and the son of a senior judge who had served in Panama and Quito, was appointed alcalde mayor of Chiapa.[58] His successor, Licenciado Cristóbal Ortiz de Avilés, was also a degree-holding lawyer.[59] Yet upon arrival in Chiapa, Gómez de Andrade, who had not purchased the position, immediately had difficulties, precisely because he was beholden to no one. The local royal officials in Ciudad Real delayed his assumption of the office on the grounds that his guarantors lacked the necessary assets. This was quickly shown to be false, and Gómez de Andrade assumed his position, but it was a sign of the problems that those who did not purchase their offices could have.[60]

Between 1780 and 1800, during the last decade of the reign of Charles III and the first of Charles IV, it became increasingly common for the crown to appoint men with law degrees as magistrates. Such was the case of the alcaldes mayores of Totonicapán, Verapaz, Sonsonate, Chimaltenango, and Atitlán.[61] All of the tenientes letrados–asesores (legal lieutenants and assessors) in the four intendancies, as we have seen in chapter 2, were lawyers. The first intendant of Chiapas,

Francisco Saavedra y Carbajal, was also a lawyer and at the time of his appointment was serving as the criminal prosecutor (*fiscal del crimen*) of the Audiencia of Guatemala. Having served his term in Chiapas, he was then promoted to the prestigious post of criminal prosecutor under the fiscal of the Audiencia of Mexico. His successor, although not a lawyer, came from the treasury department rather than from the military.[62] The first intendant of El Salvador, Josef Ortiz, was no less than a judge of the Audiencia of Guatemala.[63]

The crown stuck with military officers, however, for the more militarily significant intendancies of Honduras and Nicaragua. Moreover, after less than a decade in power, Charles IV's government reverted to the old policy of appointing soldiers to all the intendancies and virtually all of the magistracies. Only the assistants to the intendants—the tenientes letrados–asesores—continued to be lawyers, since the post demanded knowledge of the law. Had the crown stuck to appointing lawyers, a whole new era of royal bureaucracy would have emerged. As it turned out, however, it was only for a brief time that men with law degrees and possible future careers in the legal profession, perhaps even in the audiencias, served as magistrates. Nevertheless, the crown thought there were good reasons to believe that the quality of the magistrates in Central America was improving, and even officials not connected to the reformers around Gálvez or Charles III believed that there had indeed been improvement. The political consequences of preferring Europeans over Americans, however, were apparently ignored.

VI

It is important to note that the apparent improvement in the quality of the magistrates took place even though salaries did not rise until the 1790s. Nevertheless, violations of the prohibition against repartimientos continued, although the abuses had diminished.[64] Moreover, the customary gift-giving to the audiencia judges continued until 1798, when that august body voluntarily decided to dispense with the old custom of accepting gifts of foodstuffs like cacao and fish. Known locally as "gifts of the table," these called into question the honesty of the judges. It is likely that there was some pressure for the judges to give up their gifts, since the fiscal of the Council of the Indies noted that the king, Charles IV, was very pleased with the judges' decision.[65]

In 1799 a new effort was made to provide proper salaries for the magistrates. As noted above, in Mexico viceregal resistance to the new intendancy system had been based to a great extent on the lack of such salaries for the new subdelegados who were to replace the old alcaldes mayores.[66] The Audiencia of Guatemala decided to address the issue by taking 2 percent of the Indians' community tax, normally paid to the village government for community expenses, and assigning it to the magistrates as a supplement to their official salaries. To make it easier for the indigenous people, payment was permitted in maize or wheat (which, it was thought, Indians would find easy to produce). This measure was put into effect, the king ordering the audiencia to report on how it was working out before he would grant his definitive approval.[67] It is likely that the 2 percent from the community tax helped some of the magistrates achieve a greater income, but, as we shall see, it did not solve the problems of all the alcaldes mayores and corregidores.

In 1802, while preparing a more thorough reform of salaries, the audiencia took further steps to provide income for the magistrates. It proclaimed eight new revenue sources, mostly based on new taxes imposed on increased agricultural production and stock raising by Indians, on agriculture carried out by non-Indian squatters, and on new looms, factories, and mills established in the provinces under the jurisdiction of the magistrates. This measure was almost certainly unworkable because of the difficulty, or impossibility, of collecting the taxes. No one was likely to report any increased production or new industrial establishments, and the magistrates did not have the resources to find out about any. Much more realistic were two direct taxes not on production but on people: (1) a flat tax of one real per year on each tributary, to replace the old supposedly abusive system of community labor; and (2) a tax paid by landowners of one-half real for every Indian laborer provided by the magistrate through a revived system of short-term forced labor drafts, called *mandamientos*. These were justified on the grounds that they would not be an additional burden on the indigenous people because they would replace the community labor formerly demanded. Moreover, it was asserted, the labor was good for society as a whole.[68] Members of Spanish society, of course, were not required to work. In a colonial system, what was good for the native people was not good for the colonists.

These two measures produced some revenue for all the magistrates, although the amount varied depending on the population and the level of commercial agriculture on private estates. It probably was enough for some magistrates—especially those in regions with many haciendas like the intendancies of Nicaragua and El Salvador and the corregimiento of Chiquimula—but clearly not for others. For example, in 1802–1803 the government found it difficult to get anyone to serve as alcalde mayor of Suchitepéquez. One appointee showed up and quit after only five months, and his successor immediately tried to resign and requested the position as intendant of San Salvador instead. The president pointed out to the treasury department in Spain that it was the repartimiento system that had made posts like Suchitepéquez (a producer of cacao) "desirable and very juicy." Since magistrates could no longer carry out that business, they could no longer make any money.[69]

Unfortunately for good government and honest administration, the latest measures to fund larger incomes for magistrates were introduced when the late colonial economy was in crisis and decline. The economic decline would affect all members of society and probably make it more difficult for the indigenous people to pay their tribute, although it is not possible to determine in any precise way what the overall impact was.

First, severe locust plagues caused havoc throughout the kingdom from the 1770s on. An especially bad outbreak began in 1797 and lasted until at least 1805. Grain shortages became endemic, meat became scarce, and in 1803 wheat flour had to be imported all the way from Chile.[70] Gravely affected by the locusts, which seemed to eat anything of vegetable material, was San Salvador, the region producing indigo, the commercial lifeblood of the colony. Production and exports declined, causing commercial disruption and bankruptcy.[71]

Second, in the late colonial period the silver mining economy of Tegucigalpa, part of the new intendancy of Honduras, began to go

into decline, thereby depriving the kingdom of one of its few valuable exports. This was caused by the exhaustion of the old silver
lodes, the lack of capital to exploit new ones or to introduce new
mining equipment or technology, and a shortage of labor. In addition, not enough mercury was being provided by the government,
and in some places there was even a shortage of salt, necessary for
amalgamation and smelting. Some new lodes were discovered, but
these were further away from the main roads and thus the cost of
transportation went up. Some new grinding equipment introduced
by the intendant did not prove very effective, and efforts to establish institutions of credit to lend money to mine operators failed.[72] A
second region of the kingdom thus went into decline. Silver was not
as important as indigo as an export, but decreased silver production in Honduras, on the back of declining indigo exports from El
Salvador, meant that the kingdom's economy suffered two severe
blows from which the region had difficulty recovering.

    Third, the outbreak of war in 1797 and the resulting British block-
ade of Spanish ports severely disrupted commerce.[73] Peace was
declared briefly in 1802, but in 1803 the war was resumed, and by
1805 the price of European goods was reported to have quadrupled
in some cases.[74] The disruption of commerce, of course, meant a sharp
decline in royal revenues, which were derived to a great extent from
taxes on trade. The late-colonial wars soon produced other negative,
long-lasting results. After 1797 the Spanish government opened the
ports of the Spanish empire to neutral shipping, and although this
measure was soon reversed, the damage was done: British cotton cloth
carried in U.S. ships began to arrive in significant quantities in Central America. Soon the goods were being smuggled in on British ships.
When the Spanish government collapsed in 1808 and Great Britain
became Spain's ally in the war against France, the smuggled textiles
became a flood. Goods made in Guatemala could not compete with
the cheaper foreign-made cloth, and the cotton textile industry began
to decline. The work of Indian women—who had done practically
all of the spinning of thread and most of the weaving—correspond-
ingly declined in value as well. As the consulado lamented—in its
plea for protectionism—in 1823, an industry that in Guatemala City,
Antigua, and Quezaltenango alone had produced goods valued at

over one million pesos eventually collapsed, and "all has been lost, and consequently has fallen into desolation and poverty."[75]

A fourth blow to the economy would fall shortly after 1804, when the royal government, desperate for money to finance the latest war against Great Britain and to pay a large cash subsidy to Napoleon, proclaimed what was known as the *consolidación de vales reales*. This measure required the sale of Church-owned real estate, the proceeds going to the government in the form of a loan. However, the consolidación also ordered the calling-in of all loans made by or owed to the Church, including those in the form of *capellanías* (chantries). The latter, however, were rarely the result of money loaned to individuals but rather were simply legally binding promises to pay the ecclesiastical establishment a specified amount of money per year in return for masses said for the souls of the founders of the chantries. In addition, the government also took village community funds, allegedly because they frequently were used to pay for religious festivals. All funds were supposedly loans to the crown that would eventually be returned with interest. Needless to say, the crown never repaid any of the money.[76]

The implementation of the consolidación soon had the effect of depriving the villages of their hard-earned revenues and of forcing the Hispanic elite to sell property to pay debts.[77] By 1809 more than a hundred thousand pesos had been taken from the Indian community funds, while the consolidación as a whole brought in well over a million pesos in cash, most of which was sent to Spain. The deflationary effect of the measure on the economy as a whole and on the indigenous people in particular can well be imagined. The president pointed out to the treasury office in Spain that given the kingdom's poverty, the cash remittance was the equivalent of removing twenty million pesos from the economy of New Spain.[78] The city council of Guatemala City complained that the consolidación, when combined with the decline of indigo exports, was causing severe economic problems and leading to falling land values. Of course, it was also a major factor leading to the crown's loss of support and loyalty among the creole elite, whose economic interests were gravely affected by the consolidación.[79]

Finally, the more rigorous enforcement since 1782 of the prohibition on repartimientos by government officials also disrupted the
economy. This had always been predicted by those who had supported the old way of providing income for the magistrates. Those
people had argued that the repartimiento system was necessary to
force the Indians to work. Viceroy Bucareli of New Spain had argued
back in 1774 that Indians were lazy by nature and only worked if
compelled to do so. The magistrates, by advancing credit or goods
to the indigenous people, got them into debt, and then, using the
political powers of their office—that is, compulsion backed up by the
threat, and sometimes application, of flogging—forced them to pay
those debts.[80] Thus the Indians, who if given the choice would have
produced much less and remained isolated from the commercial
economy, were compelled to participate in commerce, to the benefit
of all—or so it was argued.

Government officials in Guatemala described the repartimiento
system in the same way. As the audiencia explained in 1784, the
crucial point was the ability of the magistrates to make the Indians pay
their debts; this they accomplished either by taking money from the
village community funds or by making the indigenous people work
on haciendas.[81] As the various royal provisions banning repartimientos
went into effect in the kingdom between 1779 and 1782, magistrates
found it impossible to carry out business openly in the old way, and
risky to do so surreptitiously. The result was much less credit advanced
to the indigenous people, who in turn chose to enjoy their freedom
from debt rather than engage in nonessential production for the market
for personal gain.[82]

The assumption about the "natural laziness" of the Indians survived the repartimiento system and became the basis of what turned
out to be the last effort to provide the magistrates with better salaries.
In 1803 the audiencia reported that its plans of 1799 and 1802 had not
produced the desired effect, for the income being generated during
a time of economic decline was insufficient.[83] As a result, some of the
alcaldes mayores had resumed carrying out repartimientos. Still, these
were on a much lower level than before because the magistrates were
by now afraid to violate the law on a scale significant enough to attract
the attention of higher-ups. Moreover, the officials resorted to the

repartimientos not to line their pockets, because the income generated was much too small for that. Rather, they did it to stimulate the economy.

The audiencia then restated the old justifications that defenders of the repartimiento had used throughout the eighteenth century. Although taking cognizance of the impact of war and locust plagues, and refusing to recommend a return to the old system known to be unpopular in Spain, the judges stated that the major cause of the economic decline of the kingdom was the laziness of the Indians. As they explained the matter, the problem was "the Indians' lack of necessities." They were "accustomed to nudity, to bad times, to a scarce and simple diet, and to sleeping on the ground or on a simple straw mat." The only things that forced them to work beyond a subsistence level were tribute, community taxes, the contributions owed to their priests, mandatory labor drafts euphemistically referred to as "service," and the demands placed on them by their religious brotherhoods. The Indians fulfilled these obligations with very little work, and paid a good deal of what they were required to pay in kind, that is, in their own products such as maize, chickens, eggs, firewood, fodder, and in some places, beans, fish, or cheese. As a result, since the end of the repartimientos they were said to have fallen into "pernicious idleness." Indigenous festivals, paid for with *cofradía* funds, ended up bankrupting most of the Indians elected to run the brotherhoods. The people liked their festivals, however, "being their only sources of diversion and relief, which end up generally in drunkenness."

In the past, the business activities of the alcaldes mayores had solved these problems: "forced repartimientos by the magistrates, with profits more or less excessive depending on greed, which was the only rule for the setting of prices, because there was no fear of competition," got the Indians into debt. The debts were not collected by the magistrate, however, but by the officials of the Indian government. This meant that the debts were collected "without fail." This forced the indigenous people to work, although the latter received none of the benefits. Moreover, there were abuses: "the profits generated by this monopoly were exorbitant; some of the items sold to the Indians were useless to them; and debt collection was heavy-handed. And it was because of this accumulation of injustices inseparable from the repartimientos" that the king ordered their abolition, "leaving the Indians with complete freedom to trade," and granting private merchants the right to trade with them to provide them with their necessities.

The result, however, as the audiencia pointed out, was not exactly what had been intended. As noted, some of the magistrates, "lacking income . . . have continued to carry out repartimientos, by themselves or through go-betweens, with an effort more or less to disguise them, in accordance with their character or circumstances." A few Indians have improved themselves, but no merchants have been willing to do business with the indigenous people, "because, it being necessary to extend credit, they would expose their interests, as is well known, with little or no probability of getting anything back." The fate of the Indians and the magistrates therefore was linked, for without credit the former could not purchase anything and the latter could not make enough money to support themselves. As the audiencia put it, "the Indians need hoes, machetes, and some other things that they can only buy on credit; no outsider provides it because of the well-known risk; the poorly paid magistrate is at the ready, and with the danger of being discovered and punished being very remote, and with such an abundance of means for avoiding and making a mockery of all investigations," the result was predictable.

This detailed report by the audiencia has been worth analyzing in detail because it reveals once more the reality of the repartimiento system. Moreover, it was submitted not by a critic of that system reflecting a purely partisan point of view. Rather, the audiencia had never been one of the critics of the repartimiento, but on the contrary had largely seen it as a necessary evil. Indeed, analysis of the report suggests that if people in Spain were more open to the idea of restoring the system, the audiencia would go along with them.

In any case, the report reveals the following truths regarding the repartimiento:

(1) It was "forzado" (forced), that is, non-voluntary. As evidence from chapter 4 also demonstrates, the argument that the repartimiento was voluntary in the case of the Kingdom of Guatemala cannot be sustained. Evidence proves the contrary. When finally

given a choice in the matter, the indigenous people chose not to accept repartimientos.

(2) From an economic perspective it was essentially a system of credit. The indigenous people were advanced money or goods, and they paid their debts at a later time. As such, it stimulated both production and consumption by the Indians.

(3) Debt collection was carried out not directly by the magistrate but by village government officials. Without the cooperation of those officials, the system could not work. With their cooperation, collection was "without fail."

(4) The prices of goods sold on credit or bought in advance were determined by the magistrate, who could set prices because he exercised a monopoly. Because of this monopoly, he sold goods at high prices and bought goods at below-market prices. The profits from the transactions were to a certain extent disguised loans.

(5) Even though private merchants were not officially prohibited from loaning money to the Indians, they were in fact prevented from doing so by market conditions. Indians paid virtually no price for defaulting on their debts because the private merchant had no means of forcing them to pay what they owed. The magistrate, of course, faced different conditions, because he could compel debt collection. That is why he could operate as a monopolist. Weak commercial institutions thus favored the man-on-the-spot with the political power necessary to collect the debts owed to him.

From a modern point of view, it could be concluded that the indigenous people, unlike the Spanish, were not motivated by the desire to accumulate wealth in order to raise their social status. They were perfectly happy to be subsistence producers, and they produced a surplus only because they were forced to do so. The colonialist mentality therefore declared the colonized people to be lazy. This assumption about the Indians led naturally to a solution. The audiencia put forward a plan according to which village government funds—bienes de comunidad—would be used to extend credit to the Indians, who would have to increase production in order to pay their debts. The credit would be used to purchase goods the Indians needed (which formerly had been provided through the repartimiento). But with the magistrates being excluded from the business, the Indians would be able to buy the goods at market prices, rather than at the high prices charged by the magistrates in the past. It was hoped, for example, that a hoe that cost the indigenous consumers between thirty and thirty-six reales in the past would cost only between eighteen and twenty-two reales under the new plan. The profits resulting from the increased production would be split between the village government, which was to get 50 percent, and the magistrates, who would get 30 percent, the remaining 20 percent to be reinvested in the same community funds used to make the loans. The audiencia thought everyone would benefit, and therefore the Indians would be willing to work and produce goods for the market. This plan was put into effect pending approval by the crown.

Because the audiencia understood that good local administration was necessary for the program to work, it also recommended a new policy regarding Spanish magistrates in the kingdom: that the practice of rarely reappointing officials to a second term in office be discarded in favor of a policy of reappointment for the good performance of duty. This, it was hoped, would encourage the magistrates to see themselves as career officials rather than as temporary placeholders.[84] The audiencia's program therefore was a manifestation in Central America of a more modern view of bureaucracy, in which government positions were no longer seen as rewards. Rather, officials were to start at a low level and either hold their positions for some time or work their way up, motivated in part by the real possibility of career advancement for good performance in office. The Spanish empire, in short, was showing signs of moving toward a governmental system based on modern conceptions of bureaucracy.

In Spain the crown officials took up this plan, already being implemented in the Kingdom of Guatemala, in 1805. Pedro de Aparici, the head of contaduría and an ardent advocate of rooting out corruption by eliminating the repartimiento,[85] reported that, given the natural laziness of the Indians—even the reformers accepted that as a truism—the plan was acceptable, as long as the credit advanced to the Indians by their own village government from community funds was truly voluntary. Moreover, with respect to the prices to be charged for goods sold on credit to the Indians, Aparici warned that prices should be openly stated in advance; otherwise the magistrates might overcharge and use the community funds to pay for the same abusive practices as had been perpetrated through the repartimiento system. An independent judge should therefore be appointed to oversee the setting of prices. Finally, Aparici found the idea of a career ladder for the magistrates to be "admissible."[86]

In Spain itself, then, modern ideas of bureaucracy were making considerable headway. The concept of a bureaucratic career ladder certainly existed throughout the Spanish empire, although in colonial capitals like Buenos Aires it did not work: since positions other than those of provincial magistrates were frequently lifetime appointments, and since few people resigned or were removed for malfeasance, only death opened up positions for aspiring underlings, and death for superiors sometimes came later than it did for those seeking to climb the bureaucratic ladder.[87] Upward movement, therefore, was rare.

The fiscal of the Council of the Indies, however, was skeptical about the audiencia's plan. He did not object to the idea of a bureaucratic career ladder, but he pointed out that it would work only if the funding scheme also worked. He thought it likely, however, that village community funds in fact would be dissipated and debts unpaid, thereby causing the system to collapse. Everything depended, he emphasized, on the actions of the village government officials, who were to be put in charge of both the distribution of the community funds and the collection of the debts. But experience showed that the community government might instead introduce new abuses and cover up what were in fact involuntary loans, such as had been made through the old repartimiento system. In that case, the indigenous people would once again have no choice in the matter, and advances of money would once again be involuntarily accepted. If the credit were truly voluntary and the people were not forced to accept it, then the Indians, rather than produce more and pay off their debts, might defy their leaders and refuse to pay. The leaders, in turn, might not be as insistent on collecting as they had been when the debts had been owed to an alcalde mayor possessing political power. This would bankrupt the community chest and leave the indigenous people worse off than before. The fiscal concluded that the audiencia had acted too hastily in implementing the plan before receiving royal approval.[88]

Nevertheless, even though the program had never been approved by the Council of the Indies, the Ministry of the Indies, or the king, it was in effect and stayed in effect for some time. Its chances of success, however, were practically nonexistent because the money supposed to be used to provide credit to the Indians quickly disappeared. This was because the consolidación proclaimed in 1804 resulted in the transfer to the government of all Indian community funds. By 1809, as we have seen, more than a hundred thousand pesos in cash from these funds had been remitted to Spain. This would have left little in the village treasuries, and as noted, the money was never repaid. It was a permanent loss for the Indians.[89] In an economy continually short of cash, the consolidación had a deflationary effect, further lowering the level of the commercial activity that provided the government with a large part of its revenues. No money was available to provide credit in accordance with the audiencia's plan. The magistrates would therefore have received no income at all from the scheme.

In any case, the Spanish government did not even consider the issue again until 1815 (because more important matters were in mind during the French invasion of 1808–14). In that year the fiscal of the Council of the Indies discovered that the crown had never approved the plan and that the audiencia had never reported on how it was working out. He ordered the audiencia to report.[90] As far as is known, it never did.

VII

Despite the lack of a clear program or plan for the reform of the bureaucracy in the Kingdom of Guatemala, the crown succeeded to a significant, and even surprising, extent in diminishing corruption and increasing honesty in government in the region. This was accomplished in part by the introduction of the intendancy system in Chiapas, El Salvador, Honduras-Comayagua, and Nicaragua. It was accomplished in Guatemala proper without the intendancy by terminating the practice of selling offices, improving the quality of magistrates, eliminating some of the practices that had gotten royal officials into debt, raising the incomes of some of the corregidores and alcaldes mayores (although not enough was accomplished in this area), and prohibiting the repartimiento system and threatening to punish severely those officials who engaged in it. As we have seen, the reforms did not completely eliminate the repartimiento. But they did reduce it significantly in scale, thereby leading to less consumption and production by the Indians. This, of course, was a factor that contributed to the economic decline evident in the Kingdom of Guatemala since the end of the eighteenth century.

Of course, one can always dispute the real success achieved. Honesty is impossible to measure, and the absence of references to corruption in government in the archival sources does not prove that it did not exist. Yet it should be noted that in its own secret correspondence, the Spanish government had never before tried to hide the existence of corruption in its bureaucracy in America. Indeed, the evidence proves convincingly that the crown was informed of it, knew about it, lamented it, and rarely did anything about it. Therefore when the royal officials themselves started to take pride in their accomplishments in the 1790s and later, it is hard to believe that they had suddenly decided to cover up corruption or fool themselves about it. For them, there had been a real improvement in government, and they had succeeded substantially, if not completely, in rooting out corruption.

The reforms, however, had been carried out on the backs, as it were, of the Indians. True, the virtual end of the repartimiento system freed the indigenous people from one form of traditional exploitation and abuse. However, the program implemented by the audiencia to raise salaries for the magistrates would have reintroduced the repartimiento to a certain extent, this time financed by village community funds. More research needs to be done to study the effects of this change, although the expropriation by the government of the community funds probably meant that the audiencia's measure had no impact at all.

On the other hand, it is clear that the smuggling of English cotton textiles—which began to enter Central America after 1797—first undermined and then destroyed the local textile industry that had been the single most important branch of the repartimiento system. In other words, the old way of carrying out business with the Indians was doomed anyway. New abuses, however, were likely to emerge from the parts of the audiencia's plan that taxed the Indians and recreated the old system of forced labor drafts—under the new name of mandamientos—in order to provide better salaries for the magistrates. This is in fact where the money to pay the officials came from, and this was hardly accidental, since the same methods were being used in nearby Yucatan at the same time.[91] Mandamientos then became an important feature of the colonial regime, survived changes after Independence, and remained in force until the 1930s.[92] Thus the rooting out of corruption depended, as colonialism itself depended, on the labor of the Indians.

Even so, it was with pride that one of the last governors–captain generals of the Kingdom of Guatemala wrote to his superiors that the old days of corrupt officeholders had passed, hopefully never to be revived. He attributed this to the change in policy in appointing magistrates, noting that it had been a very bad idea to appoint people in Spain—as in the past—whose only desire was to get rich quick and return home as fast as possible.[93]

Of course, the favoring of Europeans over Americans for appointments was, in the long run, also a bad idea for the preservation of the Spanish empire. It should be emphasized, however, that in the Kingdom of Guatemala, the crown did continue to appoint creoles to positions, including the magistracies, even though it did so on a smaller scale than before. Moreover, in 1815—five years after the outbreak of the war for independence in Mexico and elsewhere—the Audiencia of Guatemala's oidores included three Americans and only two Europeans.[94]

Nevertheless, in Spain, the Council of the Indies paid close attention to the homeland of the candidates for office, and it obviously preferred the Spanish-born. This created in American society the feeling that Americans were being treated as inferiors and were considered unworthy to hold positions of power. One suspects that many, if not most, Europeans believed in their inherent superiority. Paradoxically, the Enlightenment, which was spreading ideas of tolerance throughout the Western world, contributed significantly to the strengthening of old attitudes that held everything in America in contempt. This certainly happened not just in Spain but also in England and France. Many Enlightenment figures believed that America corrupted plants, animals, and people.[95] As a result, old prejudices against creoles, based to a great extent on environmental determinism, were strengthened by the very intellectual movement that undermined prejudice against women and Jews and destroyed the old justification of slavery. Those who suffered from these prejudices were the Americans, who increasingly resented being ruled by a bureaucracy composed to a great extent of Europeans. All of this, of course, helps explain the increasingly bitter conflicts between creoles and peninsulars in the late colonial period, as manifested in the struggles between the Cabildo of Santiago and of the new capital of Guatemala City with the peninsular-dominated Consulado of Guatemala over such issues as smuggling, commercial contact with the English on the Caribbean coast, and the establishment of a bank to serve the interests of the indigo producers.[96] The creole-peninsular issue was not the only cause of these conflicts, it is important to point out.[97] Yet the disagreements between the two were evident in virtually any political issue that came up.

From the point of view of European Spaniards, however, it was no coincidence that the bureaucracy became more honest once the Americans were diminished in numbers. Still, it would be too much to conclude that the American Spaniards were the cause of corruption. Clearly, European Spaniards for centuries had come to America not to serve their king but to serve themselves. What changed in the late eighteenth century was not so much the replacement of Americans by Europeans as the improved conditions of government (better checks on corruption and better salaries) and the quality of the officeholders, who were sometimes trained lawyers making the bureaucracy their career and motivated in many cases by genuine desire to serve their king. On the other hand, the return to the old policy of appointing mostly soldiers to positions in the bureaucracy may have undermined the reforms. It did, however, bring the Kingdom of Guatemala into line with the practice at the same time in Spain, where regional government was also in the hands of soldiers rather than lawyers.[98] Similarly, even in the capital of the Viceroyalty of Río de la Plata, there was a strong tendency for the crown to appoint soldiers rather than lawyers to most posts.[99]

For these changes, the kings themselves—Charles III and Charles IV—were to a great extent responsible. They had instituted policies that led to greater honesty in government while also stimulating American Spaniards to think of themselves as a sovereign people deserving of independence from an increasingly autocratic, and indeed foreign, monarchy.

Conclusion

There was one point on which both defenders and critics of the repartimiento system agreed: the Indians were lazy. Coercion in various forms was thus an essential feature of colonialism and an essential feature of the repartimiento system in colonial Central America.[1] We see this clearly in the arguments presented early in the eighteenth century by the bishops of Chiapa over the business carried out by the alcalde mayor of the province. In 1712 Bishop Juan Álvarez de Toledo reported that the magistrate made a great deal of money at the expense of the Indians by forcing them to pay their tribute in kind and then reselling the goods at market prices. Even if they tried to pay in cash, they were forced to pay much more than their tribute assessment. As a result of this business, the bishop reported, the alcalde mayor earned between four and six thousand pesos per year. If tribute goods were assessed at market prices, or if the indigenous people were allowed to pay in cash, they would pay less and therefore avoid such exploitation. Álvarez de Toledo argued that the Indians should be allowed to pay their tribute in money.[2] The crown eventually agreed, and by the 1740s, in most parts of the kingdom, the indigenous people were allowed to pay in money.

These allegations are typical of statements critical of the business activities of the magistrates, and like all such allegations, they should be put in context. Álvarez de Toledo had recently announced that he would carry out another episcopal inspection, which usually ended up forcing the indigenous people to pay money to have the bishop

approve the accounts of their cofradías. Having already suffered
through one such episcopal pillaging expedition, and fearful of another,
the Tzeltal Mayas rebelled, and their rebellion became one of the largest-
scale indigenous revolts in the history of colonial Central America.[3]
The bishop's report was motivated by his desire to show the king his
great concern for the Indians, as well as to attack the alcalde mayor,
Pedro Gutiérrez de Mier y Terán, who had written to the crown
blaming the expensive uprising on the bishop's greed.

One might reject Álvarez de Toledo's report out of hand, given the
political context. Yet his allegations were confirmed by the next bishop,
Jacinto de Olivera Pardo, who was asked to investigate the matter.
The new diocesan leader, who had served for years in the Diocese
of Guadalajara (New Galicia), reported the same facts as his predecessor: the Indians were being required to pay in kind with goods
evaluated below market prices. Olivera Pardo, however, unlike his
predecessor, defended the alcalde mayor's practices. First, the benefi-
ciaries of the system—the magistrate and his associates—charitably
gave money and food to the Church and to the bishop's family. Second,
and most importantly, if the Indians were allowed to pay their tribute
in money, they would have to pay less, and thus "because of their
innate laziness," they would certainly work less. The Council of the
Indies did not like the practice but merely ordered the Audiencia of
Guatemala to take steps to prevent the alcalde mayor from reselling
the goods. This had no effect at all.[4] The function of the system, according to an insider with well-formed ideas regarding Indians, was to
force the indigenous people to produce a larger surplus, which they
would not have done if given the choice.

Bishop Olivera Pardo's predictions of what would happen if
reforms were implemented allowing tribute payment in cash soon
proved to be true in the alcaldía mayor of San Antonio Suchitepéquez. In 1732 the Audiencia of Guatemala reported that the alcalde
mayor of that province was carrying out the same kind of business
as the magistrate of Chiapa, forcing the indigenous people to pay
their tribute in kind (in this case cacao) and making a big profit by
reselling it at market prices. The audiencia issued an order allowing
the Indians to pay their tribute in money should they wish to do so.
The indigenous people found that they could pay their tribute debt

with less cacao than before, and so they scaled back their production to the level necessary to pay their tribute and no more. As a result, it was reported that over the next several decades, cacao production plummeted in what had been a cacao-rich province. Tribute was being paid, but exports to Mexico and sales taxes collected on cacao had fallen.[5] In other words, the indigenous people continued to produce the surplus necessary to pay their taxes but chose not to produce beyond that, causing total production to decline. Their level of production, after all, did not depend on credit. Formerly, the Indians had been forced to produce more than they had wanted because it was the only way permitted to pay their tribute.

The defenders of the business activities that magistrates carried out with the indigenous people in contravention of the law thus made a point often missed in the historiography of the repartimiento: the system worked to stimulate Indian production and thereby to stimulate the economy. At the same time, it is misleading to conclude that the repartimiento system was nothing more than economic exchange resulting from the extension of credit to Indians who would otherwise have been unable to participate in the economy as buyers of valuable consumer goods. As we have seen, coercion was sometimes used to force the indigenous people to accept money, credit, or goods and was always a threat when it came time to pay debts. Since the system was involuntary, coercion in one form or another was part of the repartimiento in highland Guatemala, and probably in many other places as well. And most importantly, the people who reported this were not idealistic reformers trying to eliminate the system by resorting to exaggeration in a partisan conflict. The people who favored the continuation of the repartimiento openly admitted and justified the use of coercion.

All these points were made clear in 1749 in a secret report by the president of the Audiencia of Guatemala, Captain General José de Araujo.[6] He informed the king that all the alcaldes mayores of the kingdom carried out repartimientos, of which there were several kinds. Most of the time, money or goods were advanced to the indigenous people as a means of stimulating trade, and the debts were repaid at a later time in kind at values "somewhat below current prices." In other places, cotton was distributed to be made into thread, which was then distributed among other people to be woven into cloth. All magistrates also sold mules, oxen, tools, and other goods. This was done, however, "without violence and at comfortable prices." Therefore, if there were any complaints lodged in court by the Indians, "this was not because of any tyranny exercised against them but because the alcalde mayor had punished them for their vices or because they did not want to pay for what they had received or because someone who did not like the alcalde mayor had put them up to it." In any case, the repartimiento "method," as the president referred to it, had been in existence "since the conquest, and would continue without remedy despite the law prohibiting it." This was true and was known to all the royal officials charged with stopping it. The same was true, he pointed out, "in both Americas," that is, North and South.

The president went on to state that formal charges against alcaldes mayores would always fail as long as the officials "make sure that their backs are well guarded in the capital." Charges therefore are always dropped, except in the cases of the magistrates who "fail to follow that maxim from the time they take office." Only then were there consequences for breaking the law.

Araujo then came to the crucial point: the repartimiento system was necessary to ensure that the indigenous people paid their tribute. Without it, "the Indians would fall into the idleness that characterizes them all," and commerce in all the provinces would suffer a decline. Once again, the alleged laziness of the Indians reared its head. Toleration of the repartimiento should continue, he stated, and in order that the indigenous people get the credit they need, it is "necessary that commerce be accompanied by authority, because without sales being carried out in return for kind rather than cash over a six- to twelve-month period or paid for in labor, the private merchant would not be able to sell because he lacks the authority to collect."

Given this reality, President Araujo argued for the creation of a board in the capital that would oversee the repartimiento to ensure that Indians were not underpaid for the goods that they delivered to repay their debts or overcharged for the goods that they acquired on credit. That, of course, meant the legalization of what had been illegal. The result would be not just fair prices but the opening up of a whole branch of commerce to taxation, thereby raising royal income. It would also be beneficial to the alcaldes mayores because the latter, the president reported, were paying considerable quantities of money "to the judges and their agents for the toleration of their repartimientos." In other words, fewer bribes would have to be paid if the business were legal.

The crown had asked for the president's opinion because it was carrying out a policy review on the issue of repartimientos throughout its American kingdoms. The result was an important royal order in 1751. The king noted that the business activities of the royal magistrates in America were abusive. At the same time, however, he accepted the basic position of the supporters of the repartimiento: without it the Indians, because of their natural laziness, would not work and thus could not pay their tribute. Private merchants were reluctant to loan money to the indigenous people because of the difficulty of debt collection; this was why alcaldes mayores and corregidores—armed with political power—were the only ones who could engage in business with the Indians. The magistrates advanced credit for the payment of tribute, but then demanded repayment not in money but in kind. The problem, the king noted, was in the evaluation of the goods being delivered to repay the debts: the goods were being evaluated at below market prices, thereby allowing the alcaldes mayores to profit by reselling those goods at their true value. The crown therefore accepted the position put forward by President Araujo: a board should be set up to regulate repartimientos, establishing fair prices more favorable to the Indians and limits to the volume of business permitted to the magistrates.[7] As a result, after 1751 the repartimiento was finally, although only temporarily, legal. It is worth noting once again that the assumption behind this policy was the nature of the Indians: they were lazy.

When the repartimiento process began as the allocation of credit for the payment of tribute, compulsion was not always needed. Repartimiento was still somewhat involuntary, but since it was connected to tribute, it could not easily be resisted or avoided. Other forms of repartimiento, however, apparently did require force. That is why the Audiencia of Guatemala made its ruling of March 24, 1759, permitting coercion in order to compel the Indians to participate.[8] Thus, in some cases, for the indigenous people the cost of nonparticipation was just as severe as the cost of default: incarceration and the physical pain of flogging. This did not have to occur often, and indeed President Araujo had noted almost twenty years earlier that the repartimientos were normally carried out "without violence." All that a magistrate had to do was to threaten to use the power entrusted to him. The village government felt compelled to obey, and the Indians usually followed their leaders.

The underlying assumptions that had justified the legalization of the repartimiento were then reiterated in the titles of office given to succeeding presidents of the audiencia. Thus Brigadier Pedro de Salazar's title, dated November 14, 1764, stated that even though the business dealings of the magistrates were "destroying the Indians," they were necessitated by the "laziness" of the indigenous people. The king even recognized that the system was "forced" (forzoso), not voluntary, but he also noted that only the alcaldes mayores and corregidores could carry out commerce with the indigenous people because private merchants lacked the means of making the Indians pay up. A board had been set up in the capital to oversee the repartimientos (although there is no other documentary evidence of its existence). As a result, the king concluded that he had to give permission to the president to engage in the same business, but the president was instructed to keep within the limits set by "the Viceroy to whom you belong."[9] That meant the viceroy of New Spain.

Meanwhile, in New Spain itself, Viceroy Bucareli opposed the introduction of the intendancy system that was partly designed to root out the repartimiento. Bucareli thought the existing system worked quite well, and he offered as evidence Mexico's huge increase in silver production. But the system would work better, he wrote, if the regulated repartimiento system, with agreed upon commutation rates and quantities, were kept in effect. He thought the intendancies to be unnecessary, but the repartimientos were "required in most of the alcaldías of the Kingdom because of the Constitution of the Country, due to the laziness of the wretched Indians."[10] The justification for the use of a coercive system of unequal economic exchange was thus widely accepted.

The abolition of the repartimiento everywhere in the Spanish empire after 1782 had economic effects that the supporters of the system had correctly predicted. The magistrates no longer had a mechanism to guarantee tribute collection, and although tribute continued to be paid for the most part, commercial activity declined. While payment of taxes was still mandatory, commercial exchange was voluntary. The system had worked in the past in a way such that not only was tribute paid, but also the magistrates made a handsome profit by being paid in kind at artificially low prices and then reselling the goods on the market. Profits from the latter activity largely disappeared after the abolition of the repartimiento, and the sheer size of the surplus being extracted from the indigenous people declined. That meant a decline in overall commercial activity. As noted in the previous chapter, even Pedro de Aparici, one of the most ardent of the reformers who wanted to root out the repartimiento, accepted this reality. He thought that "the Indians, being lazy by nature," needed some kind of a stimulus, and thus he supported the idea of using indigenous community funds "to counteract the natural laziness of the Indians."[11]

Thus, once the crown made commercial participation by the Indians voluntary, by prohibiting the magistrates from compelling them to accept allocations of goods or credit, the repartimiento collapsed. This is still more proof of the involuntary nature of the system. Although whipping and what former President Araujo had called "violence" were rare occurrences, the repartimiento could not function without some form of coercion, whether to compel indigenous participation or to collect debts.[12] Therefore, business and government worked together in Spanish America to control economic exchange between the indigenous people and the wider world. At the same time, once colonial coercion was relaxed, the indigenous people cut back on production. Commerce declined and the late colonial economy declined as well.

In other words, the system worked not because of market forces but because of colonialism. The repartimiento in highland Guatemala and lowland Nicaragua involved the indigenous people in a system that required them to pay off their debts through work, especially by spinning and weaving the textiles that were a vital part of world trade and economic integration. It was therefore a system of forced labor, which could not have existed without the repressive power of the colonial state. Wallerstein's interpretation of the colonial Spanish American economy as a system of "coerced cash-crop" production must be turned on its head: the repartimiento made it "coerced industrial production." In fact, it ceased to exist once the Spanish government prevented its officials from engaging in business with the Indians under their jurisdiction.

Yet forced labor, of course, had a purpose, and the repartimiento system accomplished the goal of incorporating the Indians into the world economy more effectively than market forces alone would have done. The goods produced as a result of the repartimiento were a vital part of the world economy. Most importantly, the indigenous people made most of the textiles that clothed not only the people of the colonial cities, but also those in the mining camps producing the precious metal that was the lifeblood of world trade, and those on the plantations producing the indigo that was Central America's major export. Mexican and Peruvian (and even Honduran) silver led to the creation, for the first time in history, of a true world economy, for it was in the Philippines that Spanish merchants, supplied with silver from America shipped across the Pacific on the Nao de Manila, came into direct contact with Chinese merchants in Manila. This encounter almost immediately fueled the massive expansion of world trade resulting from the equally massive increase first of Chinese and later of Indian exports.[13] Floods of American silver also flowed eastward to Europe, giving the British, Dutch, and French merchants the precious metals needed to go to Asia and purchase Chinese and Indian goods directly. Finally, the indigenous people of highland Guatemala produced textiles that united them with the cultivators of raw cotton on the Guatemalan Pacific coast, the manufacturers of iron tools in Mexico, the Salvadoran producers of indigo, and the manufacturers and workers who used American-made dyes in Europe.

These commercial networks even incorporated the slaves and slave traders caught up or engaged in a commerce financed in part by the profits made in highland Guatemala by merchants like Juan Montes de Oca. The forced labor system known as the repartimiento in Huehuetenango-Totonicapán—and in hundreds of other places in America under the control of Spanish colonial officials like Juan Bacaro—thus played a vital integrating role in the world economy. It was thanks to the traditional cotton manufactures of places like this, as well as Quezaltenango, Verapaz, and Atitlán-Tecpanatitlán in Guatemala, and Chiapas, Yucatan, Oaxaca, the Philippines, China, and India—and therefore *not* Lancashire or Massachusetts—that the workers in silver and gold mines; sugar, tobacco, and indigo plantations; spice-yielding tropical islands; and the African economies that were engaged in the slave trade found the light, easy-to-wash, and relatively cheap clothing that they desired.

Parts of the non-Western world, therefore, became more, not less, industrial in the era following the incorporation of America into the world economy. To be sure, these traditional structures of production were doomed, for they would collapse as the result of the Industrial Revolution. This was happening in Central America in the early nineteenth century, and much industry had already collapsed as early as 1823, as the Consulado of Guatemala pointed out in a pamphlet arguing for protectionism.[14] As industry increasingly came to be concentrated in Western Europe and the United States, the rest of the world suffered through the long and painful process of de-industrialization.[15] Traditional spinners and weavers had a much reduced place in the new world order that emerged in the nineteenth century.

At the same time, industry in America was not necessarily like that in Europe. A large working class had yet to emerge, and the people who inhabited places like Huehuetenango and Nicaragua were of non-European culture. The Indians therefore operated with different goals in mind, did not respond to European incentives, and even resisted colonialism by resorting to what James Scott has called "the weapons of the weak," that is, non-cooperation, foot-dragging, sabotage, and the like (which of course led to the myth of the "lazy native").[16] This is not to say that indigenous people sought to isolate themselves entirely from market activities. In most of Mesoamerica, Indians had been accustomed to marketing for centuries before the arrival of Europeans and continued to engage in commerce during and after the colonial period. But they tended to do so when they perceived market conditions to be favorable to them, and thus sold goods over which they maintained full control of production and marketing.[17] The repartimiento system, of course, was not of that type. Consequently the colonial masters resorted to coercion, sometimes, but not always, to get the Indians to accept the deals, but frequently to get them to fulfill their contracts; that is, to pay their debts. The same method, of course, was used to get the indigenous people to pay their taxes, and as we have seen, the collection of repartimiento debts was frequently related to the collection of tribute.

It is important to emphasize the cultural difference between the colonizers and the colonized. A close analysis of the indigenous side of the commercial exchange reveals that Indians behaved in terms of their own, non-Western, cultural norms. These, of course, had a logic all of their own. Most importantly, the Spanish reported, the Indians did not respond to economic incentives the way Europeans would, because they had no desire to accumulate property to demonstrate their social superiority; on the contrary, they were content to remain as they were. They did not believe that their debts to magistrates or merchants involved any moral obligation on their part, and they did not care about legalities. Moreover, repayment might be avoided altogether as a result of the death of the debtor, and in any case the indigenous people felt that they possessed the right to resist each and every payment demanded by their colonial masters. From the Spanish legalistic perspective, however, the Indians were obligated to pay their debts, and this gave the alcaldes mayores the right to demand repayment. This was the justification for coercion, which the Spaniards used to counteract indigenous resistance—manifested in laziness according to Hispanic society—to the terms of commercial exchange involved in the repartimiento. The Spanish conclusion that the Indians were lazy, therefore, is proof positive of indigenous resistance to the repartimiento in particular and to colonialism in general.

TRIBUTARIES AND INDIGENOUS POPULATION, 1746

Province	Tributaries	Approximate indigenous population
Chiapa	13,646	54,000
Soconusco	3,709	15,000
Quezaltenango	4,983	20,000
Huehuetenango-Totonicapán	6,810	27,000
Atitlán-Tecpanatitlán	7,049	28,000
Amatitanes and Chimaltenango	21,665	87,000
Verapaz	8,413	34,000
Chiquimula de la Sierra	7,921	32,000
Suchitepéquez	3,793	15,000
Escuintla-Guazacapán	2,873	11,000
Sonsonate	3,709	15,000
San Salvador	6,552	26,000
Honduras-Comayagua	3,659	15,000–17,000
Tegucigalpa	1,046	4,000–5,000
Sébaco-Chontales	1,375	5,000–8,000
Sutiaba	1,447	6,500
Realejo	458	1,800–2,000
Nicaragua	5,249	21,000–23,600
Nicoya	50	250
Costa Rica	?	?

Source: AGI, Escribanía de Cámara 361A, Quaderno 2, Testimonio de la Cuenta y Liquidación de todas las entradas y salidas de la Real Caja de esta Corthe, 1746.
Note: A conversion factor of 4.0 is used to convert tributaries to total population.

Tributaries and Estimated Population, 1768

Province	Number of villages or barrios	Tributaries	Population
Urban barrios	10	459	2,111
Chimaltenango	21	10,024	46,110
Amatitlanes	42	7,266	33,424
Soconusco	23	825	3,795
San Salvador	118	8,413	38,700
Chiapa	116	14,642	67,353
Quezaltenango	29	3,995	8,377
Totonicapán	53	7,951	36,575
Suchitepéquez	30	4,457	20,502
Chiquimula	30	7,591	34,919
Verapaz	13	9,124	41,970
Atitlán	40	6,264	28,814
Escuintla	28	3,153	14,504

Source: Guatemala 547, Expediente 25, Testimonio de la Liquidación formada por Don Miguel Mariano de Yturvide, Contador de cuentas reales de este Reyno, del ingreso y salidas de estas Reales Caxas, dando razón por maior de las foráneas, 1768.
Note: A conversion factor of 4.6 is used to convert tributaries to total population.

APPENDIX C

Tributaries and Laboríos, c. 1773

Province	Tributaries	Laboríos
Urban barrios	422	0
Nicaragua	1,968	943
Comayagua	5,121	71
Quezaltenango	4,222	21
Chiquimula	8,045	0
Sutiaba	1,466	0
Matagalpa	2,375	599
San Salvador	12,567	288
Sololá	5,720	0
Sonsonate	4,450	0
Verapaz	9,783	0
Tegucigalpa	795	33
Totonicapán	9,556	11
Escuintla	3,010	0
Realejo	396	129
Nicoya	88	0
Costa Rica	274	27
Ciudad Real	7,675	682
Tuxtla	3,363	271
Soconusco	1,081	177
Suchitepéquez	3,047	8
Chimaltenango	8,609	0
Amatitlán	8,972	0

Source: AGI, Guatemala 560, Audiencia al Rey, December 6, 1778.

Tributaries and Estimated Population, 1797

Province	Tributaries	Laboríos	Population
León	10,285	1,288	53,236
Comayagua	6,758	436	33,092
San Salvador	13,493	476	64,257
Ciudad Real	15,737	621	75,247
Suchitepéquez	2,324	82	11,068
Quezaltenango	4,642	10	21,399
Totonicapán	9,933	19	45,779
Sololá	5,747	0	26,436
Chimaltenango	7,834	0	36,036
Sacatepéquez	9,517	0	43,778
Escuintla	3,101	0	14,265
Chiquimula	7,675	0	35,305
Verapaz	11,061	0	50,881
Sonsonate	4,750	2	21,859

Source: AGI, Indiferente General 1699, Quaderno 4, Testimonio de los autos sobre la creación de una Contaduría Gral. de Proprios, arvitrios y Bienes de Comunidades de Yndios en el Reyno de Guatemala, 1797.

Note: A conversion factor of 4.6 is used to convert tributaries to total population.

APPENDIX E

Tributaries and Estimated Population, 1803

Province	Number of villages	Tributaries	Population
Nicaragua (I) (10 subdelegaciones)		10,322	47,481
Costa Rica (G)		328	1,509
El Salvador (I)		12,375	56,925
Honduras-Comayagua (I) (7 subdelegaciones)		9,283	42,702
Chiapas (I) (2 subdelegaciones)		16,790	77,234
Quezaltenango	27	6,148	28,281
Chiquimula	31	7,578	34,859
Chimaltenango	21	8,316	38,254
Escuintla	34	2,051	9,435
Sacatepéquez	48	1,054	4,848
Sonsonate	21	4,558	20,967
Verapaz	14	11,311	52,031
Totonicapán	49	11,803	54,294
Suchitepéquez	16	2,558	11,767
Sololá	31	6,860	31,556

Source: AGI, Guatemala 441, Audiencia al Rey, June 3, 1803.

Notes: A conversion factor of 4.6 is used to convert tributaries to total population.

G = Gobernación

I = Intendancy

NOTES

INTRODUCTION

1. Immanuel Wallerstein, *The Modern World-System: Capitalist Agriculture and the Origins of the European World Economy in the Sixteenth Century* (New York: Academic Press, 1976).

2. For an argument putting the traditional interpretation on its head, see Andre Gunder Frank, *ReOrient: Global Economy in the Asian Age* (Berkeley: University of California Press, 1998). While polemical, self-promoting, and exaggerated, this book provides a great deal of information regarding the period before the Industrial Revolution when China and India were the most important producers of industrial goods for the world economy. See also Om Prakash, *European Commercial Enterprise in Pre-colonial India* (Cambridge: Cambridge University Press, 1998); Kenneth Pomeranz, *The Great Divergence* (Princeton, N.J.: Princeton University Press, 2000); Dipesh Chakrabarty, *Provincializing Europe: Postcolonial Thought and Historical Difference* (Princeton, N.J.: Princeton University Press, 2000).

3. Wallerstein, *Modern World-System*, 68.

4. For the obrajes, see especially Richard J. Salvucci, *Textiles and Capitalism in Mexico: An Economic History of the Obrajes, 1539–1840* (Princeton, N.J.: Princeton University Press, 1987); Manuel Miño Grijalva, *La manufactura colonial: La constitución técnica del obraje* (Mexico: El Colegio de México, 1992); Manuel Miño Grijalva, *La protoindustria colonial hispanoamericana* (Mexico: El Colegio de México, 1993); Manuel Miño Grijalva, *Obrajes y tejedores de Nueva España, 1700–1810* (Mexico: El Colegio de México, 1998); Aurora Gómez-Galvarriato, ed., *La industria textil en México* (Mexico: Instituto Mora, El Colegio de Michoacán, El Colegio de México, Instituto de Investigaciones Historicas-UNAM, 1999); Carmen Ramos Escandón, *Industrialización, género y trabajo femenino en el sector textil mexicano: El obraje, la fábrica y la compañía industrial* (Mexico: CIESAS, Casa Chata, 2004);

Javier Ortiz de la Tabla Ducasse, "El obraje colonial ecuatoriano: Aproximación a su estudio," *Revista de Indias*, 149–50 (July–December 1977): 471–551.

5. Consulado Nacional [Guatemala], *Memorial sobre el estado actual del comercio de Guatemala: Obstáculos que impiden su progreso y medios de removerlos* (Guatemala: Beteta, 1823), 13–14. For the incorporation of the colonial indigenous textile sector into the world economy, see Carlos Sempat Assadourian, *El sistema de la economía colonial: El mercado interior, regiones y espacio económico* (Lima: Instituto de Estudios Peruanos, 1982); Robert W. Patch, *Maya and Spaniard in Yucatan, 1648–1812* (Stanford: Stanford University Press, 1993), 30–32, 81–93; Robert W. Patch, "Imperial Politics and Local Economy in Colonial Central America, 1670–1770," *Past and Present*, no. 143 (May 1994), especially 101–106.

6. See Patch, "Imperial Politics and Local Economy," for the case of colonial Central America.

7. José Manuel Santos Pérez, "Los comerciantes de Guatemala y la economía de Centroamérica en la primera mitad del siglo XVIII," *Anuario de Estudios Americanos* 56, no. 2 (1999): 463–84.

8. Jorge Juan and Juan de Ulloa, *Noticias secretas de América*, 2 vols. (Madrid: Editorial-América, 1918), 1:252, 253, 261, 266.

9. Alfredo Moreno Cebrián, *El corregidor de indios y la economía peruana del siglo XVIII (Los repartos forzosos de mercancías)* (Madrid: Consejo Superior de Investigaciones Científicas, 1977); Stanley J. Stein, "Bureaucracy and Business in the Spanish Empire, 1759–1804: Failure of a Bourbon Reform in Mexico and Peru," *Hispanic American Historical Review* 61 (February 1982): 2–28.

10. Moreno Cebrián, *El corregidor de indios*, 167–264; Stein, "Bureaucracy and Business"; Jürgen Golte, *Repartos y rebeliones: Túpac Amaru y las contradicciones de la economía colonial* (Lima: Instituto de Estudios Peruanos, 1980).

11. Horst Pietschmann, "'Alcaldes mayores,' 'corregidores' und 'subdelegados': Zum Problem der Distriktsbeamtenschaft im Vizekönigsreich Neuspanien," *Jahrbuch für Geschichte von Staat, Wirtschaft und Gesellschaft Lateinamerikas* 9 (1972): 173–270.

12. Jeremy Baskes, "Coerced or Voluntary? The *Repartimiento* and Market Participation of Peasants in Late Colonial Oaxaca," *Journal of Latin American Studies* 28, pt. 1 (February 1996): 1–28; Jeremy Baskes, *Indians, Merchants, and Markets: A Reinterpretation of the Repartimiento and Spanish-Indian Economic Relations in Colonial Oaxaca* (Stanford: Stanford University Press, 2000). Both of these works include citation of most of the literature about the repartimiento.

13. María de los Ángeles Romero Frizzi, *Economía y vida de los españoles en la Mixteca Alta: 1519–1720* (Mexico: Instituto Nacional de Antropología e Historia, 1990), 250; Baskes, *Indians, Merchants, and Markets*, 65–66.

14. Arij Ouweneel, *Shadows over Anáhuac: An Ecological Interpretation of Crisis and Development in Central Mexico, 1730–1800* (Albuquerque: University of New Mexico Press, 1996); Baskes, *Indians, Merchants, and Markets*, 20–38; Patch, *Maya and Spaniard*, 81–93; Patch, "Imperial Politics and Local Economy," 101–106.

15. Baskes, *Indians, Merchants, and Markets*, 39–61.

16. Marcello Carmagnani, "Una institución económica colonial: Repartimiento de mercancías y libertad de comercio," *Historia Mexicana* 54, no. 1 (July–September 2004): 249–62.

17. Baskes, *Indians, Merchants, and Markets*, 4, 190.

18. Ibid., 5.

19. Juan Carlos Solórzano Fonseca, "Las comunidades indígenas de Guatemala, El Salvador y Chiapas durante el siglo XVIII: Los mecanismos de la explotación económica," *Anuario de Estudios Centroamericanos* 11, no. 2 (1985): 111–15.

20. See in particular the work of James Lockhart and his students at the University of California, Los Angeles, especially James Lockhart, *The Nahuas after the Conquest: A Social and Cultural History of the Indians of Central Mexico, Sixteenth through Eighteenth Centuries* (Stanford: Stanford University Press, 1992). For the Mayas, see Robert M. Hill, *Colonial Cakchiquels: Highland Maya Adaptations to Spanish Rule, 1600–1700* (Fort Worth, Texas: Harcourt Brace Jovanovich, 1992); Matthew Restall, *The Maya World: Yucatec Culture and Society, 1550–1850* (Stanford: Stanford University Press, 1997); Matthew Restall, *Maya Conquistador* (Boston: Beacon Press, 1998); Owen Jones, "Colonial K'iche' in Comparison with Yucatec Maya: Language, Adaptation, and Intercultural Contact" (PhD. diss., University of California, Riverside, 2009).

21. For what follows, see Robert W. Patch, *Maya Revolt and Revolution in the Eighteenth Century* (Armonk, N.Y.: M. E. Sharpe, 2002). For the concept of the "hidden transcript," see James C. Scott, *Domination and the Arts of Resistance: Hidden Transcripts*. New Haven, Conn.: Yale University Press, 1990.

22. Patch, *Maya Revolt and Revolution*, 23–62. For the concept of the moral economy, see E. P. Thompson, "The Moral Economy of the English Crowd in the Eighteenth Century," *Past and Present*, no. 50 (February 1971): 76–136; James C. Scott, *The Moral Economy of the Peasant: Rebellion and Subsistence in Southeast Asia*. New Haven, Conn.: Yale University Press, 1976.

23. Patch, *Maya Revolt and Revolution*, 65–88.

24. Ibid., 89–125.

25. Ibid., 69–74, 77–80, 84, 99, 193.

26. Ibid., 26, 34, 36–37, 40–41, 49, 50, 82, 102, 188, 192. For "weapons of the weak," see James C. Scott, *Weapons of the Weak: Everyday Forms of Peasant Resistance* (New Haven, Conn.: Yale University Press, 1985).

27. The superb monographs by Charles Gibson and Murdo MacLeod have frequently been interpreted to be representative of this approach. See Charles Gibson, *The Aztecs under Spanish Rule: A History of the Indians of the Valley of Mexico, 1521–1821* (Stanford: Stanford University Press, 1964), and Murdo J. MacLeod, *Spanish Central America: A Socioeconomic History, 1524–1720* (Berkeley and Los Angeles: University of California Press, 1971). However, a close reading of these works reveals a much greater awareness of the dynamic nature of the indigenous society on those authors' part. Both Gibson and MacLeod were writing

at a time when Indians were not the focus of research, and therefore they tended to emphasize the exploitative and destructive features of colonialism, which was something of a scholarly revolution at the time. Later scholars have focused even more on the indigenous people and have provided a more nuanced interpretation of the Indians during the colonial period.

28. Three of the earliest in-depth studies of indigenous dynamism during the colonial era include Steve J. Stern, *Peru's Indian Peoples and the Challenge of Spanish Conquest: Huamanga, to 1640* (Madison: University of Wisconsin Press, 1982); Nancy Farriss, *Maya Society under Colonial Rule: The Collective Enterprise of Survival* (Princeton, N.J.: Princeton University Press, 1984); and Karen Spalding, *Huarochirí, an Andean Society under Inca and Spanish Rule* (Stanford: Stanford University Press, 1984). For more on the Maya area, see Patch, *Maya and Spaniard*; Pedro Bracamonte y Sosa and Gabriela Solís Robleda, *Espacios mayas de autonomía: El pacto colonial en Yucatán* (Mérida, Yucatán: Universidad Autónoma de Yucatán, Facultad de Ciencias Antropológicas, 1996).

29. See Linda A. Newson, *The Cost of Conquest: Indian Decline in Honduras under Spanish Rule* (Boulder, Colo.: Westview Press, 1986); Linda A. Newson, *Indian Survival in Colonial Nicaragua* (Norman: University of Oklahoma Press, 1987).

30. Archivo General de Indias (hereinafter AGI), Guatemala 947, Expediente sobre los estatutos y reglas formados por el Arzobispo de Guatemala (1785), Testimonio de los autos de la Visita canónica de esta Santa Metropolitana Yglesia de Santiago (1770).

1. People and Taxes in the Eighteenth Century

1. For overviews of colonial Central America and of demography, see M. MacLeod, *Spanish Central America*; Ciro Cardoso and Héctor Pérez Brignoli, *Centro América y la economía occidental (1520–1930)* (San José: Editorial Universidad de Costa Rica, 1979); Murdo J. MacLeod, "An Outline of Central American Colonial Demographics: Sources, Yields, and Possibilities," in *The Historical Demography of Highland Guatemala*, ed. Robert Carmack, John Early, and Christopher Lutz (Albany: Institute for Mesoamerican Studies, State University of New York, 1982), 3–18; Víctor Hugo Acuña Ortega and Iván Molina Jiménez, *Historia económica y social de Costa Rica (1750–1950)* (San José, Costa Rica: Editorial Porvenir, 1991), 21–68; Elizabeth Fonseca Corrales, "Economía y sociedad en Centroamérica (1540–1680)," in Julio Pinto Soria, ed., *El régimen colonial (1524–1750)*, vol. 2 of *Historia general de Centroamérica* (Madrid: Comunidades Europeas / Sociedad Estatal Quinto Centenario / FLACSO, 1993), 95–150.

2. AGI, Guatemala 542, Expediente 1, Audiencia al Rey, February 25, 1764.

3. AGI, Guatemala 575, Expediente 4, Gobernador Intendente de Nicaragua al Rey (January 20, 1788); Informe de la Contaduría (August 7, 1788); and Informe del Fiscal (August 18, 1788).

4. In addition to the sources cited in the appendices, see Gustavo Palma Murga, "Economía y sociedad en Centroamérica (1680–1750)," in Julio Pinto Soria, ed., *El régimen colonial (1524–1750)*, vol. 2 of *Historia general de Centroamérica* (Madrid: Comunidades Europeas / Sociedad Estatal Quinto Centenario / FLACSO, 1993), 230.

5. Jorge Arias de Blois, "Demografía," in *Historia general de Guatemala*, ed. Jorge Luján Muñoz and Cristina Zilbermann de Luján (Guatemala: Asociación de Amigos del País, Fundación para la Cultura y el Desarrollo, 1994–95), 3:103–19.

6. Newson, *Indian Survival in Colonial Nicaragua*, 319.

7. Newson, *Cost of Conquest*, 306.

8. Juan Carlos Solórzano Fonseca, "Los años finales de la dominación española (1750–1821)," in Héctor Pérez Brignoli, ed., *De la Ilustración al Liberalismo (1750–1870)*, vol. 3 of *Historia general de Centroamérica* (Comunidades Europeas / Sociedad Estatal Quinto Centenario / FLACSO, 1993), 26–27; Germán Romero Vargas, *Las estructuras sociales de Nicaragua en el siglo XVIII* (Managua: Editorial Vanguardia, 1988), 296–306.

9. It has been suggested that the total population increased moderately from 19,293 in 1700 to 24,022 in 1751, and then rapidly to 52,591 in 1801. See Mario Fernández, Anabel Schmidt, and Víctor Basauri, "La Población de Costa Rica," in *Población de Costa Rica y orígenes de los costarricenses*, ed. Joaquín Gutiérrez (San José: Editorial Costa Rica, 1977), 2:226, cited in María de los Ángeles Acuña León and Doriam Chavarría López, "Cartago colonial: Mestizaje y patrones matrimoniales, 1738–1821," *Mesoamérica* 31 (June 1996): 163. I find these figures much too large to believe, given what we know about the population of the surrounding provinces.

10. Solórzano Fonseco, "Los años finales de la dominación española," 26.

11. See appendices.

12. Elizabeth A. Fenn, *Pox Americana: The Great Smallpox Epidemic of 1775–82* (New York: Hill and Wang, 2001).

13. Newson, *Indian Survival in Colonial Nicaragua*, 329.

14. AGI, Guatemala 568, Audiencia al Rey, June 6, 1783; Testimonio de los Autos sobre Perdón de tributos, 1783; AGI Guatemala 574, Expediente 7, Alcalde Mayor de Amatitanes al Rey, December 31, 1787; AGI, Guatemala 587, Expediente 14, Intendente Gobernador de Honduras al Príncipe de la Paz, August 25, 1798; Newson, *Cost of Conquest*, 316–18; Newson, *Indian Survival in Colonial Nicaragua*, 329.

15. AGI, Guatemala 714, Oficio 380, Presidente al Secretario de Hacienda, December 3, 1803; Guatemala 620 (1803).

16. The best overviews of the period are Miles L. Wortman, *Government and Society in Central America, 1680–1840* (New York: Columbia University Press, 1982); Palma Murga, "Economía y sociedad en Centroamérica (1680–1750)"; Solórzano Fonseca, "Los años finales de la dominación española (1750–1821)," 13–71.

17. Christopher H. Lutz, *Santiago de Guatemala, 1541–1773: City, Caste, and the Colonial Experience* (Norman: University of Oklahoma Press, 1994), 79–112.

18. Jorge Luján Muñoz, "Fundación de villas de ladinos en Guatemala en el último tercio del siglo XVIII," *Revista de Indias* 36 (1976): 51–81.

19. Ibid., 52–53.

20. AGI, Escribanía de Cámara 358C, Residencia de Joseph González de Rancaño y Rivera, 1744; Guatemala 596, Expediente diario 2, 1769; Guatemala 441, Título del corregimiento de Chiquimula de la Sierra, Consulta, March 17, 1769.

21. Wortman, *Government and Society in Central America*, 113–16.

22. For the cacao economy before 1720, see M. MacLeod, *Spanish Central America*, 68–95, 235–52, 330–40.

23. *Colección de documentos antiguos del archivo del ayuntamiento de la ciudad de Guatemala, formada por su secretario Don Rafael Arévalo.* Edición del Museo Guatemalteco (Guatemala: Imprenta de Luna, 1857), March 9, 1709, 128–46; M. MacLeod, *Spanish Central America*, 241–50; Wortman, *Government and Society in Central America*, 23, 89, 98, 194; Newson, *Indian Survival in Colonial Nicaragua*, 107–108, 139.

24. AGI, Guatemala 641, Sumario hecho en el Consejo de Indias, April 24, 1764. For a different interpretation, see Solórzano Fonseca, "Las comunidades indígenas de Guatemala," 102.

25. Newson, *Indian Survival in Colonial Nicaragua*, 138–40, 264.

26. Philip MacLeod, "Auge y estancamiento de la producción de cacao en Costa Rica, 1660–95," *Anuario de Estudios Centroamericanos* 22, no. 1 (1996): 83–107; Juan Carlos Solórzano Fonseca, "Costa Rica en la primera mitad del siglo XVIII: Análisis regional de una sociedad en transición," *Anuario de Estudios Centroamericanos* 19, no. 1 (1993): 59.

27. Santos Pérez, "Los comerciantes de Guatemala," 463–84.

28. Robert S. Smith, "Forced Labor in the Guatemalan Indigo Works," *Hispanic American Historical Review* 36, no. 3 (August 1956): 31828; Robert S. Smith, "Indigo Production and Trade in Colonial Guatemala," *Hispanic American Historical Review* 39, no. 1 (February 1959): 181–211; Troy S. Floyd, "The Indigo Merchant: Promoter of Central American Economic Development, 1750–1808," *Business History Review* 39, no. 4 (Winter 1965): 466–88; M. MacLeod, *Spanish Central America*, 176–203; José Antonio Fernández Molina, *Pintando el mundo de azul: El auge añilero y el mercado centroamericano, 1750–1810* (San Salvador: Biblioteca de Historia Salvadoreña, 2003); Robert W. Patch, "Cura y empresario: Los préstamos financieros de Mateo Cornejo y la producción de añil en El Salvador, 1764–1789," *Mesoamérica* 48 (2006): 47–67.

29. Consulado Nacional [Guatemala], *Memorial sobre el estado actual del comercio*, 13.

30. Troy S. Floyd, "The Guatemalan Merchants, the Government, and the Provincianos, 1750–1800," *Hispanic American Historical Review* 41, no. 1 (February 1961): 90–110; Newson, *Indian Survival in Colonial Nicaragua*, 265–68.

31. See chapter 3.

32. Stanley J. Stein and Barbara H. Stein, *Silver, Trade, and War: Spain in the Making of Early Modern Europe* (Baltimore, Md.: Johns Hopkins University Press, 2000), 180–99; Stanley J. Stein and Barbara H. Stein, *Apogee of Empire: Spain and New Spain in the Age of Charles III, 1759–1789* (Baltimore, Md.: Johns Hopkins University Press, 2003), 74–75.

33. *Colección de documentos antiguos del archivo del ayuntamiento*, 124–27.

34. AGI, Guatemala 423, Cédula, February 22, 1718; Wortman, *Government and Society in Central America*, 20–24.

35. *Colección de documentos antiguos del archivo del ayuntamiento*, 50–53, 76–77.

36. Stanley J. Stein, "Francisco Ignacio de Yraeta y Azcárate, almacenero de la ciudad de México, 1732–1797: Un ensayo de microhistoria," *Historia Mexicana* 50, no. 3 (January–March 2001): 465–67.

37. AGI, Guatemala 555, Diputación del Comercio al Rey, October 1, 1772; Testimonio del expediente instruido a instancia de los diputados del comercio de esta Ciudad, sobre el modo, términos, y circunstancias, 1772, fols. 43–52, 62–63.

38. Carmelo Sáenz de Santa María, "Inglaterra y el reino de Guatemala," *Revista de Indias* 42 (1982): 109–201.

39. AGI, Guatemala 640, Instancia de Partes 1747, Orden-en-Consejo, December 2, 1747.

40. Guatemala 642, Presidente (Arcos y Moreno) al Secretario de Indias, January 31, 1756; Compañía de Goathemala al Presidente, January 30, 1756; Instancia de la Compañía de Goathemala al Rey, November 26, 1750; Instancia de la Audiencia al Rey, January 9, 1749; Instancia del Presidente (Araujo) al Rey, January 12, 1749.

41. S. Stein and B. Stein, *Apogee of Empire*, 72.

42. S. Stein, "Francisco Ignacio de Yraeta," 484.

43. Barbara H. Stein and Stanley J. Stein, *Edge of Crisis. War and Trade in the Spanish Atlantic, 1789–1808* (Baltimore, Md.: Johns Hopkins University Press, 2009), 130–61; Ralph Lee Woodward, *Class Privilege and Economic Development: The Consulado de Comercio of Guatemala, 1793–1871* (Chapel Hill: University of North Carolina Press, 1966).

44. For Spain's commercial reforms relating to its colonies, see the three books by Stein and Stein: *Silver, Trade, and War*; *Apogee of Empire*; and *Edge of Crisis*.

45. For an overview of the Bourbon Reforms in Central America, see Wortman, *Government and Society in Central America*. See also José Manuel Santos Pérez, *Élites, poder local y régimen colonial: El cabildo y los regidores de Santiago de Guatemala, 1700–1787* (Salamanca, Spain: Servicios de Publicaciones de la Universidad de Cádiz, Plumsock Mesoamerican Studies, and Centro de Investigaciones Regionales de Mesoamérica, 1999), 243–74, and the chapters in Jordana Dym and Christophe Belaubre, eds. *Politics, Economy, and Society in Bourbon Central America, 1759–1821* (Boulder, Colo.: University Press of Colorado, 2007).

46. For the establishment of the encomienda in Central America, see Salvador Rodríguez Becerra, *Encomienda y conquista: Los inicios de la colonización en Guatemala* (Seville: Publicaciones del Seminario de Antropología Americana, Universidad de Sevilla, 1977); Wendy Kramer, *Encomienda Politics in Early Colonial Guatemala, 1524–1544: Dividing the Spoils* (Boulder, Colo.: Westview Press, 1994).

47. Wortman, *Government and Society in Central America*, 25–27; Solórzano Fonseca, "Las comunidades indígenas de Guatemala," 99.

48. For a summary of the development of the encomienda in Guatemala, see AGI, Guatemala 582, Expedientes de Cartas, no. 4, Testimonio de las Diligencias instruidas en virtud de Real Cédula de 9 de julio de 1775 sobre liquidar el número de tributarios de encomiendas (1775).

49. For the complicated subject of forced labor, see William L. Sherman, *Forced Native Labor in Sixteenth-Century Central America* (Lincoln: University of Nebraska Press, 1979). For the seventeenth century, see Stephen Webre, "El trabajo forzoso de los indígenas en la política colonial guatemalteca (siglo XVII)," *Anuario de Estudios Centroamericanos* 13, no. 2 (1987): 49–61. For the eighteenth century, see Solórzano Fonseca, "Las comunidades indígenas de Guatemala," 116–18.

50. AGI, Guatemala 542, Expedientes y Cartas, no. 3, Audiencia al Rey, April 30, 1764.

51. Pilar Hernández Aparicio, "Problemas socioeconómicos en el Valle de Guatemala (1670–1680)," *Revista de Indias* 37 (1977): 585–637.

52. For a good overview of tribute in the eighteenth century, see Solórzano Fonseca, "Las comunidades indígenas de Guatemala," 99–103.

53. AGI, Guatemala 340, Presidente (Pedro de Rivera) al Rey, January 28, 1737.

54. Solórzano Fonseca, "Los años finales de la dominación española," 22.

55. AGI, Guatemala 550, Cartas y Expedientes, no. 26, Representación del Administrador de Alcabalas de Guatemala al Secretario de Indias (Julián de Arriaga), September 30, 1769.

56. Wortman, *Government and Society in Central America*, 141–53.

57. Jorge H. González, "State Reform, Popular Resistance, and Negotiation of Rule in Late Bourbon Guatemala: The Quetzaltenango Aguardiente Monopoly, 1785–1807," in *Politics, Economy, and Society in Bourbon Central America, 1759–1821*, ed. Jordana Dym and Christophe Belaubre (Boulder: University Press of Colorado, 2007), 129–55.

58. AGI, Escribanía de Cámara 361A, Quaderno 2, Testimonio de la Cuenta y Liquidación de todas las entradas y salidas de la Real Caja de esta Corthe, 1746, fol. 2.

59. AGI, Guatemala 541, Expediente 21, Carta no. 2 del Escribano de Cámara y Gobierno al Secretario de Indias (Julián de Arriaga), August 15, 1763.

60. AGI, Guatemala 607, Expediente 14, Estracto de Notas . . . puestas por el contador de cuentas . . . en las cuentas de 1763.

61. AGI, Guatemala 560, Expediente 1, Testimonio de la Real Orden en que S[u] M[ajestad] manda, se exija de Oficiales Reales el informe, 1763.

62. AGI, Guatemala 545, Expediente 19, Cura de Xalapa al Rey, March 30, 1767.

63. AGI, Guatemala 340, Informe del Consejo al Rey, March 1756.

64. AGI, Guatemala 340, Informe del Fiscal del Consejo, March 1, 1748; Informe del Fiscal del Consejo, March 1756.

65. AGI, Guatemala 541, Carta 1 del Escribano de Cámara y Gobierno al Secretario de Indias (Julián de Arriaga), August 15, 1763.

66. AGI, Guatemala 560, Expediente 1, Presidente (Fernández de Heredia) al Secretario de Indias, October 30, 1763; Presidente (Mayorga) al Rey, June 30, 1775; Informe de la Contaduría, October 23, 1777; Informe del Fiscal, July 10, 1778.

67. AGI, Guatemala 560, Expediente 1, Informe de la Contaduría, October 22, 1778; Audiencia al Rey, December 6, 1778.

68. AGI, Guatemala 560, Expediente 1, Informe del Fiscal, July 20, 1781.

69. AGI, Guatemala 564, Expediente sobre los tributos de Negros, Mulatos, Mestizos, Laboríos, Naboríos y Ladinos, Audiencia al Rey, December 22, 1779; Audiencia, 1780, Quaderno 1, Testimonio del Pedimento del Señor Dr. Don Francisco Saavedra, Fiscal de lo Civil de la Real Audiencia de Guatemala, sobre que se declare que los Negros, Negras . . . ; Informe de la Contaduría, June 1782.

70. AGI, Guatemala 575, Expediente 4, Gobernador Intendente de Nicaragua al Rey, January 20, 1788.

71. AGI, Guatemala 575, Expediente 4, Informe de la Contaduría, August 7, 1788; Informe del Fiscal, August 18, 1788.

72. AGI, Guatemala 340, Quaderno 1, 1743, Testimonio de los Autos seguidos por oficiales Reales para que por el Superior Govierno se dé providencia para la paga de tributos.

73. AGI, Escribanía de Cámara 358C, Residencia de Don Manuel de Lacunza, Alcalde Mayor de Suchitepéquez, 1748.

74. Archivo Histórico Nacional (hereinafter AHN), 20973, Pieza 1, Residencia del Capitán Pedro Lastiri, Alcalde Mayor de Verapaz, 1764, fol. 83.

75. AGI, Guatemala 558, Expediente 12, Audiencia al Rey, April 25, 1776; Expediente 14, Audiencia al Rey, April 25, 1776.

76. AGI, Guatemala 566, Expediente 2, Audiencia al Rey, March 14, 1781.

77. AGI, Guatemala 557, Expediente 11 (1775), Testimonio del Pueblo de San Mateo; 1775, Testimonio de los Naturales de Quezaltenango.

78. AGI, Guatemala 561, Expediente 8, Audiencia al Rey, July 6, 1778; Guatemala 410, Consulta, March 20, 1781.

79. AGI, Guatemala 606, Expediente 13, Francisco Xavier Aguirre al Rey, January 21, 1795; AGI, Guatemala 712, Correspondencia del Presidente, no. 309, August 3, 1803; Guatemala 717, Correspondencia del Presidente, no. 613, January 3, 1805.

80. See especially the tables in M. MacLeod, *Spanish Central America*, 98–100; Thomas T. Veblen, "Native Population Decline in Totonicapán, Guatemala," in *The Historical Demography of Highland Guatemala*, ed. Robert Carmack, John Early, and Christopher Lutz (Albany: Institute for Mesoamerican Studies, State University

of New York, 1982), 97; Newson, *Cost of Conquest*, 314; Newson, *Indian Survival in Colonial Nicaragua*, 328.

81. AGI, Guatemala 568, Audiencia al Rey, June 6, 1783; Testimonio de los Autos sobre Perdón de tributos, 1783; AGI, Guatemala 574, Expediente 7, Alcalde Mayor de Amatitanes al Rey, December 31, 1787; AGI, Guatemala 587, Expediente 14, Intendente Gobernador de Honduras al Príncipe de la Paz, August 25, 1798.

82. AGI, Guatemala 542, Expediente 3, Audiencia al Rey, April 30, 1764.

83. Luján Muñoz, "La fundación de villas de ladinos," 58–64.

84. AGI, Guatemala 557, Expediente 12, Audiencia al Rey, November 20, 1775; Testimonio 1775.

85. See Inge Langenberg, *Urbanisation und Bevölkerungsstruktur der Stadt Guatemala in der ausgehenden Kolonialzeit: eine sozialhistorische Analyse der Stadtverlegung und ihrer Ausvirkungen auf die demographische, berufliche, und soziale Gliederung der Bevölkerung (1773–1824)* (Cologne and Vienna: Böhlau, 1981). See also Oakah L. Jones, *Guatemala in the Spanish Colonial Period* (Norman: University of Oklahoma Press, 1994), 5–6, 131–40.

86. AGI, Guatemala 410, Consulta secular, May 21, 1779.

87. AGI, Guatemala 557, Expediente 19, Obispo de Comayagua al Rey, November 28, 1774.

88. AGI, Guatemala 558, Audiencia al Rey, April 30, 1776.

89. AGI, Guatemala 553, Expediente 18, Testimonio (1771); Guatemala 554, Expediente 12, Audiencia al Rey, October 31, 1772; AGI, Guatemala 410, Consulta, May 31, 1779.

90. AGI, Guatemala 554, Expediente 10, Audiencia al Rey, October 31, 1772.

91. AGI, Guatemala 443, Títulos de la Alcaldía Mayor de San Salvador, March 21, 1781.

92. Patch, *Maya and Spaniard in Yucatan*, 218–20.

93. AGI, Guatemala 712, Correspondencia del Presidente, no. 226, Informe del Presidente al Despacho Universal de Hacienda, March 3, 1803; no. 230, Informe del Presidente al Despacho Universal de Hacienda, March 3, 1803; no. 288, Informe del Presidente al Despacho Universal de Hacienda, June 3, 1803; no. 311, Oficio del Presidente al Despacho Universal de Hacienda, August 3, 1803; Guatemala 717, Correspondencia del Presidente, no. 608, Informe del Presidente al Despacho Universal de Hacienda, February 3, 1805; no. 613, January 3, 1805.

94. AGI, Guatemala 562, Expediente 9, Arzobispo al Rey, September 10, 1777; Guatemala 559, Expediente 4, Informe del Fiscal del Consejo, March 31, 1778.

95. AGI, Guatemala 561, Expediente 10, Arzobispo al Rey, July 5, 1778; Guatemala 562, Expediente 8, Presidente al Rey, July 6, 1779.

2. Government Officials and the Colonial State

1. Troy S. Floyd, *The Anglo-Spanish Struggle for Mosquitia* (Albuquerque: University of New Mexico Press, 1967), 31.

NOTES TO PAGES 43–50

2. In this book I use the term "magistrate" to refer to corregidores, alcaldes mayores, and gobernadores because all of those officials carried out the duties of a magistrate. For an overview of the bureaucratic structure of colonial Central America, see Carlos Molina Argüello, "Gobernaciones, alcaldías mayores y corregimientos en el reino de Guatemala," *Anuario de Estudios Americanos* 17 (1950): 105–32.

3. For an introduction to the nature of Spanish government in the provinces, see Woodrow Borah, ed., *El gobierno provincial en la Nueva España* (Mexico City: Universidad Nacional Autónoma de México, Instituto de Investigaciones Históricas, 1985).

4. AGI, Guatemala 690, Summation of report by Governor-Intendant of San Salvador, July 28, 1786; Pedro José Pérez de Luque al Secretario de Indias, August 23, 1786; Título de D. Diego Piloña y Ayala, August 18, 1786; Título de D. Josef Mariano Valero, February 1, 1787.

5. Héctor Humberto Samayoa Guevara, *Implantación del régimen de intendencias en el reino de Guatemala* (Guatemala: Editorial del Ministerio de Educación Pública "José de Pineda Ibarra," 1960), 62–66.

6. British Library, Ms. Additional 17583, Consulta del Consejo, September 23, 1760, fol. 226.

7. The coins in circulation in Spain in the seventeenth and eighteenth century included doubloons, ducats, escudos, reales, maravedís, and pesos. In America, only pesos and reales were in use. Official rates of exchange existed, but these changed over time and were not always in effect on both sides of the Atlantic at once. However, practically everything could be converted into pesos, which served both as currency and as money of account. I have converted all currency to pesos of account as follows:

1 doubloon = 4 pesos
1 ducat = 1.2 pesos
1 escudo = 1 peso
1 peso = 450 maravedís
1 peso = 8 silver reales
1 peso = 15 copper reales

8. See J. H. Parry, *The Sale of Public Office in the Spanish Indies under the Hapsburgs* (Berkeley: University of California Press, 1953).

9. Fernando Muro Romero, "El 'beneficio' de oficios públicos con jurisdicción en Indias: Notas sobre sus orígenes," *Anuario de Estudios Americanos* 35 (1978): 2–6; Angel Sanz Tapia, "Provisión y beneficio de cargos políticos en Hispanoamérica (1674–1700)," *Jahrbuch für Geschichte Lateinamerikas* 37 (2000): 25–26.

10. Sanz Tapia, "Provisión y beneficio de cargos políticos," 43.

11. AGI, Guatemala 274, Provisión de la Presidencia, January 11, 1711.

12. Ibid., July 13, 1733.

13. AGI, Guatemala 274, Provisiones, March 9, 1709; Oficios del Consejo de Indias, December 3, 1709, and December 13, 1709.

14. AGI, Guatemala 274, Provisiones de Oidores, April 7, 1710.

15. Ibid., April 25, 1710.

16. Ibid., May 9, 1710.

17. Ibid., August 20, 1711.

18. Ibid., August 22, 1711.

19. Ibid., July 7, 1740.

20. Ibid., April 27, 1722; August 22, 1723; April 20, 1735; September 18, 1741.

21. AGI, Guatemala 274, Provisiones de Oidores, August 27, 1745.

22. AGI, Escribanía de Cámara 362A–B.

23. AGI, Escribanía de Cámara 354A, Residencia del Presidente Francisco Rodríguez de Rivas, Segunda pieza, 1724; Guatemala 641, Tomás de Arana al Rey, December 31, 1761. This Arana was the son of the above-mentioned oidor Tomás de Arana.

24. AGI, Escribanía de Cámara 359A, Residencia del Presidente Tomás de Rivera y Santa Cruz, Cuadernos 1–4, 1747; Escribanía de Cámara 359B, Cuadernos 7–8, 1748; Escribanía de Cámara 359C, Cuadernos 9–10, 1748.

25. British Library, Ms. Additional 17583, Informe del Presidente (Pedro de Rivera) al Señor Marqués de Torre Nueva, January 2, 1738, fols. 222–26.

26. Angel Sanz Tapia, "Aproximación al beneficio de cargos políticos americanos en la primera mitad del siglo XVIII," *Revista Complutense de Historia de América*, no. 24 (1998): 155.

27. AGI, Guatemala 274, Provisiones, March 9, 1709, Oficios del Consejo de Indias, December 3, 1709, and December 13, 1709.

28. Luis Navarro García, "Los oficios vendibles en Nueva España durante la Guerra de Sucesión," *Anuario de Estudios Americanos* 32 (1975): 133–54.

29. Jeffrey A. Cole, *The Potosí Mita, 1573–1700: Compulsory Indian Labor in the Andes* (Stanford: Stanford University Press, 1985); Webre, "El trabajo forzoso de los indígenas."

30. AGI, Guatemala 278, Provisiones de empleos de la Real Hacienda, Contaduría de la Caja, 1696–1743; Tesorería de la Caxa, 1618–1751.

31. AGI, Guatemala 278, Provisiones de empleos de la Real Hacienda, Contaduría de Nicaragua, 1687–1744; Tesorería de Nicaragua, 1647–1757.

32. AGI, Guatemala 278, Provisiones de empleos de la Real Hacienda, Contaduría de Honduras, 1715–35; Tesorería de Honduras, 1694–1735; Tesorería de Costa Rica, 1618.

33. AGI, Guatemala 567, Expediente 8, Fiscal de lo Civil al Rey, May 6, 1782.

34. AGI, Guatemala 278, Provisiones de empleos de la Real Hacienda, Oficial Real de Sonsonate, 1751–54.

35. AGI, Guatemala 276, Provisiones de Corregimientos, Sutiaba, July 25, 1693; AGI, Guatemala 278, Provisiones de Empleos de la Real Hacienda, Contaduría de la Caja, 1696.

36. AGI, Guatemala 442, Título de la Alcaldía Mayor de Huehuetenango-Totonicapán, July 10, 1711; Guatemala 277, Provisión de la Alcaldía Mayor de

Verapaz, August 25, 1713; AGI, Guatemala 277, Provisiones de la Alcaldía Mayor de Atitlán, October 16, 1713.

37. AGI, Guatemala 277, Provisión de la Alcaldía Mayor de Huehuetenango-Totonicapán, February 2, 1706.

38. Sanz Tapia, "Aproximación al beneficio de cargos políticos," 165–66, 168.

39. Chiapa consisted of what are now the highlands and northern lowlands of the modern-day Mexican state of Chiapas. In 1770 the alcaldía mayor was divided in two to create a new province; the two high magistracies were then known as Chiapa and Tuxtla. In 1786 these two alcaldías mayores and the province of Soconusco on the Pacific coast were united into an intendancy, which then became known as Chiapas.

40. Sanz Tapia, "Aproximación al beneficio de cargos políticos," 168.

41. AGI, Guatemala 440, Título de la Gobernación de Soconusco, June 18, 1677.

42. Ibid., May 15, 1682.

43. AGI, Guatemala 442, Título de la Alcaldía Mayor de Chiapa, April 22, 1682.

44. AGI, Guatemala 443, Título de la Alcaldía Mayor de Suchitepéquez, May 11, 1683; and Título de la Alcaldía Mayor de Verapaz, May 6, 1683.

45. AGI, Guatemala 442, Título de la Alcaldía Mayor de Chiapa, December 19, 1685.

46. AGI, Escribanía de Cámara 358C, Residencia de Francisco López Marchán, Alcalde Mayor [Corregidor] de Quezaltenango, 1745.

47. AGI, Guatemala 440, Título de la Gobernación de Honduras, November 6, 1686.

48. AGI, Guatemala 275, Provisión del Gobierno de Soconusco, May 11, 1692.

49. AGI, Guatemala 277, Provisión de la Alcaldía Mayor de Atitlán-Tecpanatitlán, October 5, 1703.

50. AGI, Guatemala 442, Título de la Alcaldía Mayor [Corregimiento] de Nicoya, October 20, 1680.

51. AGI, Guatemala 443, Título de la Alcaldía Mayor de San Salvador, June 25, 1761, and May 26, 1769.

52. For example, Bernabé de la Torre Trassierra was removed from office as the alcalde mayor of San Salvador after coming into conflict with the city council of San Salvador and the town councils of San Vicente and San Miguel. See AGI, Guatemala 595, Expediente diario del apoderado de Bernabé de la Torre Trassierra, 1768. Captain Joseph Ventura Manso de Velasco was blamed for provoking an Indian rebellion and was removed as alcalde mayor of Atitlán-Tecpanatitlán in 1762. See AGI, Guatemala 641, Joseph Ventura Manso de Velasco al Rey, September 25, 1762.

53. AGI, Guatemala 750, Expediente 1, Audiencia al Rey, July 24, 1766.

54. AGI, Guatemala 441, Título del Corregimiento de Quezaltenango, November 2, 1689.

55. AGI, Escribanía de Cámara 356A, Residencia de Joseph Damián Fernández de Córdoba, Gobernador de Soconusco, Cuadernos 1–2 (1720).

56. AGI, Guatemala 440, Título de la Governación de Nicaragua, April 20, 1711, and July 4, 1715.

57. AGI, Guatemala 277, Provisión de la Alcaldía Mayor de San Salvador, April 3, 1707.

58. AGI, Guatemala 277, Provisión de la Alcaldía Mayor de Tegucigalpa, October 29, 1708.

59. AGI, Guatemala 276, Provisión del Corregimiento de Quezaltenango, May 20, 1713.

60. AGI, Escribanía de Cámara 357A, Residencia de Pedro de Echevers, Alcalde Mayor de San Salvador, 1730.

61. AGI, Escribanía de Cámara 358C, Residencia de Manuel Lacunza, Alcalde Mayor de Suchitepéquez, 1748.

62. AGI, Guatemala 276, Provisión del Corregimiento de Sutiava, January 31, 1735.

63. Moreno Cebrián, *El corregidor de indios*, 99–104.

64. AGI, Escribanía de Cámara 358C, Residencia de Manuel de Lacunza, Alcalde Mayor de Suchitepéquez, 1748.

65. AGI, Escribanía de Cámara 358C, Residencia de Manuel Antonio de Lazalde, Alcalde Mayor de Suchitepéquez, 1749.

66. AHN, Consejos 20977, Residencia de Isidro Díaz de Vívar, Alcalde Mayor de San Salvador, 1753.

67. AGI, Guatemala 277, Provisión de la Alcaldía Mayor de San Salvador, September 17, 1746, and August 12, 1750; Guatemala 595, Expediente diario del apoderado de Don Bernabé de la Torre Trassierra, 1768.

68. AGI, Guatemala 440, Título de la Gobernación de Soconusco, June 16, 1688.

69. Guatemala 277, Provisión de la Alcaldía Mayor de Tegucigalpa, October 29, 1708; and Provisión de la Alcaldía Mayor de Escuintla-Guazacapán, August 27, 1709.

70. AGI, Guatemala 276, Provisión del Corregimiento de Quezaltenango, May 20, 1713.

71. Guatemala 440, Título de la Gobernación de Soconusco, November 16, 1716.

72. Guatemala 276, Provisión del Corregimiento de Quezaltenango, January 13, 1716.

73. Guatemala 277, Provisión de la Alcaldía Mayor de Suchitepéquez, April 23, 1717.

74. Guatemala 277, Provisión de la Alcaldía Mayor de Verapaz, November 28, 1702; July 4, 1712, and August 25, 1713; AGI, Guatemala 443, Título de Alcalde Mayor de Verapaz, November 8, 1694, and June 22, 1718.

75. Guatemala 275, Provisiones de la Gobernación de Soconusco; Guatemala 276, Provisiones del Corregimiento de Quezaltenango; Guatemala 277, Provisiones de la Alcaldía Mayor de Suchitepéquez; Alcaldía Mayor de Verapaz; Alcaldía Mayor de Tegucigalpa; Alcaldía Mayor de Sonsonate; and Alcaldía Mayor de Chiapa; Guatemala 440, Títulos de la Gobernación de Soconusco; and

Corregimiento de Quezaltenango; Guatemala 442, Títulos de la Alcaldía Mayor de Chiapa; Guatemala 443, Títulos de la Alcaldía Mayor de Suchitepéquez; Alcaldía Mayor de Verapaz; Alcaldía Mayor de Tegucigalpa; and Alcaldía Mayor de Sonsonate.

76. Benedict Anderson, *Imagined Communities: Reflections on the Origin and Spread of Nationalism* (London: Verso, 1983; rev. ed., New York: Verso, 1991), 52–65, 114.

77. AGI, Guatemala 276, Provisiones de corregimientos, Quezaltenango, January 13, 1716.

78. Ibid., May 31, 1724.

79. AGI, Guatemala 276, Provisiones de corregimientos, Realejo, July 30, 1746, May 20, 1748, and April 8, 1756.

80. AGI, Guatemala 277, Provisiones de alcaldías mayores, Verapaz, November 28, 1702.

81. Ibid., February 7, 1755.

82. AGI, Guatemala 277, Provisiones de alcaldías mayors, Suchitepéquez, November 8, 1703.

83. Ibid., February 25, 1722.

84. Ibid., November 20, 1742.

85. For just two good examples of many, see AGI, Guatemala 277, Provisión de la Alcaldía Mayor de San Antonio Suchitepéquez, March 5, 1728; Guatemala 443, Título de la Alcaldía Mayor de Sonsonate, June 17, 1699.

86. Pablo E. Pérez-Mallaína, *Spain's Men of the Sea: Daily Life on the Indies Fleet in the Sixteenth Century* (Baltimore, Md.: Johns Hopkins University Press, 1998), 30–33.

87. Information derived from sources cited in note 75.

88. AGI, Guatemala 440, Título de la gobernación de Soconusco, June 16, 1688; Guatemala 442, Título de la alcaldía mayor de Chiapa, October 17, 1731; Guatemala 440, Título de la gobernación de Soconusco, September 9, 1771; Guatemala 441, Título de la alcaldía mayor de Chimaltenango, March 2, 1774.

89. Gerhard Masur, *Simon Bolívar* (Albuquerque: University of New Mexico Press, 1948), 678.

90. AGI, Guatemala 441, Títulos y Provisiones, Chiquimula de la Sierra, Consulta, July 30, 1800, and Consulta, October 22, 1806.

91. Susan Socolow, *The Bureaucrats of Buenos Aires, 1769–1810: Amor al real servicio* (Durham, N.C.: Duke University Press, 1987), 130–36.

92. Patch, *Maya Revolt and Revolution*, 43–47.

93. AGI, Escribanía de Cámara 358C, Residencia de Joseph González de Rancaño y Rivera, 1744.

94. AGI, Guatemala 596, Expediente diario 2, 1769.

95. AGI, Guatemala 441, Título del corregimiento de Chiquimula de la Sierra, Consulta, March 17, 1769.

96. Ibid., October 19, 1763.

97. For the Spanish empire as a whole, for the years between 1674 and 1700—when the sale of these offices was in full swing—65.5 percent of positions were given to people who had provided money or something of value to the crown in return for a post, while only 25.9 percent went to people who had nothing but merit or past service to support their requests. Sanz Tapia, "Provisión y beneficio de cargos políticos," 37.

98. Gustavo Palma Murga, "Núcleos de poder local y relaciones familiares en la ciudad de Guatemala a fines del siglo XVIII," *Mesoamérica* 12 (December 1986): 241–308.

3. Indians and the Colonial State

1. For contemporary information concerning the land, people, and economy of seventeenth-century Guatemala, see Francisco Antonio Fuentes y Guzmán, *Recordación florida. Discurso natural, material, militar y político del Reino de Goathemala*, 3 vols. (Madrid: Biblioteca de Autores Españoles, Ediciones Atlas, 1969) completed in the year 1690; and Pedro Cortés y Larraz, *Descripción geográfico-moral de la Diócesis de Goathemala*, 2 vols. (Guatemala: Biblioteca "Goathemala" de la Sociedad de Geografía e Historia de Guatemala, 1958) written in the 1760s. Useful for interpreting Cortés y Larraz is Francisco de Solano, *Los mayas del siglo XVIII: Pervivencia y transformación de la sociedad indígena guatemalteca* (Madrid: Ediciones Cultura Hispánica, 1974). Data regarding the number of villages and tributaries in 1746 are derived from AGI, Escribanía de Cámara 361A, Quaderno 2, Testimonio de la Cuenta y Liquidación de todas las entradas y salidas de la Real Caja de esta Corthe (1746). Detailed information on the economic activities of the magistrates in 1765–66 is found in AGI, Guatemala 607, Testimonio de los Autos instruidos a concecüencia de Real Cédula, dada en San Lorenzo a 16 de octubre de 1769 para que con la justificación devida, sobre los dos medios propuestos de beneficio de Alcaldías, 1780. Hereinafter this document will be cited as Guatemala 607, Testimonio de Autos instruidos, 1780. For a brief overview of repartimientos in Guatemala, Chiapas, and El Salvador, see Solórzano Fonseca, "Las comunidades indígenas de Guatemala," 111–15.

2. Details of the commercial activities of the alcaldes mayores of Chiapa are found in AGI, Guatemala 363, Obispo de Ciudad Real al Rey, April 4, 1716, and November 8, 1717; AGI, Escribanía de Cámara 360B, Pieza 50, Testimonio de las Diligencias remitidas por Don Antonio Zuazúa Alcalde Mayor de Chiapa, 1744; and Pieza 54, Testimonio de Autos seguidos contra Don Juan Baptista Garrazín, Alcalde Mayor de la Probincia de Ciudad Real de Chiapa y sus fiadores, 1750; AGI, Guatemala 607, Testimonio de Autos instruidos, 1780, fols. 132–37. For an interpretation of the business activities of the alcaldes mayores that is completely different from mine, see Robert Wasserstrom, *Class and Society in Central Chiapas* (Berkeley and Los Angeles: University of California Press, 1983), 35–37;

see also Brooke Larson and Robert Wasserstrom, "Consumo forzoso en Cocha-bamba y Chiapa durante la época colonial," *Historia Mexicana* 31, no. 3, issue 123 (1982): 383–408. For another look at the repartimiento from a cultural point of view, see Mario Humberto Ruz, *Gestos cotidianos: Acercamientos etnológicos a los mayas de la época colonial* (Campeche, Mexico: Gobierno del Estado de Campeche, Universidad Autónoma del Carmen, Universidad Autónoma de Campeche, Instituto Campechano, and Instituto de Cultura de Campeche, 1997), 151–78.

3. Historical demography of Central America is still a largely unexplored topic, and consequently factors for converting tributaries to total population have yet to be developed in a systematic way. In this essay for pre-1750 data I shall employ a rough conversion factor of 4.0, which is that suggested by the late seventeenth-century writer Fuentes y Guzmán in *Recordación florida*, 3:15–18, 22–44, and is utilized by twentieth-century demographic historians. Changes in the tributary system in 1754 exempted women from tribute, and thus conver-sion factors of between 4.5 and 4.7 should be used for data from the second half of the eighteenth century. I will use 4.6 in order not to assume the highest or the lowest number. For a pioneering effort in the field of Central American demographic history, see Carmack, Early, and Lutz, eds., *Historical Demography of Highland Guatemala*.

4. See Hamnett, *Politics and Trade*, 5–23.

5. S. Stein, "Francisco Ignacio de Yraeta," 486–88.

6. Salvucci, *Textiles and Capitalism in Mexico*.

7. British Library, Ms. Additional 17,583, Report by President Pedro de Rivera to the Señor Marqués de Torre Nueva, January 2, 1738, fols. 222–26. All subse-quent references to the report of 1738 refer to this document.

8. AGI, 607, Testimonio de Autos instruidos, 1780, fols. 132–37.

9. What follows is derived from AGI, Escribanía de Cámara 356A, Residen-cia de Joseph Damián Fernández de Córdoba, Gobernador de Soconusco, 1720, Cuadernos 1–2; Guatemala 236, Fiscal de la Audiencia al Rey, December 17, 1747; and Testimonio de las diligencias practicadas por el Sr. Fiscal para Ynfor-marse de la denumpcia, 1747.

10. M. MacLeod, *Spanish Central America*, 68–79.

11. For what follows, see AGI, Escribanía de Cámara 356A, Residencia de Juan Rodríguez de la Gala, Alcalde Mayor [Corregidor] de Quezaltenango, 1724 and 1725; Guatemala 607, Testimonio de Autos instruidos, 1780, fols. 104–18. For a historical study of Quezaltenango, Atitlán, and Suchitepéquez provinces, see Elías Zamora Acosta, *Los mayas de las tierras altas en el siglo XVI* (Seville: Diputación Provincial, 1985).

12. AGI, Escribanía de Cámara 362B, Residencia de Francisco Antonio de Granda y de Nicolás Mencos, Alcaldes Mayores de Huehuetenango-Totonicapán, 1749; Guatemala 603, Expediente diario 1, Testimonio de la Instancia de Don Juan de Bacaro, Alcalde Mayor de Gueguetenango, 1773; Guatemala 599, Expediente

diario 1, de Juan Bacaro, 1775; AGI, Guatemala 607, Testimonio de Autos instruidos, 1780, fols. 80–93. For the historical geography of part of Huehue-tenango-Totonicapán, see W. George Lovell, *Conquest and Survival in Colonial Guatemala: A Historical Geography of the Cuchumatán Highlands, 1500–1821* (Kingston and Montreal: McGill-Queen's University Press, 1985).

13. AGI, Escribanía de Cámara 351A, Residencia de Cristóbal Ortiz de Letona, Alcalde Mayor de Atitlán-Tecpanatitlán, 1694; Guatemala 641, Testimonio de la real Cédula y demás diligencias prácticas en el Pueblo de Santa Catharina Istaguacam de la Jurisdicción de Sololá, sobre repartimientos, 1746; Guatemala 607, Testimonio de Autos instruidos, 1780, fols. 9–21. For a study of part of Atitlán-Tecpanatitlán, see Sandra L. Orellana, *The Tzutujil Mayas: Continuity and Change, 1250–1630* (Norman: University of Oklahoma Press, 1984).

14. AGI, Guatemala 441, Título del Corregidor de Chiquimula, Consulta, March 17, 1769.

15. AGI, Guatemala 340, Informe del Consejo al Rey, March 1756; AHN, 20950, 1768, fols. 1–21; AHN, 20952, Residencia de Alonso Fernández de Heredia, Presidente, Pieza 56, 1769.

16. Nicole Percheron, "Producción agrícola y comercio de la Verapaz en la época colonial," *Mesoamérica* 20 (December 1990): 243–45.

17. AGI, Escribanía de Cámara 358A, Residencia de Manuel de Barrueta, Alcalde Mayor de Verapaz, 1738–39; Escribanía de Cámara 362B, Residencia de Ignacio Buenvecino, Alcalde Mayor de Verapaz, 1753 [in fact 1756 or 1757]; Guatemala 607, Testimonio de Autos instruidos, 1780, fols. 30–41.

18. Nahua was the language of many Indians of central Mexico. A variation of this language, introduced somewhat later in history, was Náhuatl, spoken by the Mexicas (Aztecs), from whom the name Mexico is derived. Various groups in the Kingdom of Guatemala were the descendants of people of Mexican Indian origin who had been migrating into Central American since the ninth or tenth centuries. They were called "Mexican" in colonial documents, but they were not of Mexica origin.

19. Percheron, "Producción agrícola y comercio de la Verapaz," 243–45.

20. Chiquimula de la Sierra included a section called Acasaguastlán until the middle of the eighteenth century, and then another section called Zacapa. The following discussion is based on AGI, Escribanía de Cámara 358C, Residencia de Joseph González Rancaño, Corregidor de Chiquimula, 1744; Guatemala 596, Expediente diario 2, 1769; Guatemala 607, Testimonio de Autos instruidos, 1780, fols. 150–58.

21. AGI, Escribanía de Cámara 358C, Residencia de Manuel de Lacunza, Alcalde Mayor de Suchitepéquez, 1748; Guatemala 552, Expediente 14, Testimonio de la Sumaria instruida en virtud de Real Orden de su M[ajestad] sobre los proze-dimientos del Alcalde Mayor de la Provincia de San Antonio Suchitepéquez, 1770; Guatemala 607, Testimonio de Autos instruidos, 1780, fols. 118–28.

22. AGI, Guatemala 641, Sumario hecho en el Consejo de Indias, April 24, 1764.

23. AGI, Guatemala 607, Testimonio de Autos instruidos, 1780, fols. 93–104.

24. AGI, Escribanía de Cámara 357B, Residencia de Francisco Carranza y Menán, Alcalde Mayor de Sonsonate, 1734; Guatemala 607, Testimonio de Autos instruidos, 1780, fols. 21–29. For the historical geography of El Salvador, see David Browning, *El Salvador: Landscape and Society* (Oxford: Clarendon Press, 1971). For the late Post-Classic-period society and population of the Nahua people of Sonsonate, San Salvador, and Nicaragua, see William R. Fowler, *The Cultural Evolution of Ancient Nahua Civilizations: The Pipil-Nicarao of Central America* (Norman: University of Oklahoma Press, 1989).

25. AGI, Guatemala 607, Testimonio de Autos instruidos, 1780, fols. 41–61; AGI, Guatemala 547, Audiencia al Rey, October 10, 1768, and October 30, 1768.

26. AGI, Escribanía de Cámara 352A–C, Residencia de Enrique Logman, Gobernador de Honduras, 1716–17. For an analysis of Honduras in the colonial period, see Newson, *Cost of Conquest*.

27. For a critical view of the concept of Mesoamerica, see Winifred Creamer, "Mesoamerica as a Concept: An Archaeological View from Central America," *Latin American Research Review* 22, no. 1 (1987): 35–55.

28. For a discussion of the socioeconomic factors involved in the survival of native people in America, see Linda Newson, "Indian Population Patterns in Colonial Spanish America," *Latin American Research Review* 20, no. 3 (1985): 41–74. For a discussion of the people of Mosquitia in Nicaragua, see Flor de Oro Solórzano, "La colonización inglesa de la Costa Caribe de Nicaragua, 1633–1787," in *Persistencia indígena en Nicaragua*, ed. Germán Romero Vargas et al. (Managua: CIDCA-UCA, 1992), 33–58.

29. Derived from Newson, *Cost of Conquest*, 296–303. Newson uses a conversion factor of 4.7 to convert tributaries to total Indian population.

30. Frank Griffith Dawson, "William Pitt's Settlement at Black River on the Mosquito Shore: A Challenge to Spain in Central America, 1732–87," *Hispanic American Historical Review* 63, no. 4 (November 1983): 677–706; Barbara Potthast-Jutkeit, "Centroamérica y el contrabando por la Costa de Mosquitos en el siglo XVIII," *Mesoamérica* 36 (December 1998): 499–516.

31. Adam Szaszdi de Nagy, "El comercio ilícito en la provincia de Honduras," *Revista de Indias* 17, no. 68 (April–June 1957): 271–83.

32. AGI, Guatemala 561, Expediente 13, de Juan Ignacio Garzón, 1778; Guatemala 607, Testimonio de Autos instruidos, 1780, fols. 61–80.

33. Troy S. Floyd, "Bourbon Palliatives and the Central American Mining Industry, 1765–1800," *The Americas* 18 (October 1962): 105–106.

34. AGI, Guatemala 550, Cartas y Expedientes 26, Representación del Administrador de Alcabalas de Guatemala al Secretario de Indias (Julián de Arriaga), September 30, 1769.

35. Ibid., fols. 138–39, 148–50. A useful aid for the study of all of the provinces of colonial Nicaragua is Newson, *Indian Survival in Colonial Nicaragua*. See also Fowler, *Cultural Evolution of Ancient Nahua Civilizations*.

36. AGI, Escribanía de Cámara 363, Residencia de Fernando Martínez Pisón, Corregidor de Subtiaba, 1759; Guatemala 558, Expediente 7, 1772–78; Guatemala 607, Testimonio de Autos instruidos, 1780, fols. 141–45. See also Marcos Membreño Idiáquez, "Persistencia étnica en Sutiava y Monimbo," in *Persistencia indígena en Nicaragua*, ed. Germán Romero Vargas et al. (Managua: CIDCA-UCA, 1992), 106–43.

37. AGI, Guatemala 558, Expediente 7, 1772–78; Guatemala 607, Testimonio de Autos instruidos, 1780, fols. 139–41, 145–47; Guatemala 715, Informe 421 del Presidente al Despacho Universal de Hacienda, February 3, 1804.

38. AGI, Escribanía de Cámara 357B, Residencia de Bartolomé González Fitoria, Gobernador de Nicaragua, 1736; Guatemala 545, Alcalde Mayor Provisto de Tegucigalpa al Rey, July 1, 1767; Guatemala 553, Expediente 1, 1770; Guatemala 572, Expediente 20, 1785; AHN, Consejos 20978, Residencia de José Estachería, 1786; AHN, Consejos 20980, Residencia de José de Estachería, 1786–90; AGI, Guatemala 577, Expediente 1, 1790; Guatemala 715, Informe 421 del Presidente al Despacho Universal de Hacienda, February 3, 1804. See also Newson, *Indian Survival in Colonial Nicaragua*; Romero Vargas and Solórzano, "Las poblaciones indígenas de Nicaragua, 1492–1821," 11–30; Membreño Idiáquez, "Persistencia étnica en Sutiava y Monimbo," 106–43.

39. AGI, Guatemala 607, Testimonio de Autos instruidos, 1780, fols. 137–38, 147–48. See also Meritxell Tous Mata, *De protagonistas a desaparecidos: Las sociedades indígenas de la Gran Nicoya, siglos XIV a XVII* (Managua: Lea Grupo Editorial, 2008).

40. AGI, Escribanía de Cámara 351C, Residencia de Lorenzo Antonio de la Granda y Balbín, Gobernador de Costa Rica, 1714; Escribanía de Cámara 353B, Residencia de Joseph Lacayo de Briones, Gobernador de Costa Rica, 1719; Escribanía de Cámara 358A, Residencia de Baltazar Francisco de Balderrama, Gobernador de Costa Rica, 1737.

41. Fernández, Schmidt, and Basauri, "La población de Costa Rica," 226, cited in María de los Ángeles Acuña León and Doriam Chavarría López, "Cartago colonial: Mestizaje y patrones matrimoniales 1738–1821," *Mesoamérica* 31 (June 1996): 163.

42. Acuña León and Chavarría López, "Cartago colonial," 163.

43. Santos Pérez, "Los comerciantes de Guatemala," 463–84.

44. The business accounts of one alcalde mayor and his merchant partner in Santiago are found in AGI, Guatemala 603, Expediente diario 1, Testimonio de la Instancia de Don Juan Bacaro Alcalde Mayor de Gueguetenango, 1773. In this case, the merchant received goods from the Alcalde Mayor of Huehuetenango-Totonicapán, shipped them for sale to San Salvador, received indigo in return, exported indigo to Peru and Spain, and invested in Cádiz in a slave-trading company doing business in Africa. The case is analyzed in detail in chapter 4.

45. For the extent of the forced labor draft in highland Bolivia, see Enrique Tandeter, "Forced and Free Labor in Late Colonial Potosí," *Past and Present*, no. 92 (November 1981): 98–136.

46. A similar situation existed in Yucatan, where the Yucatec Mayas survived during the colonial period despite subjection to the repartimiento system and incorporation into the world economy. See Patch, *Maya and Spaniard in Yucatan*. For an interpretation of the survival of Maya culture in Yucatan that is somewhat the opposite of mine, see Farriss, *Maya Society under Colonial Rule*.

47. AGI, Indiferente 1713, Informe no. 195, del Visitador General del Perú al Secretario de Indias (José de Gálvez), Lima, May 16, 1780.

48. AGI, Guatemala 607, Expediente diario 14, Representación del Contador de Cuentas de Guatemala al Secretario de Indias, October 20, 1764; Audiencia al Rey, April 20,1780; Informe de la Contaduría, October 31, 1781.

49. AGI, Guatemala 601, Expediente diario 9, Plan remitido por la Audiencia de Guatemala sobre la rebaxa que debe hacerse de sus salarios a los Corregidores y Alcaldes Mayores de aquel Distrito, March 22, 1777.

50. AGI, Guatemala 601, Expediente diario 9, Informe de la Contaduría, Madrid, October 24, 1777.

51. Pérez-Mallaína, *Spain's Men of the Sea*, 112–14.

52. AGI, Guatemala 601, Expediente diario 9, Respuesta del Sr. Fiscal del Consejo, August 14, 1778; Informe del Oidor Juan González Bustillo, September 14, 1778; Consulta del Consejo, October 17, 1778; Guatemala 558, Informe del Fiscal del Consejo, February 19, 1778.

4. The Business of Politics and the Politics of Business in the Highlands

1. The lawsuit is found in AGI, Guatemala 603, Expediente diario 1, Testimonio de la instancia de Don Juan Bacaro Alcalde Mayor de Gueguetenango sobre remover las existencias de la compañía de gananciales que ha tenido con Don Juan de Montes de Oca, and accompanying documents, 1773. Unless otherwise noted, all folio citations in this chapter are from this testimony, hereinafter cited as AGI, Guatemala 603, Testimonio.

2. See Susan Migden Socolow, *The Merchants of Buenos Aires, 1770–1810: Family and Commerce* (Cambridge: Cambridge University Press, 1978); John Kicza, *Colonial Entrepreneurs: Families and Business in Bourbon Mexico City* (Albuquerque: University of New Mexico Press, 1983); Christiana Renate Borchart de Moreno, *Los mercaderes y el capitalismo en la ciudad de México, 1759–1778* (Mexico City: Fondo de Cultura Económica, 1984); María Cristina Torales Pacheco, Tarsicio García Díaz, and Carmen Yuste, *La compañía de comercio de Francisco Ignacio de Yraeta, 1767–1797: Cinco ensayos* (Mexico: Instituto Mexicano de Comercio Exterior, 1985); Carmen Yuste, "Francisco Ignacio de Yraeta y el comercio transpacífico," *Estudios de Historia Novohispana* 9 (1987): 189–217; Pedro Pérez Herrero, *Plata y libranzas: La articulación commercial del México borbónico* (Mexico: El Colegio de México, 1988); Louisa Schell Hoberman, *Mexico's Merchant Elite, 1590–1660: Silver, State, and Society* (Durham, N.C.: Duke University Press, 1991). For commerce in general,

see Antonio García-Baquero González, *Cádiz y el Atlántico (1717–1778)* (Seville: Escuela de Estudios Hispano-Americanos, 1976); Geoffrey J. Walker, *Spanish Politics and Imperial Trade, 1700–1789* (Bloomington: Indiana University Press, 1979); Lutgardo García Fuentes, *El comercio español con América, 1650–1700* (Seville: Excelentísima Diputación Provincial de Sevilla, 1982).

3. Stanley J. Stein, "Tending the Store: Trade and Silver at the Real de Huautla, 1778–1781," *Hispanic American Historical Review* 77, no. 3 (August 1997): 377–407.

4. AGI, Guatemala 599, Expediente diario 1 de Juan Bacaro (1775), Carta M.

5. AGI, Guatemala 603, Testimonio, fols. 6–9.

6. AGI, Guatemala 599, Expediente diario 1 (1775), Informe de Juan Bacaro, n.d., acted upon by the Consejo de Indias on July 31, 1775.

7. See Patch, "Imperial Politics and Local Economy"; AGI, Guatemala 277, Provisiones de Alcaldes Mayores, Huehuetenango-Totonicapán, July 13, 1750.

8. Sanz Tapia, "Aproximación al beneficio de cargos políticos," 165–66, 168.

9. AGI, Guatemala 603, Testimonio, fols. 11, 25–27, 57, 72.

10. Ibid., fols. 14–15, 17–18, 36, 39.

11. Ibid., fols. 98–99.

12. Ibid., fols. 34, 36. For information on the cotton repartimiento in the coastal province of San Antonio Suchitepéquez, see AGI, Escribanía de Cámara 358C, Residencia de Manuel Lacunza, Alcalde Mayor de Suchitepeques, 1748; see also AHN, Consejos 20950, Residencia del Presidente Alonso Fernández de Heredia, fols. 1–21 (1768); and Consejos 20952, Pieza 56 (1769). For shipments of raw cotton from Nicaragua to Guatemala through the port of Acajutla into the early nineteenth century, see AGI, Guatemala 715, no. 421, Oficio del Presidente al Secretario de Hacienda, February 3, 1804.

13. AGI, Guatemala 603, Testimonio, fols. 80–84.

14. Ibid., fols. 80–82, 147–51.

15. Ibid., fols. 5, 11, 101.

16. AGI, Guatemala 554, Expediente 10 (1772).

17. AGI, Guatemala 603, Testimonio, fols. 139, 142–44.

18. Ibid., fols. 10–11, 97, 103, 144–45, 271.

19. Ibid., fols. 5, 27–30.

20. Ibid., fol. 97.

21. For shipments of thread and textiles from the highlands to Honduras-Tegucigalpa, see AGI, Guatemala 561, Expediente 13, de Juan Ignacio Garzón, 1778; Guatemala 607, Testimonio de los Autos instruidos a concecüencia de Real Cédula, dada en San Lorenzo a 16 de octubre de 1769 para que con la justificación devida, sobre los dos medios propuestos de beneficio de Alcaldías, 1780, fols. 61–80. For the alcalde mayor's control of cloth imports into San Salvador, see fols. 21–29 in the same source. The specialization in indigo in San Salvador caused the cotton textile industry there virtually to disappear. See AGI, Guatemala 690, Informe del Gobernador-Intendente de San Salvador, July 28, 1786. For the study of a merchant-priest who imported cotton goods for sale in the San

Vicente area of San Salvador, see Patch, "Cura y empresario," 47–67. For imports from China into San Salvador, see AGI, Guatemala 555, Diputación de Comercio al Rey, October 1, 1772; Testimonio del expediente instruido a instancia de los Diputados del Comercio de esta Ciudad sobre el modo, terminos, y circunstancias, 1772, fols. 43–52.

22. AGI, Guatemala 603, Testimonio, fols. 7, 22, 39.

23. Arturo Taracena Arriola, *Invención criolla, sueño ladino, pesadilla indígena. Los Altos de Guatemala: De región a estado, 1740–1850* (San José, Costa Rica: Editorial Porvenir / CIRMA, 1997), 33.

24. AGI, Guatemala 603, Testimonio, fols. 80–82, 148–51.

25. Ibid., fol. 11; Patch, "Imperial Politics and Local Economy," 102; S. Stein, "Francisco Ignacio de Yraeta," 486–88.

26. AGI, Guatemala 603, Testimonio, fols. 5, 53.

27. Ibid., fols. 53, 76.

28. Ibid., fols. 10–11.

29. Ibid.

30. Ibid., fols. 102, 139, 152.

31. Jordana Dym, *From Sovereign Villages to National States: City, State, and Federation in Central America, 1759–1839* (Albuquerque: University of New Mexico Press, 2006), 11, table 1.1.

32. AGI, Guatemala 603, Testimonio, fol. 139.

33. Ibid., fols. 139–42.

34. Ibid., fols. 5, 10–14.

35. Ibid., fols. 8–9.

36. Ibid., fols. 5, 10, 11.

37. Ibid., fols. 5, 10, 83, 139, 152.

38. AGI, Guatemala 599, Expediente diario 1, 1773, Cuaderno B, Testimonio de los autos respectivos . . . que da principio con la Real Provicion de 24 de marzo de 59 por la que se declararon libres del repartimiento de Algodón a los Yndios; AHN, Consejos 20979, Residencia del Barón de Riperdá y de Francisco Aibar, Gobernadores de Comayagua, Pieza 1, 1784, fols. 9–24; AHN, 20982, Residencia de José Alvarado, Alcalde Mayor de San Antonio Suchitepeques, 1796, and Residencia de Agustín de las Cuentas Zayas, Gobernador-Intendente de Chiapas, Cuaderno 2, 1803.

39. AGI, Guatemala 599, Expediente diario 1 (1775), Informe de Juan Bacaro, n.d., acted upon by the Consejo de Indias on July 31, 1775.

40. For the archbishop's side of the conflict, see Cortés y Larraz, *Descripción geográfico-moral*, 2:98–126.

41. AGI, Guatemala 599, Expediente diario 1 (1775), Carta F (1773), Carta G (1773), Representación de Juan Bacaro al Rey, n.d., Informe del Fiscal del Consejo de Indias, November 4, 1774; Guatemala 603, Expediente diario 1, Respuesta del Fiscal del Consejo, January 14, 1787.

42. AGI, Guatemala 603, Testimonio, fols. 108–109.

43. Ibid., fol. 144.

44. Ibid.

45. Ibid., fol. 11.

46. Ibid., fols. 122–23.

47. Ibid., fols. 120–21, 125.

48. Ibid., fols. 119, 121, 124–25.

49. Ibid., fols. 118, 122, 124.

50. AGI, Guatemala 599, Expediente diario 1 de Juan Bacaro (1775), Informe del Fiscal, November 4, 1774.

51. AGI, Guatemala 603, Testimonio, fol. 161.

52. Ibid., fols. 59, 119, 126–29.

53. Ibid., fols. 153–56, 160–61.

54. Ibid., fols. 18, 23.

55. For the charges and countercharges, see AGI, Guatemala 603, Testimonio, fols. 15–25, 37–42, 54–72, 87–95, 125–32, 152–56, 160–63, 179–80.

56. Ibid., fol. 22.

57. Ibid., fols. 53, 143.

58. Ibid., fols. 30–31.

59. Ibid., fols. 129–32.

60. Ibid., fol. 135.

61. AGI, Guatemala 603, Expediente diario 1, Juan Bacaro al Rey, August 22, 1774; Consulta del Consejo, July 31, 1775; Informe del Fiscal del Consejo, August 14, 1775; Juan Bacaro al Rey, July 15, 1786; Respuesta del Fiscal, January 14, 1787.

62. This is one of the main points in Margarita Menegus, *El repartimiento forzoso de mercancías en México, Perú y Filipinas* (Mexico City: Instituto de Investigaciones Dr. José María Luis Mora, Centro de Estudios sobre la Universidad-UNAM, 2000).

63. See Patch, *Maya Revolt and Revolution*, for a further exposition of the concepts of moral polity and moral economy in the Maya region.

64. AGI, Audiencia de Lima, 1119, Informe de la Contaduría, y Respuestas Fiscales correspondientes al Expediente de Intendencias, Informe de los Señores Contadores Generales, December 30, 1800, parags. 344–46.

5. Government and Business in the Lowlands

1. Once again, indispensable for a discussion of colonial Nicaragua is Newson, *Indian Survival*.

2. Solórzano, "La colonización inglesa de la Costa Caribe de Nicaragua, 1633–1787," 33–58.

3. But see Membreño Idiáquez, "Persistencia étnica en Sutiava y Monimbo," 106–43, for an interpretation arguing for substancial cultural survival.

4. Patch, *Maya Revolt and Revolution*, 50.

5. Roberto Trigueros, "Las defensas estratégicas del Río de San Juan de Nicaragua," *Anuario de Estudios Americanos*, 11 (1954): 427–76.

6. Trigueros, "Las defensas estratégicas," 479–81; Floyd, *Anglo-Spanish Struggle for Mosquitia*, 115–16.

7. For the war in Nicaragua, see Trigueros, "Las defensas estratégicas," 490–93; Floyd, *Anglo-Spanish Struggle for Mosquitia*, 132–62.

8. John Sugden, *Nelson: A Dream of Glory, 1758–1797* (New York: Holt, 2004), 149–75.

9. AGI, Guatemala 440, Título de Gobernador de Nicaragua, August 16, 1782.

10. AGI, Guatemala 440, Título de Presidente de José de Estachería, August 28, 1783.

11. AGI, Guatemala 440, Título de Presidente de Bernardo Troncoso, July 12, 1789.

12. José Joaquín Pardo, *Miscelánea histórica, Guatemala, siglos 16 a 19: Vida, costumbres, sociedad* (Guatemala: Editorial Universitaria, 1978), 132–34. This was first posted on the website of the Asociación para el Fomento de los Estudios Históricos en América Central (AFEHC.org) as ficha 2471, Banquete del Recibimiento del Capitán General don José de Estachería. I thank Christophe Belaubre for bringing it to the attention of scholars.

13. AGI, Guatemala 569, Expediente 16, Representación de la Provincia de Nicaragua al Rey, November 1, 1783.

14. AGI, Guatemala 569, Expediente 16, Parecer del Fiscal, July 22, 1784.

15. AGI, Guatemala 569, Expediente 16, Acuerdo del Consejo, July 29, 1784.

16. AGI, Guatemala 569, Expediente 11, 1783.

17. AGI, Guatemala 572, Expediente 20, Cabildo de Granada al Rey, April 24, 1785.

18. AGI, Guatemala 572, Expediente 20, Informe de la Contaduría, October 2, 1789; Informe del Fiscal, November 17, 1789; Consulta del Consejo, November 23, 1789.

19. AHN, Consejos 20978, Residencia de José de Estachería, Piezas 1–5 (1786).

20. AGI, Guatemala 572, Nota del Señor Secretario, 1789.

21. AGI, Guatemala 440, Título de la Intendencia de San Salvador, September 17, 1785.

22. Smith, "Forced Labor in the Guatemalan Indigo Works," 319–20; Smith, "Indigo Production and Trade," 191–92.

23. Floyd, "Bourbon Palliatives and the Central American Mining Industry," 121.

24. AGI, Guatemala 690, Informe del Gobernador-Intendente de San Salvador, July 28, 1786.

25. AGI, Guatemala 576, Expediente 14, 1788–89.

26. A maestre de campo was the commander of a *tercio*, the largest military unit of the Spanish army from the late fifteenth century to the early eighteenth century. This was about the size of a later large regiment or brigade, so the rank was equivalent to that of colonel or brigadier. It should be noted that neither a maestre de campo nor a later *mariscal de campo* was a field marshal, as some

Anglophone authors of the Spanish empire have erroneously assumed. The rank of mariscal de campo was between the ranks of brigadier and lieutenant general; it was therefore the modern equivalent of a major general or of a *general de división*.

27. Information from the 1730s is from AGI, Escribanía de Cámara 357B, Residencia de Maestre de Campo Don Bartolomé González Fitoria, Gobernador de Nicaragua, 1736.

28. Romero Vargas, *Las estructuras sociales de Nicaragua*, 302.

29. AGI, Guatemala 553, Expediente 1, Testimonio de las diligencias practicadas por Don Manuel de Montenegro en virtud de comisión, fol. 16 (1770).

30. Information on the Estachería repartimientos when he was governor of Nicaragua is in AGI, Guatemala 577, Expediente 1, Testimonio de los Autos de Pesquisa Ynstruidos por el Señor Don Josef Ortiz de la Peña, fols. 21–97 (1790).

31. Estachería's salary of 2,000 pesos is specified in AGI, Guatemala 440, Título de Governador de Nicaragua, August 16, 1782.

32. AGI, Guatemala 577, Expediente 1, Testimonio de los Autos de Pesquisa Ynstruidos por el Señor Don Josef Ortiz de la Peña, fols. 45–46 (1790).

33. AGI, Guatemala 545, Expediente 21, Alcalde Mayor Provisto de Tegucigalpa, Don Geronimo de la Vega y Lacayo al Rey, July 1, 1767, fol. 5.

34. AGI, Guatemala 553, Expediente 1, Testimonio de las diligencias practicadas por Don Manuel de Montenegro en virtud de comisión (1770).

35. AGI, Guatemala 577, Expediente 1, Testimonio de los Autos de Pesquisa Ynstruidos por el Señor Don Josef Ortiz de la Peña, fols. 29–30 (1790).

36. Guy C. P. Thomson, *Puebla de los Angeles: Industry and Society in a Mexican City, 1700–1850* (Boulder, Colo.: Westview Press, 1989).

37. AGI, Guatemala 577, Expediente 1, Informe del Oydor Comisionado Don Josef Ortiz, December 2, 1790.

38. AGI, Guatemala 577, Expediente 1, Testimonio de los Autos de Pesquisa Ynstruidos por el Señor Don Josef Ortiz de la Peña, fols. 29–31 (1790).

39. Ibid., fols. 45, 48.

40. Ibid., fol. 50.

41. Ibid., fol. 60.

42. Ibid., fol. 69.

43. Ibid., fol. 54.

44. Ibid., fols. 51–52.

45. Ibid., fols. 59, 61.

46. Ibid., fol. 68.

47. Ibid., fols. 45–46.

48. Ibid., fol. 48.

49. The residencia is in AHN, Consejos 20980.

50. For information about just the Rivas (Villa de Nicaragua) area, see AGI, Guatemala 556, Representación del Procurador Síndico de Rivas al Secretario de Indias (Arriaga), June 27, 1774; AGI, Guatemala 584, Expediente 7, Cabildo de Rivas al Rey, November 12, 1795.

51. For the Philippines see Luis Alonso Álvarez, *El costo del imperio asiático: La formación colonial de las Islas Filipinas bajo dominio español, 1565–1800* (La Coruña and México: Universidade da Coruña and El Instituto Mora, 2009), especially 223–60.

52. AGI, Guatemala 577, Expediente 1, Informe del Oydor Comisionado Don Josef Ortiz, December 2, 1790.

53. AHN, Consejos 20981, Residencia de Juan de Ayza, Gobernador e Intendente de Nicaragua, 1794.

6. Imperial Reform and Political Conflict in the Eighteenth Century

1. AGI, 607, Expediente 14, Informe del Fiscal y Consulta del Consejo, June 30, 1796.

2. AGI, Guatemala 525, Presidente al Secretario de Gracia y Justicia, October 24, 1810.

3. For works dealing mostly with reforms at the level of the provincial magistrates, see John Lynch, *Spanish Colonial Administration, 1782–1810: The Intendant System in the Río de la Plata* (London: University of London Press, Athlone Press, 1958); J. R. Fisher, *Government and Society in Colonial Peru: The Intendant System, 1784–1814* (New York: Oxford University Press, 1970); D. H. Brading, *Miners and Merchants in Bourbon Mexico, 1763–1810* (Cambridge: Cambridge University Press, 1971); Brian R. Hamnett, *Politics and Trade in Southern Mexico, 1750–1821* (Cambridge: Cambridge University Press, 1971); Pedro A. Vives, "Intendencias y poder en Centroamérica: La reforma incautada," *Anuario de Estudios Centroamericanos* 13, no. 2 (1987): 37–47; Josefina Zoraida Vázquez, ed., *Interpretaciones del siglo XVIII mexicano: El impacto de las reformas borbónicas* (Mexico: Nueva Imagen, 1992); Anthony McFarlane, *Colombia before Independence: Economy, Society, and Politics under Bourbon Rule* (New York: Cambridge University Press, 1993), 216–19 (which treats a case where, like Guatemala, the crown did not introduce intendancies); Kenneth J. Andrien, ed., *The Political Economy of Spanish America in the Age of Revolution, 1750–1850* (Albuquerque: University of New Mexico Press, 1994); Luis Navarro García, *Las reformas borbónicas en América: El plan de intendencias y su aplicación* (Seville: Universidad de Sevilla, 1995); Ignacio del Río, *La aplicación regional de las reformas borbónicas en Nueva España: Sonora y Sinaloa, 1768–1787* (Mexico: Universidad Nacional Autónoma de México, Instituto de Investigaciones Históricas, 1995); Horst Pietschmann, *Las reformas borbónicas y el sistema de intendencias en Nueva España: Un estudio político-administrativo* (Mexico City: Fondo de Cultura Económica, 1996); Celia María Parcero Torre, *La pérdida de La Habana y las reformas borbónicas en Cuba, 1760–1773* (Valladolid, Spain: Junta de Castilla y León, Consejería de Educación y Cultura, 1998), 259–77; Carmen Castañeda, "Los intendentes en el gobierno de Guadalajara, 1790–1809," *Revista de Indias*, 59, no. 1 (January–June 2002): 67–80; Jordana Dym, "Bourbon Reform and City Government

in Central America, 1759–1808," in *Politics, Economy, and Society in Bourbon Central America, 1759–1821*, ed. Jordana Dym and Christophe Belaubre (Boulder: University Press of Colorado, 2007), 75–100.

4. The literature on the Bourbon Reforms is too lengthy to cite here. For Central America, see Wortman, *Government and Society*, 129–83; Vives, "Intendencias y poder en Centroamérica"; and Dym and Belaubre, eds., *Politics, Economy, and Society in Bourbon Central America*.

5. AGI, Guatemala 641, Fiscal de la Audiencia al Rey, January 6, 1749.

6. AGI, Guatemala 641, Fiscal de la Audiencia al Rey, January 6, 1749; and Testimonio de la Real Cédula y demás diligencias practicadas en el Pueblo de Santa Catharina Istaguacam de la Jurisdicción de Solola, sobre repartimientos, 1746.

7. AGI, Guatemala 641, Tomás de Arana al Rey, December 31, 1761.

8. AGI, Escribanía de Cámara 359B, Residencia del Presidente Tomás de Rivera y Santa Cruz, Cuadernos 7–8 (1748); Escribanía de Cámara 359C, Cuadernos 9–10 (1748).

9. Patch, *Maya Revolt and Revolution*, 63–88.

10. AGI, Escribanía de Cámara 362B, Residencia de Francisco Antonio de Granda y Nicolás de Mencos, 1749.

11. AGI, Guatemala 544, Expediente 9, Audiencia al Rey, February 28, 1767.

12. AGI, Guatemala 545, Expediente 18, Obispo de Nicaragua al Rey, January 28, 1767.

13. Mark A. Burkholder and D. S. Chandler, "Creole Appointments and the Sale of Audiencia Positions in the Spanish Empire under the Early Bourbons, 1701–1750," *Journal of Latin American Studies* 4, no. 2 (1972): 187–206.

14. British Library, Ms. Additional 17,583, Consulta del Consejo, September 23, 1760, fol. 226.

15. AGI, Guatemala 642, Audiencia al Rey, March 30, 1769; and Audiencia al Rey, December 20, 1769.

16. This is revealed in AGI, Guatemala, 442, Títulos de las Alcaldías Mayores; Guatemala 443, Títulos de Alcaldías Mayores.

17. AHN, Consejos 20981, Residencia de Juan de Ayza, Pieza 1, 1794, fol. 82.

18. AHN, Consejos 20979, Residencia del Barón de Riperdá y de Francisco Aibar, Gobernadores de Comayagua, Pieza 1, 1784, fols. 9–24.

19. AGI, Guatemala 569, Expediente 16, Representación de la Provincia de Nicaragua al Rey, November 1, 1783; Guatemala 572, Expediente 20, Informe de la Contaduría, October 2, 1789; Informe del Fiscal, November 17, 1789; Consulta del Consejo, November 23, 1789; and Nota del Secretario del Despacho de Indias al Consejo de Indias, 1789; AHN, Consejos 20980, Residencia del Brigadier Josef de Estachería, gobernador de Nicaragua, 1790; Guatemala 582, Expedientes de Cartas, no number, Testimonio del expediente sobre Recaudazion i remizion a España de 1200 pesos que se impusieron de multas en la Residencia de Don Josefph Estachería Presidente que fue de Guatemala (1795).

20. AGI, Guatemala 442, Título del Alcalde Mayor de Amatitan-Sacatepéquez, August 20, 1801.

21. AHN, Consejos 20979, Residencia del Barón de Riperdá y de Francisco Aibar, Gobernadores de Comayagua, Pieza 1, 1784, fols. 9–24.

22. AGI, Indiferente General 1714, Informe 1330 del Virrey de Nueva España (Bucareli) al Secretario de Indias (Arriaga), March 27, 1774.

23. AGI, Guatemala 599, Expediente diario 1, 1775.

24. AGI, Guatemala 607, Expediente 14, Representación del Contador de Cuentas (Manuel Herrarte) al Secretario de Indias, October 20, 1764.

25. For a discussion of the commercial prospects of the magistrates, see Patch, "Imperial Politics," 92–101.

26. AGI, Guatemala 607, Expediente 14, Informe de la Contaduría, October 31, 1781.

27. AGI, Guatemala 607, Expediente 14, Audiencia al Rey, April 20, 1780; Guatemala 423, Informe de la Audiencia, October 31, 1781.

28. AGI, Guatemala 582, Expedientes de Cartas, no. 5, Audiencia al Rey, March 22, 1777; Guatemala 601, Expedientes diarios, no. 9, Informe del Fiscal del Consejo de Indias, August 14, 1778.

29. AGI, 558, Expediente 7, Informe del Fiscal del Consejo de Indias, February 19, 1778; Consulta del Consejo, May 11, 1778.

30. AGI, 558, Expediente 7, Informe del Fiscal del Consejo de Indias, February 19, 1778; Consulta del Consejo, May 11, 1778.

31. AGI, Guatemala 549, Expediente 6, Representacion del Presidente al Secretario de Indias, November 1, 1769.

32. AGI, Guatemala 340, Informe del Consejo al Rey, March 1765; AGI, Guatemala 442, Títulos de Alcaldes Mayores, Amatitan y Sacatepequez, October 27, 1759; AGI, Guatemala 443, Títulos de Alcaldes Mayores, October 27, 1759.

33. AGI, Guatemala 442, Títulos de Alcaldías Mayores, June 12, 1774, and August 20, 1801.

34. AGI, Guatemala 593, Expedientes diarios, no. 2, 1760.

35. AGI, Guatemala 596, Expediente diario 2, 1769.

36. AGI, Guatemala 440, Títulos de gobernadores, Soconusco, September 9, 1771.

37. AGI, Guatemala 440, Títulos de presidentes, August 28, 1783, and July 12, 1789.

38. AGI, Guatemala 552, Expediente 13, 1771, Informe del Fiscal del Consejo, August 15, 1771, and Testimonio, 1771.

39. AGI, Guatemala 600, Expedientes diarios 10, 11, 17, 19 (1776).

40. Wortman, *Government and Society*, 138–39.

41. AGI, Guatemala 641, Capitán de Infantería Joseph Ventura Manso de Velasco, alcalde mayor de Atitlán, al Rey, September 25, 1762.

42. AGI, Guatemala 545, Cura de Xalapa al Rey, March 30, 1767.

43. AHN, Consejos 20952, Pieza 101, Informe de la Audiencia, November 25, 1765.

44. For a good example of early conflict between creoles and peninsulars, see John Frederick Schwaller, "The Cathedral Chapter of Mexico in the Sixteenth Century," *Hispanic American Historical Review* 61, no. 4 (1981): 651–74.

45. *Colección de documentos antiguos del archivo del ayuntamiento*, 46–49.

46. Ibid., 121–22. For a study of the alternation of power within the religious orders, see Antonine S. Tibesar, "The *Alternativa*: A Study in Spanish-Creole Relations in Seventeenth-Century Peru," *The Americas* 11, no. 3 (1955): 229–83.

47. AGI, Guatemala 605, no. 1, Religiosos Criollos al Rey, August 2, 1792.

48. Maynard Geiger, "The Mallorcan Contribution to Franciscan California," *The Americas* 4, no. 2 (1947): 141–50; Isidro Félix de Espinosa, ed., *Misioneros valencianos en Indias*, 2 vols. (Valencia: Generalitat Valenciana, 1989), 1: 11–58.

49. AGI, Guatemala 607, Expediente 14, Provincial de la Orden de Santo Domingo al Secretario del Consejo de Indias, December 31, 1794.

50. Ibid.

51. AGI, Guatemala 609, Expediente 13, Arzobispado al Secretario del Consejo de Indias, October 2, 1796.

52. AGI, Guatemala 609, Expediente 13, Presidente al Secretario del Consejo de Indias, November 30, 1796.

53. AGI, Guatemala 609, Expediente diario 13, Consulta del Consejo de Indias, April 29, 1797.

54. Santos Pérez, "La práctica del autogobierno en Centroamérica," 69–94.

55. AGI, Indiferente General 1714, Informe no. 1330 del Virrey de la Nueva España (Bucareli) al Secretario de Indias (Arriaga), March 27, 1774.

56. AGI, Guatemala 577, Expediente 9, Presidente (Troncoso) al Secretario de Indias (Porlier), May 30, 1790.

57. AGI, Guatemala 602, Expediente diario 3, Solicitud de don Manuel Antonio Freixanes Pereira, October 4, 1781.

58. AGI, Guatemala 442, Títulos de alcaldías mayores, June 2, 1764.

59. Ibid., January 20, 1772.

60. AGI, Guatemala 544, Expediente 8, Audiencia al Rey, February 25, 1767; Testimonio de los autos seguidos en la Real Audiencia de Goathemala por don Fernando Gomez de Andrade, provisto Alcalde Mayor de la Provincia de Ciudad Real de Chiapas, 1766.

61. AGI, Guatemala 443, Títulos de alcaldías mayores, Totonicapán, September 3, 1800; Verapaz, September 3, 1800; Sonsonate, May 5, 1800; AGI, Guatemala 441, Títulos de alcaldías mayores, Chimaltenango, March 10, 1800; AGI, Guatemala 442, Títulos de alcaldías mayores, Atitlán, January 26, 1801.

62. AGI, Guatemala 440, Título del Intendente de Chiapas, September 20, 1786, and March 21, 1789.

63. AGI, Guatemala 440, Título del Intendente de El Salvador, September 17, 1785.

64. AGI, Guatemala 584, Expediente 10, Audiencia al Rey, June 3, 1796.

65. AGI, Guatemala 587, Audiencia al Rey, August 3, 1798; Informe del Fiscal del Consejo de Indias, July 2, 1799.

66. AGI, Indiferente General 1714, Informe no. 1330 del virrey de Nueva España (Bucareli) al Secretario de Indias (Arriaga), March 27, 1774.

67. AGI, Guatemala 421, Minutos de Cédulas Seculares, Cédula, October 9, 1802.

68. AGI, Guatemala 525, Expedientes e Instancia de la Audiencia, 450 (1810), Testimonio del Estado demostratibo de los corregimientos y alcaldías mayores de este Reino, sueldos que gozan, y tiempo en que se posecionaron de ellas, October 11, 1811.

69. AGI, Guatemala 713, Informe no. 323, del Presidente (González Sarabia) al Despacho Universal de Hacienda, September 3, 1803.

70. AGI, Guatemala 712, Informe no. 226, del Presidente (González Sarabia) al Despacho Universal de Hacienda, March 3, 1803; Informe no. 288, del Presidente (González Sarabia) al Despacho Universal de Hacienda, June 3, 1803; Guatemala 715, Informe no. 390, del Presidente (González Sarabia) al Despacho Universal de Hacienda, January 3, 1804; Guatemala 717, Informe no. 608, del Presidente (González Sarabia) al Despacho Universal de Hacienda, February 3, 1805.

71. Wortman, *Government and Society*, 184–94; Bernabé Fernández Hernández, *El reino de Guatemala durante el gobierno de Antonio González Saravia, 1801–1811* (Guatemala: Comisión Interuniversitaria Guatemalteca de Conmemoración del Quinto Centenario del Descubrimiento de América, 1992), 126–52; Fernández Molina, *Pintando el mundo de azul*, 299–338; AGI, Guatemala 628, Audiencia al Rey, no. 340, November 3, 1803.

72. Floyd, "Bourbon Palliatives and the Central American Mining Industry"; Bernabé Fernández Hernández, "Crisis de la minería de Honduras a fines de la época colonial," *Mesoamérica* 24 (December 1992), 365–83; Bernabé Fernández Hernández, *El gobierno del intendente Anguiano en Honduras, 1796–1812* (Seville: Universidad de Sevilla, 1997).

73. See Gustavo Palma Murga, "Between Fidelity and Pragmatism: Guatemala's Commercial Elite Responds to Bourbon Reforms in Trade and Contraband," in Dym and Belaubre, *Politics, Economy, and Society in Bourbon Central America*, 101–27, for the response of merchants to the late-colonial commercial crisis resulting from war and smuggling.

74. AGI, Guatemala 717, Informe no. 632, del Presidente (González Sarabia) al Despacho Universal de Hacienda, May 3, 1805.

75. Consulado Nacional [Guatemala], *Memoria sobre el estado actual del comercio*, 17–18.

76. For an overview of the consolidación in all of Spanish America, see Reinhard Liehr, "Endeudamiento estatal y crédito privado: La consolidación de vales reales en Hispanoamerica," *Anuario de Estudios Americanos* 41 (1984): 553–78.

77. For resistance to the crown's policies of taking control of Church revenues, see Christophe Belaubre, "In the Shadow of the Great: Church Financiers' Everyday Resistance to the Bourbon Reforms, Guatemala City, 1773–1821," in Dym and Belaubre, *Politics, Economy, and Society in Colonial Central America*, 47–73.

78. AGI, Guatemala 525, Presidente (González Sarabia) al Despacho Universal de Gracia y Justicia, November 3, 1809.

79. Geoffrey A. Cabat, "The Consolidation of 1804 in Guatemala," *The Americas* 28, no. 1 (1971): 20–38; Wortman, *Government and Society*, 64.

80. AGI, Indiferente 1444, Informe no. 1330, del Virrey de Nueva España (Bucareli) al Secretario de Indias (Arriaga), March 27, 1774.

81. AHN, Consejos 20979, Residencia del Barón de Riperdá y de Don Francisco Aibar, Gobernadores de Comayagua, Pieza 1, Informe del Fiscal del Consejo de Indias, October 26, 1786.

82. AGI, Guatemala 628, Expedientes, 1815, Carta no. 340, de la Audiencia al Rey, November 3, 1803.

83. Ibid.

84. Ibid.

85. S. Stein, "Bureaucracy and Business," 20–21; Stein and Stein, *Edge of Crisis*, 20.

86. AGI, Guatemala 628, Expedientes, 1815, Informe del Contador (Aparici), July 27, 1805.

87. Socolow, *Bureaucrats of Buenos Aires*, 109–53.

88. AGI, Guatemala 628, Informe del Fiscal, January 19, 1806.

89. AGI, Guatemala 525, Presidente (González Sarabia) al Despacho Universal de Gracia y Justicia, November 3, 1809.

90. AGI, Guatemala 525, Consulta del Consejo, January 31, 1815; Real Cédula, June 23, 1815.

91. Patch, *Maya and Spaniard*, 166–67.

92. David McCreery, *Rural Guatemala, 1760–1940* (Stanford: Stanford University Press, 1994), 93–101, 220–23.

93. AGI, Guatemala 525, Carta no. 450, del Presidente de la Audiencia (González) al Secretario de Gracia y Justicia, October 24, 1810.

94. AGI, Guatemala 421, Minutas y Consultas Seculares y Eclesiásticos, unsigned note, October 18, 1815.

95. Arthur P. Whitaker, *The Western Hemisphere Idea: Its Rise and Decline* (Ithaca, N.Y.: Cornell University Press, 1954), 16–19; Jorge Cañízares-Esguerra, "New World, New Stars: Patriotic Astrology and the Invention of Indian and Creole Bodies in Colonial Spanish America, 1600–1650," *American Historical Review* 104, no. 1 (February 1999): 36–68; Fred Anderson, *Crucible of War: The Seven Years' War and the Fate of Empire in British North America, 1754–1766* (New York: Alfred A. Knopf, 2000), 155–56.

96. Evelyne Sánchez, "Las élites de Nueva Guatemala, 1770–1821: Rivalidades y poder colonial," *Mesoamérica* 31 (June 1996): 129–56; Potthast-Jutkeit, "Centroamérica y el contrabando por la Costa de Mosquitos," 499–516.

97. José Manuel Santos Pérez, "La práctica del autogobierno en Centroamérica: Conflictos entre la Audiencia de Guatemala y el Cabildo de Santiago en el siglo XVIII," *Mesoamérica* 40 (December 2000): 69–94.

98. Charles Esdaille, *The Peninsular War: A New History* (New York: Palgrave Macmillan, 2003), 40–41.

99. Socolow, *Bureaucrats of Buenos Aires*, 58–59.

CONCLUSION

1. A similarly coercive repartimiento system existed in Yucatan. See Patch, *Maya and Spaniard in Yucatan*, 163–64; Jorge I. Castillo Canché, "Ocioso, pobre e incivilizado: Algunos conceptos e ideas acerca del maya yukateko a finales del siglo XVIII," *Mesoamérica* 39 (June 2000): 239–53.

2. AGI, Guatemala 363, Obispo de Ciudad Real al Rey, June 13, 1712.

3. See Kevin Gosner, *Soldiers of the Virgin: The Moral Economy of a Colonial Maya Rebellion* (Tucson: University of Arizona Press, 1992).

4. AGI, Guatemala 363, Obispo de Ciudad Real al Rey, April 4, 1716, and November 8, 1717; Consulta del Consejo, March 14, 1718.

5. AGI, Guatemala 641, Sumario hecho en el Consejo de Indias, April 24, 1764.

6. AGI, Audiencia de Lima, 1119, Informe de la Contaduría, y Respuestas Fiscales correspondientes al Expediente de Intendencias, Informe de los Señores Contadores Generales, December 30, 1800, parags. 344–46.

7. British Library, Ms. Additional 17,583, Medio que providencio S[u] M[ajestad] por cédula de 15 de junio de 1751 a representación de los Virreyes del Peru y Nueva España, para evitar los perjuicios y vejaciones que los corregidores y alcaldes mayores hacían a los Yndios, 1751, fols. 228–38.

8. AGI, Guatemala 599, Expediente diario 1 (1775), Carta F (1773), Carta G (1773), Representacion de Juan Bacaro al Rey, n.d., Informe del Fiscal del Consejo de Indias, November 4, 1774; Guatemala 603, Expediente diario 1, Respuesta del Fiscal del Consejo, January 14, 1787.

9. AHN, Consejos 20978, Residencia de Pedro de Salazar, Pieza 1 (1771), fols. 21–23.

10. AGI, Indiferente General 1714, Informe no. 1330 del Virrey de Nueva España (Bucareli) al Exmo. Sr. Don Julián de Arriaga (Secretario del Despacho Universal de Indias), March 27, 1774.

11. AGI, Guatemala 628, Informe del Contador (Pedro de Aparici), July 27, 1805.

12. For the collapse of the repartimiento system in Yucatan once participation became voluntary, see Patch, *Maya and Spaniard in Yucatan*, 163–68.

13. Dennis O. Flynn and Arturo Giráldez, "Born with a 'Silver Spoon': World Trade's Origin in 1571," *Journal of World History* 6, no. 2 (September 1995); Dennis O. Flynn and Arturo Giráldez, "Silk for Silver: Trade via Manila and Macao in the 17th Century," *Philippine Studies* 44 (1st Quarter 1996): 52–68.

14. Consulado Nacional [Guatemala], *Memorial sobre el estado actual del comercio*.

15. The literature on de-industrialization is lengthy. For recent studies that review that literature, see David Clingingsmith and Jeffrey G. Williamson, "Deindustrialization in Eighteenth- and Nineteenth-Century India: Mughal Decline,

Climate Shocks, and British Industrial Ascent," *Explorations in Economic History* 45 (July 2008): 209–34; Indrajit Ray, "Identifying the Woes of the Cotton Textile Industry in Bengal: Tales of the Nineteenth Century," *Economic History Review*, n.s., 62, no. 4 (November 2009): 857–92; Robert C. Allen, "Agricultural Productivity and Rural Incomes in England and the Yangtze Delta, c.1620–c.1820," *Economic History Review*, n.s., 62, no. 3 (August 2009): 525–50.

16. James C. Scott, *Weapons of the Weak* (New Haven, Conn.: Yale University Press, 1987).

17. Robert W. Patch, "Dependency and the Colonial Heritage in Southeastern Mesoamerica," in *Colonial Legacies: The Problem of Persistence in Latin American History*, ed. Jeremy Adelman (New York: Routledge, 1999), 91–106.

Bibliography

Archives and Manuscript Collections

Archivo General de Indias (Seville)
Audiencia de Guatemala, Audiencia de Lima, Audiencia de México, Escribanía de Cámara, Indiferente General
Archivo Histórico Nacional (Madrid)
Consejos
Bancroft Library (Berkeley)
British Library (London)
Additional Manuscripts

Books and Articles

Acuña León, María de los Ángeles, and Doriam Chavarría López. "Cartago colonial: Mestizaje y patrones matrimoniales, 1738–1821." *Mesoamérica* 31 (June 1996): 157–79.

Acuña Ortega, Víctor Hugo, and Iván Molina Jiménez. *Historia económica y social de Costa Rica (1750–1950)*. San José, Costa Rica: Editorial Porvenir, 1991.

Allen, Robert C. "Agricultural Productivity and Rural Incomes in England and the Yangtze Delta, c.1620–c.1820." *Economic History Review*, n.s., 62, no. 3 (August 2009): 525–50.

Alonso Álvarez, Luis. *El costo del imperio asiático: La formación colonial de las Islas Filipinas bajo dominio español, 1565–1800*. La Coruña and Mexico: Universidade da Coruña and Instituto Mora, 2009.

Anderson, Benedict. *Imagined Communities: Reflections on the Origin and Spread of Nationalism*. London: Verso, 1983. Rev. ed., New York: Verso, 1991.

Anderson, Fred. *Crucible of War: The Seven Years' War and the Fate of Empire in British North America, 1754–1766*. New York: Alfred A. Knopf, 2000.

Andrien, Kenneth J., ed. *The Political Economy of Spanish America in the Age of Revolution, 1750–1850*. Albuquerque: University of New Mexico Press, 1994.

Arias de Blois, Jorge. "Demografía." In *Historia general de Guatemala*, edited by Jorge Luján Muñoz and Cristina Zilbermann de Luján. Vol. 3, *Siglo XVIII hasta la Independencia*, 103–19. Guatemala: Asociación de Amigos del País, Fundación para la Cultura y el Desarrollo, 1994–95.

Assadourian, Carlos Sempat. *El sistema de la economía colonial: El mercado interior, regiones y espacio económico*. Lima: Instituto de Estudios Peruanos, 1982.

Baskes, Jeremy. "Coerced or Voluntary? The *Repartimiento* and Market Participation of Peasants in Late Colonial Oaxaca." *Journal of Latin American Studies* 28, pt. 1 (February 1996): 1–28.

———. *Indians, Merchants, and Markets: A Reinterpretation of the Repartimiento and Spanish-Indian Economic Relations in Colonial Oaxaca*. Stanford: Stanford University Press, 2000.

Belaubre, Christophe. "In the Shadow of the Great: Church Financiers' Everyday Resistance to the Bourbon Reforms, Guatemala City, 1773–1821." In Dym and Belaubre, *Politics, Economy, and Society in Bourbon Central America*, 47–73.

Borah, Woodrow, ed. *El gobierno provincial en la Nueva España*. Mexico City: Universidad Nacional Autónoma de México, Instituto de Investigaciones Históricas, 1985.

Borchart de Moreno, Christiana Renate. *Los mercaderes y el capitalismo en la ciudad de México, 1759–1778*. Mexico City: Fondo de Cultura Económica, 1984.

Bracamonte y Sosa, Pedro, and Gabriela Solís Robleda. *Espacios mayas de autonomía: El pacto colonial en Yucatán*. Mérida, Yucatán: Universidad Autónoma de Yucatán, Facultad de Ciencias Antropológicas, 1996.

Brading, D. H. *Miners and Merchants in Bourbon Mexico, 1763–1810*. Cambridge: Cambridge University Press, 1971.

Browning, David. *El Salvador: Landscape and Society*. Oxford: Clarendon Press, 1971.

Burkholder, Mark A., and D. S. Chandler. "Creole Appointments and the Sale of Audiencia Positions in the Spanish Empire under the Early Bourbons, 1701–1750." *Journal of Latin American Studies* 4, no. 2 (1972): 187–206.

———. *From Impotence to Authority: Spanish Crown and American Audiencias, 1687–1808*. Columbia: University of Missouri Press, 1977.

Cabat, Geoffrey A. "The Consolidation of 1804 in Guatemala." *The Americas* 28, no. 1 (1971): 20–38.

Cañizares-Esguerra, Jorge. "New World, New Stars: Patriotic Astrology and the Invention of Indian and Creole Bodies in Colonial Spanish America, 1600–1650." *American Historical Review* 104, no. 1 (February 1999): 36–68.

Cardoso, Ciro, and Héctor Pérez Brignoli. *Centro América y la economía occidental (1520–1930)*. San José: Editorial Universidad de Costa Rica, 1979.

Carmack, Robert, John Early, and Christopher Lutz, eds. *The Historical Demography of Highland Guatemala*. Publication no. 6. Albany: Institute for Mesoamerican Studies, State University of New York, 1982.

Carmagnani, Marcello." Una institución económica colonial: Repartimiento de mercancías y libertad de comercio." *Historia Mexicana* 54, no. 1 (July–September 2004): 249–62.

Castañeda, Carmen. "Los intendentes en el gobierno de Guadalajara, 1790–1809." *Revista de Indias* 59, no. 1 (January–June 2002): 67–80.

Castillo Canché, Jorge I. "Ocioso, pobre e incivilizado: Algunos conceptos e ideas acerca del maya yukateko a finales del siglo XVIII." *Mesoamérica* 39 (June 2000): 239–53.

Chakrabarty, Dipesh. *Provincializing Europe: Postcolonial Thought and Historical Difference*. Princeton, N.J.: Princeton University Press, 2000.

Clingingsmith, David, and Jeffrey G. Williamson. "Deindustrialization in Eighteenth- and Nineteenth-Century India: Mughal Decline, Climate Shocks, and British Industrial Ascent." *Explorations in Economic History* 45 (July 2008): 209–34.

Cole, Jeffrey A. *The Potosí Mita, 1573–1700: Compulsory Indian Labor in the Andes*. Stanford: Stanford University Press, 1985.

Colección de documentos antiguos del archivo del ayuntamiento de la ciudad de Guatemala, formada por su secretario Don Rafael Arévalo. Edición del Museo Guatemalteco. Guatemala: Imprenta de Luna, 1857.

Consulado Nacional [Guatemala]. *Memorial sobre el estado actual del comercio de Guatemala: Obstáculos que impiden su progreso y medios de removerlos*. Guatemala: Beteta, 1823.

Cortés y Larraz, Pedro. *Descripción geográfico-moral de la Diócesis de Goathemala*. 2 vols. Guatemala: Biblioteca "Goathemala" de la Sociedad de Geografía e Historia de Guatemala, 1958.

Creamer, Winifred. "Mesoamerica as a Concept: An Archaeological View from Central America." *Latin American Research Review* 22, no. 1 (1987): 35–55.

Dawson, Frank Griffith. "William Pitt's Settlement at Black River on the Mosquito Shore: A Challenge to Spain in Central America, 1732–87." *Hispanic American Historical Review* 63, no. 4 (November 1983): 677–706.

Dym, Jordana. "Bourbon Reform and City Government in Central America, 1759–1808." In Dym and Belaubre, *Politics, Economy, and Society in Bourbon Central America*, 75–100.

———. *From Sovereign Villages to National States: City, State, and Federation in Central America, 1759–1839*. Albuquerque: University of New Mexico Press, 2006.

Dym, Jordana, and Christophe Belaubre, eds. *Politics, Economy, and Society in Bourbon Central America, 1759–1821*. Boulder: University Press of Colorado, 2007.

Esdaille, Charles. *The Peninsular War: A New History*. New York: Palgrave Macmillan, 2003.

Espinosa, Isidro Félix de, ed. *Misioneros valencianos en Indias*. 2 vols. Valencia, Spain: Generalitat Valenciana.

Farriss, Nancy. *Maya Society under Colonial Rule: The Collective Enterprise of Survival*. Princeton, N.J.: Princeton University Press, 1984.

Fenn, Elizabeth A. *Pox Americana: The Great Smallpox Epidemic of 1775–82*. New York: Hill and Wang, 2001.

Fernández, Mario, Anabel Schmidt, and Víctor Basauri. "La población de Costa Rica." In *Población de Costa Rica y orígenes de los costarricenses*, edited by Joaquín Gutiérrez. Vol. 2. 20 vols. Biblioteca Patria 2. San José: Editorial Costa Rica, 1977.

Fernández Hernández, Bernabé. "Crisis de la minería de Honduras a fines de la época colonial." *Mesoamérica* 24 (December 1992): 365–83.

———. *El gobierno del intendente Anguiano en Honduras, 1796–1812*. Seville: Universidad de Sevilla, 1997.

———. *El reino de Guatemala durante el gobierno de Antonio González Saravia, 1801–1811*. Guatemala: Comisión Interuniversitaria Guatemalteca de Conmemoración del Quinto Centenario del Descubrimiento de América, 1992.

Fernández Molina, José Antonio. *Pintando el mundo de azul: El auge añilero y el mercado centroamericano, 1750–1810*. San Salvador: Biblioteca de Historia Salvadoreña, 2003.

Fisher, J. R. *Government and Society in Colonial Peru: The Intendant System, 1784–1814*. New York: Oxford University Press, 1970.

Floyd, Troy S. *The Anglo-Spanish Struggle for Mosquitia*. Albuquerque: University of New Mexico Press, 1967.

———. "Bourbon Palliatives and the Central American Mining Industry, 1765–1800." *The Americas* 18 (October 1962): 103–25.

———. "The Guatemalan Merchants, the Government, and the Provincianos, 1750–1800." *Hispanic American Historical Review* 41, no. 1 (February 1961): 90–110.

———. "The Indigo Merchant: Promoter of Central American Economic Development, 1750–1808." *Business History Review* 39, no. 4 (Winter 1965): 466–88.

Flynn, Dennis O., and Arturo Giráldez. "Born with a 'Silver Spoon': World Trade's Origin in 1571." *Journal of World History* 6, no. 2 (September 1995): 201–21.

———. "Cycles of Silver: Global Economic Unity through the Mid-Eighteenth Century." *Journal of World History* 13, no. 2 (Fall 2002): 391–427.

———. "Silk for Silver: Trade via Manila and Macao in the 17th Century." *Philippine Studies* 44, (1st Quarter 1996): 52–68.

Fonseca Corrales, Elizabeth. "Economía y sociedad en Centroamérica (1540–1680)." In *El régimen colonial (1524–1750)*, edited by Julio Pinto Soria, 95–150. Vol. 2 of *Historia general de Centroamérica*. 6 vols. Madrid: Comunidades Europeas / Sociedad Estatal Quinto Centenario / FLACSO, 1993.

Fowler, William R. *The Cultural Evolution of Ancient Nahua Civilizations: The Pipil-Nicarao of Central America*. Norman: University of Oklahoma Press, 1989.

Frank, Andre Gunder. *ReOrient: Global Economy in the Asian Age*. Berkeley: University of California Press, 1998.

Fuentes y Guzmán, Francisco Antonio. *Recordación florida. Discurso natural, material, militar y político del Reino de Goathemala*. 3 vols. Madrid: Biblioteca de Autores Españoles, Ediciones Atlas, 1969.

García-Baquero González, Antonio. *Cádiz y el Atlántico (1717–1778)*. Seville: Escuela de Estudios Hispano-Americanos, 1976.

García Fuentes, Lutgardo. *El comercio español con América, 1650–1700*. Seville: Excelentísima Diputación Provincial de Sevilla, 1982.

Geiger, Maynard. "The Mallorcan Contribution to Franciscan California." *The Americas* 4, no. 2 (1947): 141–50.

Gibson, Charles. *The Aztecs under Spanish Rule: A History of the Indians of the Valley of Mexico, 1521–1821*. Stanford: Stanford University Press, 1964.

Golte, Jürgen. *Repartos y rebeliones: Túpac Amaru y las contradicciones de la economía colonial*. Lima: Instituto de Estudios Peruanos, 1980.

Gómez-Galvarriato, Aurora, ed. *La industria textil en México*. Mexico: Instituto Mora, El Colegio de Michoacán, El Colegio de México, Instituto de Investigaciones Históricas-UNAM, 1999.

González, Jorge H. "State Reform, Popular Resistance, and Negotiation of Rule in Late Bourbon Guatemala: The Quetzaltenango Aguardiente Monopoly, 1785–1807." In Dym and Belaubre, *Politics, Economy, and Society in Bourbon Central America*, 129–55.

Gosner, Kevin. *Soldiers of the Virgin: The Moral Economy of a Colonial Maya Rebellion*. Tucson: University of Arizona Press, 1992.

Gutiérrez, Joaquín, ed. *Población de Costa Rica y orígenes de los costarricenses*. 20 vols. San José: Editorial Costa Rica, 1977.

Hamnett, Brian R. *Politics and Trade in Southern Mexico, 1750–1821*. Cambridge: Cambridge University Press, 1971.

Hernández Aparicio, Pilar. "Problemas socioeconómicos en el Valle de Guatemala (1670–1680)." *Revista de Indias* 37 (1977): 585–637.

Hill, Robert M. *Colonial Cakchiquels: Highland Maya Adaptations to Spanish Rule, 1600–1700*. Fort Worth, Texas: Harcourt Brace Jovanovich, 1992.

Hoberman, Louisa Schell. *Mexico's Merchant Elite, 1590–1660: Silver, State, and Society*. Durham, N.C.: Duke University Press, 1991.

Jones, Oakah L. *Guatemala in the Spanish Colonial Period*. Norman: University of Oklahoma Press, 1994.

Jones, Owen. "Colonial K'iche' in Comparison with Yucatec Maya: Language, Adaptation, and Intercultural Contact." PhD diss., University of California, Riverside, 2009.

Juan, Jorge, and Juan de Ulloa. *Noticias secretas de América*. 2 vols. Madrid: Editorial-América, 1918.

Kicza, John. *Colonial Entrepreneurs: Families and Business in Bourbon Mexico City*. Albuquerque: University of New Mexico Press, 1983.

Kramer, Wendy. *Encomienda Politics in Early Colonial Guatemala, 1524–1544: Dividing the Spoils*. Dellplain Latin American Studies, no. 31. Boulder, Colo.: Westview Press, 1994.

Langenberg, Inge. *Urbanisation und Bevölkerungsstruktur der Stadt Guatemala in der ausgehenden Kolonialzeit: eine sozialhistorische Analyse der Stadtverlegung und ihrer Ausvirkungen auf die demographische, berufliche, und soziale Gliederung der Bevölkerung (1773–1824).* Cologne and Vienna: Böhlau, 1981.

Larson, Brooke, and Robert Wasserstrom. "Consumo forzoso en Cochabamba y Chiapa durante la época colonial." *Historia Mexicana* 31, no. 3, issue123 (1982): 361–408.

Liehr, Reinhard. "Endeudamiento estatal y crédito privado: La consolidación de vales reales en Hispanoamérica." *Anuario de Estudios Americanos* 41 (1984): 553–78.

Lockhart, James. *The Nahuas after the Conquest: A Social and Cultural History of the Indians of Central Mexico, Sixteenth through Eighteenth Centuries.* Stanford: Stanford University Press, 1992.

Lovell, W. George. *Conquest and Survival in Colonial Guatemala: A Historical Geography of the Cuchumatán Highlands, 1500–1521.* Kingston and Montreal: McGill-Queen's University Press, 1985.

Luján Muñoz, Jorge. "Fundación de villas de ladinos en Guatemala en el último tercio del siglo XVIII." *Revista de Indias* 36 (1976): 51–81.

Luján Muñoz, Jorge, and Cristina Zilbermann de Luján, eds. *Historia general de Guatemala.* 6 vols. Vol. 3, *Siglo XVIII hasta la Independencia.* Guatemala: Asociación de Amigos del País, Fundación para la Cultura y el Desarrollo, 1994–95.

Lutz, Christopher H. *Santiago de Guatemala, 1541–1773: City, Caste, and the Colonial Experience.* Norman: University of Oklahoma Press, 1994.

Lynch, John. *Spanish Colonial Administration, 1782–1810: The Intendant System in the Río de la Plata.* London: University of London Press, Athlone Press, 1958.

McCreery, David. *Rural Guatemala, 1760–1940.* Stanford: Stanford University Press, 1994.

McFarlane, Anthony. *Colombia before Independence: Economy, Society, and Politics under Bourbon Rule.* New York: Cambridge University Press, 1993.

MacLeod, Murdo J. "An Outline of Central American Colonial Demographics: Sources, Yields, and Possibilities." In *The Historical Demography of Highland Guatemala,* edited by Robert Carmack, John Early, and Christopher Lutz, 3–18. Albany: Institute for Mesoamerican Studies, State University of New York, 1982.

———. *Spanish Central America: A Socioeconomic History, 1524–1720.* Berkeley and Los Angeles: University of California Press, 1971.

MacLeod, Philip. "Auge y estancamiento de la producción de cacao en Costa Rica, 1660–95." *Anuario de Estudios Centroamericanos* 22, no. 1 (1996): 83–107.

Masur, Gerhard. *Simon Bolivar.* Albuquerque: University of New Mexico Press, 1948.

Membreño Idiáquez, Marcos. "Persistencia étnica en Sutiava y Monimbo." In Romero Vargas et al., *Persistencia indígena en Nicaragua,* 106–43.

Menegus, Margarita. *El repartimiento forzoso de mercancías en México, Perú y Filipinas.* Mexico City: Instituto de Investigaciones Dr. José María Luis Mora, Centro de Estudios sobre la Universidad-UNAM, 2000.

Miño Grijalva, Manuel. *La manufactura colonial: La constitución técnica del obraje.* Mexico: El Colegio de México, 1992.

———. *Obrajes y tejedores de Nueva España, 1700–1810.* Mexico: El Colegio de México, 1998.

———. *La protoindustria colonial hispanoamericana.* Mexico: El Colegio de México, 1993.

Molina Argüello, Carlos. "Gobernaciones, alcaldías mayores y corregimientos en el reino de Guatemala." *Anuario de Estudios Americanos* 17 (1950): 105–32.

Moreno Cebrián, Alfredo. *El corregidor de indios y la economía peruana del siglo XVIII (Los repartos forzosos de mercancías).* Madrid: Consejo Superior de Investigaciones Científicas, 1977.

Muro Romero, Fernando. "El 'beneficio' de oficios públicos con jurisdicción en Indias: Notas sobre sus orígenes." *Anuario de Estudios Americanos* 35 (1978): 1–67.

Navarro García, Luis. "Los oficios vendibles en Nueva España durante la Guerra de Sucesión." *Anuario de Estudios Americanos* 32 (1975): 133–54.

———. *Las reformas borbónicas en América: El plan de intendencias y su aplicación.* Seville: Universidad de Sevilla, 1995.

Newson, Linda A. *The Cost of Conquest: Indian Decline in Honduras under Spanish Rule.* Boulder, Colo.: Westview Press, 1986.

———. "Indian Population Patterns in Colonial Spanish America." *Latin American Research Review* 20, no. 3 (1985): 41–74.

———. *Indian Survival in Colonial Nicaragua.* Norman: University of Oklahoma Press, 1987.

Orellana, Sandra L. *The Tzutujil Mayas: Continuity and Change, 1250–1630.* Norman: University of Oklahoma Press, 1984.

Ortiz de la Tabla Ducasse, Javier. "El obraje colonial ecuatoriano: Aproximación a su estudio." *Revista de Indias* 149–50 (July–December 1977): 471–551.

Ouweneel, Arij. *Shadows over Anáhuac: An Ecological Interpretation of Crisis and Development in Central Mexico, 1730–1800.* Albuquerque: University of New Mexico Press, 1996.

Palma Murga, Gustavo. "Between Fidelity and Pragmatism: Guatemala's Commercial Elite Responds to Bourbon Reforms in Trade and Contraband." In Dym and Belaubre, *Politics, Economy, and Society in Bourbon Central America,* 101–27.

———. "Economía y sociedad en Centroamérica (1680–1750)." In *El régimen colonial (1524–1750),* edited by Julio Pinto Soria, 219–306. Vol. 2 of *Historia general de Centroamérica.* 6 vols. Madrid: Comunidades Europeas / Sociedad Estatal Quinto Centenario / FLACSO, 1993.

———. "Núcleos de poder local y relaciones familiares en la ciudad de Guatemala a fines del siglo XVIII." *Mesoamérica* 12 (December 1986): 241–308.

Parcero Torre, Celia María. *La pérdida de La Habana y las reformas borbónicas en Cuba, 1760–1773.* Valladolid, Spain: Junta de Castilla y León, Consejería de Educación y Cultura, 1998.

Pardo, José Joaquín. *Miscelánea histórica, Guatemala, siglos 16 a 19: Vida, costumbres, sociedad.* Guatemala: Editorial Universitaria, 1978.

Parry, J. H. *The Sale of Public Office in the Spanish Indies under the Hapsburgs.* Berkeley: University of California Press, 1953.

Patch, Robert W. "Cura y empresario: Los préstamos financieros de Mateo Cornejo y la producción de añil en El Salvador, 1764–1789." *Mesoamérica* 48 (2006): 47–67.

———. "Dependency and the Colonial Heritage in Southeastern Mesoamerica." In *Colonial Legacies: The Problem of Persistence in Latin American History,* edited by Jeremy Adelman, 91–106. New York: Routledge, 1999.

———. "Imperial Politics and Local Economy in Colonial Central America, 1670–1770." *Past and Present,* no. 143 (May 1994): 79–107.

———. *Maya and Spaniard in Yucatan, 1648–1812.* Stanford: Stanford University Press, 1993.

———. *Maya Revolt and Revolution in the Eighteenth Century.* Armonk, N.Y.: M. E. Sharpe, 2002.

Percheron, Nicole. "Producción agrícola y comercio de la Verapaz en la época colonial." *Mesoamérica* 20 (December 1990): 231–48.

Pérez Brignoli, Héctor, ed. *De la Ilustración al Liberalismo* (1750–1870). Vol. 3 of *Historia general de Centroamérica.* 6 vols. Madrid: Comunidades Europeas / Sociedad Estatal Quinto Centenario / FLACSO, 1993.

Pérez Herrero, Pedro. *Plata y libranzas: La articulación comercial del México borbónico.* Mexico: El Colegio de México, 1988.

Pérez-Mallaína, Pablo E. *Spain's Men of the Sea: Daily Life on the Indies Fleet in the Sixteenth Century.* Baltimore, Md.: Johns Hopkins University Press, 1998.

Pietschmann, Horst. "'Alcaldes mayores,' 'corregidores' und 'subdelegados': Zum Problem der Distriktsbeamtenschaft im Vizekönigreich Neuspanien." *Jahrbuch für Geschichte von Staat, Wirtschaft und Gesellschaft Lateinamerikas* 9 (1972): 173–270.

———. *Las reformas borbónicas y el sistema de intendencias en Nueva España: Un estudio político-administrativo.* Mexico City: Fondo de Cultura Económica, 1996.

Pinto Soria, Julio, ed. *El régimen colonial (1524–1750).* Vol. 2 of *Historia general de Centroamérica.* 6 vols. Madrid: Comunidades Europeas / Sociedad Estatal Quinto Centenario / FLACSO, 1993.

Pomeranz, Kenneth. *The Great Divergence.* Princeton, N.J.: Princeton University Press, 2000.

Potthast-Jutkeit, Barbara. "Centroamérica y el contrabando por la Costa de Mosquitos en el siglo XVIII." *Mesoamérica* 36 (December 1998): 499–516.

Prakash, Om. *European Commercial Enterprise in Pre-colonial India.* Cambridge: Cambridge University Press, 1998.

Ramos Escandón, Carmen. *Industrialización, género y trabajo femenino en el sector textil mexicano: El obraje, la fábrica y la compañía industrial.* Mexico: CIESAS, Casa Chata, 2004.

Ray, Indrajit. "Identifying the Woes of the Cotton Textile Industry in Bengal: Tales of the Nineteenth Century." *Economic History Review*, n.s., 62, no. 4 (November 2009): 857–92.

Restall, Matthew. *Maya Conquistador*. Boston: Beacon Press, 1998.

———. *The Maya World: Yucatec Culture and Society, 1550–1850*. Stanford: Stanford University Press, 1997.

Río, Ignacio del. *La aplicación regional de las reformas borbónicas en Nueva España: Sonora y Sinaloa, 1768–1787*. Mexico: Universidad Nacional Autónoma de México, Instituto de Investigaciones Históricas, 1995.

Rodríguez Becerra, Salvador. *Encomienda y conquista: Los inicios de la colonización en Guatemala*. Seville: Publicaciones del Seminario de Antropología Americana, Universidad de Sevilla, 1977.

Romero Frizzi, María de los Ángeles. *Economía y vida de los españoles en la Mixteca Alta: 1519–1720*. Mexico: Instituto Nacional de Antropología e Historia, 1990.

Romero Vargas, Germán. *Las estructuras sociales de Nicaragua en el siglo XVIII*. Managua: Editorial Vanguardia, 1988.

Romero Vargas, Germán, and Flor de Oro Solórzano. "Las poblaciones indígenas de Nicaragua, 1492–1821." In Romero Vargas et al., *Persistencia indígena en Nicaragua*, 11–30.

Romero Vargas, Germán, et al. *Persistencia indígena en Nicaragua*. Managua: CIDCA-UCA, 1992.

Ruz, Mario Humberto. *Gestos cotidianos: Acercamientos etnológicos a los mayas de la época colonial*. Campeche, Mexico: Gobierno del Estado de Campeche, Universidad Autónoma del Carmen, Universidad Autónoma de Campeche, Instituto Campechano, and Instituto de Cultura de Campeche, 1997.

Sáenz de Santa María, Carmelo. "Inglaterra y el reino de Guatemala." *Revista de Indias* 42 (1982): 109–201.

Salvucci, Richard J. *Textiles and Capitalism in Mexico: An Economic History of the Obrajes, 1539–1840*. Princeton, N.J.: Princeton University Press, 1987.

Samayoa Guevara, Héctor Humberto. *Implantación del régimen de intendencias en el reino de Guatemala*. Guatemala: Editorial del Ministerio de Educación Pública "José de Pineda Ibarra," 1960.

Sánchez, Evelyne. "Las élites de Nueva Guatemala, 1770–1821: Rivalidades y poder colonial." *Mesoamérica* 31 (June 1996): 129–56.

Santos Pérez, José Manuel. "Los comerciantes de Guatemala y la economía de Centroamérica en la primera mitad del siglo XVIII." *Anuario de Estudios Americanos* 56, no. 2 (1999): 463–84.

———. *Élites, poder local y régimen colonial: El cabildo y los regidores de Santiago de Guatemala, 1700–1787*. Salamanca, Spain: Servicios de Publicaciones de la Universidad de Cádiz, Plumsock Mesoamerican Studies, and Centro de Investigaciones Regionales de Mesoamérica, 1999.

————. "La práctica del autogobierno en Centroamérica: Conflictos entre la Audiencia de Guatemala y el Cabildo de Santiago en el siglo XVIII." *Mesoamérica* 40 (December 2000): 69–94.

Sanz Tapia, Ángel. "Aproximación al beneficio de cargos políticos americanos en la primera mitad del siglo XVIII." *Revista Complutense de Historia de América*, no. 24 (1998): 147–76.

————. "Provisión y beneficio de cargos políticos en Hispanoamérica (1674–1700)." *Jahrbuch für Geschichte Lateinamerikas* 37 (2000): 24–47.

Schwaller, John Frederick. "The Cathedral Chapter of Mexico in the Sixteenth Century." *Hispanic American Historical Review* 61, no. 4 (1981): 651–74.

Scott, James C. *Domination and the Arts of Resistance: Hidden Transcripts.* New Haven, Conn.: Yale University Press, 1990.

————. *The Moral Economy of the Peasant: Rebellion and Subsistence in Southeast Asia.* New Haven, Conn.: Yale University Press, 1976.

————. *Weapons of the Weak: Everyday Forms of Peasant Resistance.* New Haven, Conn.: Yale University Press, 1985.

Sherman, William L. *Forced Native Labor in Sixteenth-Century Central America.* Lincoln: University of Nebraska Press, 1979.

Smith, Robert S. "Forced Labor in the Guatemalan Indigo Works." *Hispanic American Historical Review* 36, no. 3 (August 1956): 318–28.

————. "Indigo Production and Trade in Colonial Guatemala." *Hispanic American Historical Review* 39, no. 1 (February 1959): 181–211.

Socolow, Susan Migden. *The Bureaucrats of Buenos Aires, 1769–1810: Amor al real servicio.* Durham, N.C.: Duke University Press, 1987.

————. *The Merchants of Buenos Aires, 1770–1810: Family and Commerce.* Cambridge: Cambridge University Press, 1978.

Solano, Francisco de. *Los mayas del siglo XVIII: Pervivencia y transformación de la sociedad indígena guatemalteca.* Madrid: Ediciones Cultura Hispánica, 1974.

Solórzano, Flor de Oro. "La colonización inglesa de la Costa Caribe de Nicaragua, 1633–1787." In Romero Vargas et al., *Persistencia indígena en Nicaragua*, 33–58.

Solórzano Fonseca, Juan Carlos. "Los años finales de la dominación española (1750–1821)." In *De la Ilustración al Liberalismo* (1750–1870), edited by Héctor Pérez Brignoli, 13–71. Vol. 3 of *Historia general de Centroamérica.* 6 vols. Madrid: Comunidades Europeas / Sociedad Estatal Quinto Centenario / FLACSO, 1993.

————. "Las comunidades indígenas de Guatemala, El Salvador y Chiapas durante el siglo XVIII: Los mecanismos de la explotación económica." *Anuario de Estudios Centroamericanos* 11, no. 2 (1985): 93–130.

————. "Costa Rica en la primera mitad del siglo XVIII: Análisis regional de una sociedad en transición." *Anuario de Estudios Centroamericanos* 19, no. 1 (1993): 55–66.

Spalding, Karen. *Huarochirí, an Andean Society under Inca and Spanish Rule.* Stanford: Stanford University Press, 1984.

Stein, Barbara H., and Stanley J. Stein. *Edge of Crisis: War and Trade in the Spanish Atlantic, 1789–1808.* Baltimore, Md.: Johns Hopkins University Press, 2009.

Stein, Stanley J. "Bureaucracy and Business in the Spanish Empire, 1759–1804: Failure of a Bourbon Reform in Mexico and Peru." *Hispanic American Historical Review* 61, no. 1 (February 1982): 2–28.

———. "Francisco Ignacio de Yraeta y Azcárate, almacenero de la ciudad de México, 1732–1797: Un ensayo de microhistoria." *Historia Mexicana* 50, no. 3 (January–March 2001): 459–512.

———. "Tending the Store: Trade and Silver at the Real de Huautla, 1778–1781." *Hispanic American Historical Review* 77, no. 3 (August 1997): 377–407.

Stein, Stanley J., and Barbara H. Stein. *Apogee of Empire: Spain and New Spain in the Age of Charles III, 1759–1789.* Baltimore, Md.: Johns Hopkins University Press, 2003.

———. *Silver, Trade, and War: Spain in the Making of Early Modern Europe.* Baltimore, Md.: Johns Hopkins University Press, 2000.

Stern, Steve J. *Peru's Indian Peoples and the Challenge of Spanish Conquest: Huamanga, to 1640.* Madison: University of Wisconsin Press, 1982.

Sugden, John. *Nelson: A Dream of Glory, 1758–1797.* New York: Holt, 2004.

Szasdi de Nagy, Adam. "El comercio ilícito en la provincia de Honduras." *Revista de Indias* 17, no. 68 (April–June 1957): 271–83.

Tandeter, Enrique. "Forced and Free Labor in Late Colonial Potosí." *Past and Present*, no. 92 (November 1981): 98–136.

Taracena Arriola, Arturo. *Invención criolla, sueño ladino, pesadilla indígena. Los Altos de Guatemala: De región a estado, 1740–1850.* San José, Costa Rica: Editorial Porvenir / CIRMA, 1997.

Thompson, E. P. "The Moral Economy of the English Crowd in the Eighteenth Century." *Past and Present*, no. 50 (February 1971): 76–136.

Thomson, Guy C. P. *Puebla de los Angeles: Industry and Society in a Mexican City, 1700–1850.* Boulder, Colo.: Westview Press, 1989.

Tibesar, Antonine S. "The *Alternativa*: A Study in Spanish-Creole Relations in Seventeenth-Century Peru." *The Americas* 11, no. 3 (1955): 229–83.

Torales Pacheco, María Cristina, Tarsicio García Díaz, and Carmen Yuste. *La compañía de comercio de Francisco Ignacio de Yraeta, 1767–1797: Cinco ensayos.* Mexico: Instituto Mexicano de Comercio Exterior, 1985.

Tous Mata, Meritxell. *De protagonistas a desaparecidos: Las sociedades indígenas de la Gran Nicoya, siglos XIV a XVII.* Managua: Lea Grupo Editorial, 2008.

Trigueros, Roberto. "Las defensas estratégicas del Río de San Juan de Nicaragua." *Anuario de Estudios Americanos* 11 (1954): 413–513.

Vázquez, Josefina Zoraida, ed. *Interpretaciones del siglo XVIII mexicano: El impacto de las reformas borbónicas.* Mexico: Nueva Imagen, 1992.

Veblen, Thomas T. "Native Population Decline in Totonicapán, Guatemala." In *The Historical Demography of Highland Guatemala*, edited by Robert Carmack, John Early, and Christopher Lutz, 81–102. Albany: Institute for Mesoamerican Studies, State University of New York, 1982.

Vives, Pedro A. "Intendencias y poder en Centroamérica: La reforma incautada." *Anuario de Estudios Centroamericanos* 13, no. 2 (1987): 37–47.

Walker, Geoffrey J. *Spanish Politics and Imperial Trade, 1700–1789*. Bloomington: Indiana University Press, 1979.

Wallerstein, Immanuel. *The Modern World-System: Capitalist Agriculture and the Origins of the European World Economy in the Sixteenth Century*. New York: Academic Press, 1976.

Wasserstrom, Robert. *Class and Society in Central Chiapas*. Berkeley and Los Angeles: University of California Press, 1983.

Webre, Stephen. "El trabajo forzoso de los indígenas en la política colonial guate-malteca (siglo XVII)." *Anuario de Estudios Centroamericanos* 13, no. 2 (1987): 49–61.

Whitaker, Arthur P. *The Western Hemisphere Idea: Its Rise and Decline*. Ithaca, N.Y.: Cornell University Press, 1954.

Woodward, Ralph Lee. *Class Privilege and Economic Development: The Consulado de Comercio of Guatemala, 1793–1871*. Chapel Hill: University of North Carolina Press, 1966.

Wortman, Miles L. *Government and Society in Central America, 1680–1840*. New York: Columbia University Press, 1982.

Yuste, Carmen. "Francisco Ignacio de Yraeta y el comercio transpacífico." *Estudios de Historia Novohispana* 9 (1987): 189–217.

Zamora Acosta, Elías. *Los mayas de las tierras altas en el siglo XVI*. Seville: Dipu-tación Provincial, 1985.

Zilbermann Morales, María Cristina, and Jorge Luján Muñoz. "Santiago de Guate-mala en vísperas de los terremotos de 1773." *Anuario de Estudios Americanos* 32 (1975): 541–71.

INDEX